FEMICIDE
IN SOUTH AFRICA

Nechama Brodie

KWELA BOOKS

Kwela Books,
an imprint of NB Publishers,
a division of Media24 Boeke (Pty) Ltd
40 Heerengracht, Cape Town, South Africa
PO Box 879, Cape Town 8000, South Africa
www.kwela.com

Copyright © Nechama Brodie 2020

All rights reserved.
No part of this book may be reproduced or transmitted in any form
or by any electronic or mechanical means, including photocopying
and recording, or by any other information storage or retrieval system,
without written permission from the publisher.

Cover design: Wilna Combrinck
Typography: Nazli Jacobs
Editor: Alison Lowry
Proof reader: Glynne Newlands
Indexer: Sanet le Roux
Set in Versailles

Printed by *novus print*, a division of Novus Holdings

First published by Kwela Books 2020

ISBN: 978-0-7957-0938-8
ISBN: 978-0-7957-0939-5 (epub)
ISBN: 978-0-7957-0940-1 (mobi)

Contents

Introduction		1
1.	Femicide Bingo	5
2.	Everywoman's femicide	10
3.	Urban legends	25
Part One: Intimate femicide		**45**
4.	'A Love Story Gone Wrong': Finding the words	47
5.	'Two Die in Tragedy': Femicide-suicide and family killings	83
6.	'Man Shoots Woman': Firearms and femicide in South Africa	102
Part Two: Non-intimate femicide		**115**
7.	'A fate worse than death': Rape and femicide	117
8.	'We only write about them when they are dead': Hate killings of black lesbians in South Africa	129
9.	'We all know who are the witches here': Witch killings	149
10.	The 'ideal victim': Elderly women and farm murders	164
Part Three: The media and the message		**181**
11.	Mega cases, race and rape: What the media gets wrong about femicide	183
12.	Fuck the hashtag	198
Acknowledgements		213
Notes		216
Index		232

Introduction

When we say South Africa has a femicide problem – a crisis, to use the words of the government – what do we mean?

Do we mean we have a problem with fatal violence against women relative to other countries, or relative to ourselves? Do we mean that fatal violence against women in South Africa, now, is different from or worse than at any other time in our country's past?

Some people argue that South Africa doesn't have a femicide problem, it has a *homicide* problem. That the real issue is our extremely high levels of inter-personal violence, the majority of victims of which are men, not women at all. This is a silly argument about a serious topic, which overlooks the unpleasant fact that both statements are true.

South Africa has one of the highest murder rates in the world (the fifth highest according to the United Nations Office on Drugs and Crime, using 2015 data). Within that, we also have a femicide rate that is five to six times the world average, depending on the year. We have a specific problem of violence against women, particularly sexual violence and fatal violence against women. Yes, these acts take place within a broader culture of brutality which becomes only sharper, harder, more vicious the closer you look at it – but these acts are also distinct within the hostels of inter-personal violence that effectively define our country's history over the past four centuries. Femicide – like the murders of children, and perhaps the elderly – carries such distinct features that, if we were to try and understand or profile these killings only in the context of male homicides, we would miss the point entirely.

The violence meted out against women has long been distinct from the violence meted out between men.

This book is based in a large part on my doctoral thesis, which looked at how South African media covered the murders of women who were killed between April 2012 and March 2013. In my research, I tried to document and analyse exactly what kind of narratives and how many stories the media crafted and published about the murders of women, in order to compare reporting on femicide with the reality of femicide, and ultimately discuss how this media coverage might have influenced public understanding of this type of violence.

Over the course of five years I built a database of more than 408 femicides, linked to over 5 700 news articles. My research showed that less than 20 per cent of femicides made it into the press at all and that, as a body of work, those that did showed little correlation with the reality of femicide across the country.

This book builds on these findings, integrated with information and data from a series of mortality and femicide studies conducted in South Africa over the last two decades, and tries to look at the phenomenon of femicide in South Africa through a much longer lens – going back 40 years and more – to see if we are better able to understand not only femicide as it is now, but also if (and how) fatal violence against women has changed over the course of the last few decades, particularly before and after 1994.

What emerges, from both the short-term and from longitudinal data, is a much broader picture of a continuum of violence against women, which, with a few exceptions, I don't believe has changed so much as we have developed new words to describe it and new ways of conceptualising it.

What this also shows is that on one level we understand femicide very well – particularly in the last 25 or so years, there has been a significant amount of good quality, peer-reviewed regional and national research into the epidemiology of fatal violence against women in South Africa. But at the same time, this has been accompanied by a mass of misinformation about crime and violence. Part of this is the legacy of an incredibly violent past and present, which makes information sometimes overwhelming, and also incomprehensible in the face of anecdote and personal experiences with crime and violence. It is also because of the state's continued reluctance to take responsibility, even going so far as to obscure crime data on more than one occasion. And, in no small part, it is due to more recent malicious players like the white right wing who have propagated myths and false claims around race and crime, including claims of a white genocide. These myths and misinformation work so well because they creep into the crevasses of our prejudices and suspicion, and then we give them guns.

This book attempts to acknowledge these narratives – the ones we have used to tell ourselves particular versions of how we think the world works – and tries to explore and explain them, using data and anecdote but distinguishing between the two, and providing essential context so we can understand how both anecdote and data can be a product of their time.

What is important to take away from this is that individual stories matter, a lot, because when women die they are not and should never be considered as just statistics. But, also, that these deaths don't happen in isolation. If we are ever really to make a meaningful difference to combating gender-based violence, we need to see and understand it for what it truly is.

1. Femicide Bingo

One Friday night, about a year before I finished my thesis, a man tried to break into the room where I was sleeping.

This happened in Franschhoek, a small town in the Cape winelands where I was a panellist at the annual literary festival. I was staying in a little guest cottage in the garden of a larger house. My room was pretty much one big bed and a generous bathroom, which had a shower and a bath. This detail is important because when I woke up to an unfamiliar noise at three in the morning, the first thing I thought was that a bird – or maybe a rat – had somehow gotten into the room and was eating the special Harry and Meghan cupcakes that were currently lying in the (empty) bathtub in anticipation of the royal wedding which was taking place that weekend. The cupcakes, together with a few royal petit fours and cookies, had been hand-delivered from Cape Town by my friend, former state prosecutor and member of parliament, Glynnis Breytenbach, who was also speaking at the festival, about the book we had written together.

The noise sounded almost like someone was walking and breathing in the bathtub. It was so nonsensical that I dismissed it at first. But the sound persisted. And eventually I got up to look in the bath, as much as I was able to see at three in the morning without my glasses, and saw that there was nothing there, except the cupcakes in their stripy cardboard box, which had not somehow magically developed feet.

The noises came again. And the second time I went to look, I noticed the bathroom blind was moving as if there was a very strong wind outside. Except there was no wind. And then I saw that, behind the blind, was a man. A man who was already more than halfway into my room, his arms and his body worked through a tiny window that, thank God, was just a little too small and a little too high to make it easy for him.

He was panting with exertion. That was what I had heard. That, and the sound of the blind tapping against the windowsill and the vase on the stand beneath it.

In that first moment of terrifying awareness and denial, there was a split second where this man breaking in through the window in my room was both impossible and inescapable. Impossible because this couldn't happen to *me*. Because I was strong. Important. Powerful. And, at the same time, it was very definitely happening to me. And part of that felt inevitable almost. The part of my brain that was going, *Ah, yes. Of course this is going to happen to you. You want to be the expert in femicide, how else did you think it was going to go?*

And that same part of my brain was also telling me that either I was going to die in that small room, or I was going to have to fight for my life. And that was also terrifying.

I have a second dan in karate and spent many years of my life learning how to fight, including a stint as a boxer. But I'm a martial artist, not a fantasist. I know that the average adult male is almost always going to be stronger than me. Fighting is a last resort, not a first choice. Plus, at three in the morning, in a tiny space that was not my own and basically blind as a bat without my glasses, what came to mind was flight.

What I needed to do was get *out* of the room that the man was trying to get into. And to do that, I needed to unlock the door using the key that was now three feet away on the stand next to my bed (I'm a Joburger, and we always lock our doors, even in the 'country'). Which meant I needed enough time to make my way back to my bed, find the key, and somehow get it to work in the unfamiliar door, all before the man could finish making his way in through the window.

I did the second thing my mind told me to do, which was to scream for help, as loud as I could.

I screamed *Help*.

I screamed *Help me*.

I screamed, *Help me, there's someone in my room.*

I screamed it again and again.

And thank God, someone answered me. In the cottage next door to me was author Rehana Rossouw and journalist Julia Grey. My screams woke them up, and bless them (truly), because they answered immediately.

I could hear them calling back to me, even while I carried on screaming.

What's wrong?

Who's in your room?

And, most important of all. *We're coming.*

The moment I heard someone say that they were coming, I knew I would be okay. I knew that there was nothing inevitable about what was happening, except my survival. And then, suddenly, Julia and Rehana were there, and I had managed to unlock the door. And the man who was already nearly in my room had run away, leaving a pair of grassy shoe marks on the ledge of the window outside. Incredibly, the police arrested him several hours later.

But here is the thing. In my head, for a long time afterwards, I kept flipping the memory of it over and over again on a loop. Because, you see, I knew this story. I knew it so well.

I knew this story because I had read tens of other stories just like it.

'. . . gained entry through a bathroom window . . .'

Men didn't break into tiny guest cottages at night thinking they were empty, and they could steal the complimentary toiletries. The man who had broken into my room had almost certainly done so knowing someone was sleeping there, done so *because* someone was sleeping there. And because, in all probability, the person sleeping in the room would be a woman.

So I knew how these stories began, and I also knew how they ended.

They ended with sentences like:

'... *found in her bathtub* ...'

'... *found on her bed* ...'

'... *raped and stabbed* ...'

There were a lot of possible endings, even if they hadn't happened to me. And it was these possibilities, probabilities, that played over and over in my mind for months afterward. This horrific femicide bingo.

Through the window.

Through the door.

Through the roof. *Through the fucking roof.*

Walking to school. Walking from school.

Going to work.

Driving.

Going to a shebeen.

Walking home from the shebeen.

Walking.

Next to the train tracks.

In a graveyard.

In an open plot.

In the bushes.

On the side of the road.

In between shacks.

In her own house.

In her mother's house.

In a hospital.

In a police station.

With a gun. With a knife. With a stick. With a sharp object. With a blunt object. With a pillow. With the victim's underwear. With his hands. With a rock. With matches.

None of these bad things had happened to me – the man climbing into my room had not, ultimately, succeeded. I was lucky not just in the big picture but in the small picture. The night before my incident, another female author at the same festival had been mugged walking home, hit in the face with a brick. All I got was a giant fright, and a temporarily lost voice (I had screamed so loudly that I couldn't speak for days after).

Even though none of these bad things had happened to me, I was still terrified. Part of me is *still* terrified. The part that knows, there but for the grace of God went I.

I had and still have a residual adrenalin response from the incident. I suppose that it is just regular post-traumatic stress, but it is intensely, physically uncomfortable when it happens, because my body is so cued for danger that it's primed to go from zero to a million in less than the space of a heartbeat. It's been triggered when I was working in Buenos Aires, two months after the incident, convinced that someone was climbing onto the balcony of my fifth-floor hotel room. It happened a year later when a young man started running away from the security guards on my street and tried to run into my open driveway, and towards my car. It happens when someone approaches me too fast from a blindspot, or when a car brakes and reverses suddenly on a street where I am standing. My mind tumbles back into that statistical mode that says, Of course.

And this is the worst part. Because it does happen, every day.

2. Everywoman's femicide

Actually, femicide doesn't just happen every day in South Africa. It currently happens around eight times a day. That means on average every three hours a woman is murdered. More than half of these women are murdered by their current or former intimate partners (including rejected lovers) – that is, every six hours a woman is killed by her husband or boyfriend or partner, or her ex-husband, ex-boyfriend, and so on. This is why sometimes you will see headlines like 'Every Six Hours a Woman is Killed', and why so many politicians and newspapers sometimes get these figures wrong. The terminology of female homicide sometimes makes the reality of the killings harder to understand. And, really, they're impossible to understand to begin with.

It is perhaps worth having a discussion here about numbers and how they are used. Whether you love numbers or you hate numbers, this part is important because numbers are something that people get wrong a lot of the time, and when we get the details wrong about femicide we start developing solutions based on errors rather than actualities.

Numbers matter a lot (five-minute read)

One of the things that you need to understand is when we write about 'every three hours' or 'eight femicides a day', we don't mean that a murder happens exactly every three hours, or that every day there are eight and only eight murders of women. These are murder rates over time, and they are calculated by taking the total number of murders for a year and averaging them out. So, between 1 April 2018 and 21 March 2019 (which is the South African Police

Service's financial reporting year, and so also their crime reporting period), the police recorded 2 771 murders of women aged 18 years and older. If you divide 2 771 by 365 (the number of days in the year) you get 7.59 which we would round up to 8. Similarly, if we have 8 murders every 24 hours, then we have one murder every three hours. But what *averages* mean is that some days you might have 12 murders and other days 6, and so on.

There is another kind of murder rate that is very important to understand, and that is the murder rate per population. This kind of data allows us to study and understand the incidence of murder relative to the size of a region or country's population.

To understand why this is important, let's look at an example that has been used previously by right-wing organisations and individuals in South Africa to mislead people about murder rates in the country.

In 1951, fewer than 2 500 murders were reported to the police. By 2000 this figure had risen to over 21 683 murders. On social media, certain people used this information to claim that murder rates in South Africa were worse under a democratic government than they had been during apartheid.

Let's set aside for a moment the fact that, before 1994, crime statistics in South Africa were unreliable outside of white areas because they did not accurately count crime in many black townships and, after the Homelands Act, excluded crimes committed in the Bantustans. What should hopefully be obvious to most of you is that, apartheid aside, we would *expect* an increase in the number of murders between 1951 and 2000 – because they are nearly 50 years apart, and our population grew during that time. In 1951 there were about 12.7 million people living in South Africa. By 2000 this had nearly quadrupled to 44.5 million.[1] Reasonably, raw crime numbers will change as population numbers change. It would be strange if they did not.

And this is why, most of the time, we don't like to use raw numbers on their own to explain crime. Because if we don't take population figures and changes into account, raw numbers can be extremely misleading.

Using crime-per-population data also allows us to study and compare crime in different regions, without letting population sizes skew the impact of the raw number data.

For example, in 2018 Jamaica recorded a total of 1 287[2] murders – this is less than the number of murders that take place in South Africa in an average month. But when we take into account that Jamaica's population was just 2 727 503[3] people compared to an estimated 57 725 600[4] people in South Africa, we can start to understand why the island country is reasonably considered to have one of the highest murder rates in the world.

To calculate a population-based rate is actually quite straightforward. For ease of use, and to avoid impossibly small numbers with lots of decimal points, we often use a population base of 100 000 people. To do this, we take the total number of crimes (let's stick with murder), divide it by the total population of the country, and then multiply that figure by 100 000. For example, if we go back to our Jamaican/South African data:

Jamaican murder rate (2018)
1 287 murders/2 727 503 = 0.00047186 x 100 000 = 47.19
Murder rate/100 000 people = 47

South African murder rate (2018/19)
21 022 murders/57 725 600 = 0.0003641 x 100 000 = 36.41
Murder rate/100 000 people = 36

So, even though Jamaica has far fewer murders, because these murders take place within a significantly smaller population base, the *rate* of murder within the Jamaican population is much higher than in South Africa.

Even within South Africa murder rates can also vary quite dramatically between provinces, between cities, and even between suburbs and precincts. For example, in 2018–2019 there were 3 965 murders reported in the Eastern Cape and 4 495 murders reported in Gauteng.[5] Gauteng had a higher *number* of murders, but a much lower murder *rate* – this is because Gauteng was home to over 14.7 million people while the Eastern Cape had less than half of that, with 6.5 million people. That meant the murder rate in the Eastern Cape was 60.8/100 000, while in Gauteng it was nearly half of that, at 30.5/100 000.

In my experience as a researcher and a teacher, crime numbers and rates are enough to make a lot of people switch off. But there is one more thing I need to explain, which is about increases and decreases between years – and the difference between raw number increases/decreases, crime rate increases/decreases, and percentage increases/decreases.

Around 2012, South Africa's murder numbers began to increase after several years of downward murder trends. This upward trend has, quite sadly, continued, and by 2018/19 we had reached numbers that had not been seen since the turn of the millennium. At the same time, because of the difference in population sizes (43.7 million in 2000 compared to 57.7 million in 2018), the murder *rates* were not the same. At the turn of the millennium, the murder rate in South Africa was 48 to 50 per 100 000, which was much higher than the 36/100 000 in 2018. So, although the raw numbers are similar between the two periods, because of population changes they should not be compared directly. Rather, we should look at the murder rate – in which case, the rate in 2018/19 is similar to what was happening in 2008/09.

And then those pesky percentages. Per cent means the part per hundred, but we also use it to calculate the part or portion or proportion of any whole. A hundred per cent of 50 is 50. Fifty per cent of 50 is 25. And so on. A lot of understanding percentages is not actually about the calculation (although those matter), but also understanding how percentage changes work, which is the other area where politicians, media and people on social media make many mistakes. If something increases by 100 per cent it means that it *doubles*. If there were 2 500 female homicides in 2017 and they increased by 100 per cent in the following year, it would mean that in 2018 there were 5 000 femicides. If the femicide numbers increased by 50 per cent, it would mean that the original number (2 500) increased by half its number (1 250), that is, 3 750.

I don't imagine this book is going to somehow slay all the false femicide information floating around, but I can promise you that femicide did *not* increase by 117 per cent two years ago, no matter what that well-meaning person told you on Twitter. Context also matters. In a country like Norway, which recorded just 25 murders in 2018, an increase of, say, ten additional murders would mean a nearly 50 per cent increase year on year. In South Africa, ten extra murders would be less than a 0.05 per cent increase.

Finally, there is also a difference between something that increases by a certain per cent, and a *percentage point* or a point increase.

Between 2017/18 and 2018/19, the murder rate increased from 35.8 per 100 000 to 36.4 (per 100 000). This means the rate increased by 0.6 points, or it increased by 1.7 per cent (the proportional change between the previous year and the next). For that same period, the murder numbers increased by 686 murders, from 20 336 to 21 022, which was a three per cent increase year on year.

We can use these figures and proportions to study the frequency and prevalence of murder in our own country, or in a province, or a city; and we can also use this information to understand these kinds of killings in a global context.

In South Africa, the femicide rate – the number of murders per 100 000 women – is currently more than six times the global average. The World Health Organisation estimated that in 2017 the global rate of 'female total homicide' was 2.3/100 000 women.[6] During the same period in South Africa, the femicide rate was 14/100 000.

Defining femicide

In a section looking at the 'gender-related killing of women and girls', the United Nations Office on Drugs and Crime's (UNODC) 2018 Global Study on Homicide uses a particular phrase, that I have repeated above: *female total homicide*. The same study also uses the term 'femicide', but does so mostly in quote marks because, as the authors correctly point out, the term 'femicide' is not actually clearly or universally defined and is still subject to a wide range of interpretation – with the exception of several countries, mostly in Latin America, that have introduced certain legal statutes that narrow the meaning of 'femicide' in that jurisdiction. Still, femicide is not a constant (in law or in research; of course, it is a global constant because women are killed everywhere). And that also makes it a little harder to know what we are really looking at, when we look at things like 'global femicide averages'.

Although men have been killing women as long as they have been killing each other, the term 'femicide' is a much more recent addition and its current and contemporary use emerged out of quite specific multi-decade movements and activism looking at women, gender, feminism, policy, violence, crime and justice. So, the murder of women is not a new phenomenon but femicide is a neologism, one which encapsulates and expresses particular understandings of violence against women and, at the same time, highlights the need for a specific word to mark these distinctions.

Before we get to femicide, let's start with murder which, broadly, can be understood to mean the unlawful killing of a person.[7] Although we often assume that murder is universally understood, legal definitions may actually vary between territories and jurisdictions, and in some territories, the word 'murder' (the illegal killing of a person) has a meaning distinct from the word 'homicide' (the killing of a person – which may not always be illegal). In this book, 'homicide' and 'murder' are used interchangeably but should be understood to imply an unlawful killing in the context of the South African legal system (which, some people may be surprised to learn, is not based on American movies) – although even here, it should be noted that the law distinguishes between 'murder' (the unlawful and intentional killing of a person) and 'culpable homicide' (the unlawful and negligent killing of a person).

The specific word 'femicide' – from the Latin for 'woman' (femina) and 'killing' (-cide) – was first used in the early nineteenth century and referred to the killing of a woman[8] in much the same way as 'homicide' refers to the killing of a man (homo). But the current iteration of the word femicide is just over 40 years old. South African-born feminist academic, author, activist and sociologist Diana Russell used it during her testimony at the International Tribunal on Crimes Against Women that was held in Belgium in 1976, to describe not only female homicide, but more specifically 'to suggest that when women are murdered, their femaleness is not incidental to the crime'.[9]

Russell, in her own words, embraced the term 'femicide' (which she, in turn, had heard from another author) as 'a substitute for the gender-neutral word "homicide"'. Russell described femicide as a hate crime against women – specifically, a 'hate killing of females perpetrated by males'. She later amended her definition of femicide to read: 'the killing of females by males because they are female'.[10]

In addition to situating violence against women firmly within the misogyny of society, Russell's deliberate use of language was designed to suggest that the murder of women by men was something distinct from and different to the ways and reasons that men killed each other.

This is borne out by studies of inter-personal violence, including studies on non-fatal injuries in South Africa, which have shown that most violent injuries between men arise from 'everyday life, most often involving strangers and including poorly defined arguments and quarrels over money, women, and drunkenness',[11] whereas most women are attacked and harmed by someone they know. Where men often participate in or even initiate violence against each other, even when they are with strangers, women are subjected to violence, and mostly by the people closest to them.

It is important to note that men make up the vast majority of perpetrators *and* victims of murder (more than 80 per cent of murder victims in South Africa are adult males), and that studying femicide as a particular phenomenon should not for one moment be taken to imply that the murder of men is in any way less important. Solving South Africa's massive homicide problem is an imperative, and an even more challenging task. What is significant, though, is that there *is* a difference in the profiles of how and why men are killed, and how and why women are killed. Whether it is due to biology, patriarchy, or any mix of these and other factors, men (as a group; there are quite obviously individual exceptions) engage in everyday behaviours that include and even encourage exchanges of inter-personal violence. This is a complex and long-standing phenomenon that I can't unpack in this book. Also because this book is about *women*, and I don't want to frame victims in relation to killers because I believe that is another form of violence – that of erasure.

What Russell did in the 1970s was draw people's attention to the fact that the profile of female homicide was different to homicide. Within that, Russell attempted to distinguish between what she labelled as 'femicides' – where a woman is killed because she is a woman – and 'female homicides', which was just where a woman is killed. For example, in Russell's view, a woman killed with her husband during the course of a supermarket robbery was not considered a femicide but a female homicide.

Influenced by this approach, many institutions[12] defined femicide as the 'killing of women [some also included girls] because of their gender', which could take the form of:

- intimate partner violence against women;
- so-called 'honour' killings, and dowry killings;[13]

- deaths related to female genital mutilation;
- the deliberate targeting and killing of women in armed conflict;
- killing women because of their sexual orientation and/or their gender identity;
- the murder of female sex workers;
- murders related to accusations of witchcraft; and
- the murders of women associated with organised crime and gangs.

Some definitions also extended to female children, and so included female infanticide and gender-based abortions of female foetuses.

All of these examples of 'femicide' could also be classified as homicides. But, under these protocols, not all homicides of women could necessarily be classified as *femicides* – because, policy makers argued, not all these acts of murder were related to the victim's gender.

But, in practice, trying to determine whether or not a woman was killed *because she is a woman* is far more complex and problematic when female homicides are studied as actual crimes rather than as social, sociological or political concepts.

During the second national study of female homicide in South Africa that was conducted in 2009[14], researchers found that the police had not identified a perpetrator in nearly 23 per cent of the cases in their system. In addition, fewer than 40 per cent of all cases resulted in convictions, which implies that the guilt of many alleged perpetrators was not conclusively determined. This leaves massive speculation as to not only the identity of the perpetrators, but also their relationship with their victims.

Within this matrix the determination of motive is impossible or ambiguous. How would one even begin to tease out or identify misogyny as a specific rather than an inherent feature of any violence against women? Writing about Marc Lépine's mass killing of fourteen women at the École Polytechnique in Canada in 1989, Andrea Dworkin commented that the women were murdered 'because they were women but also because they were engineering students; because they were learning a male science; because they wanted sacred male knowledge. They were trespassing on sacred male ground. They wanted to be engineers, and that was taken to be a militant act of aggression on their part.'[15]

Perhaps this is true for women who 'trespass' on other territories: women who have jobs outside the home; women who drive, women who stand up or who speak out ... And in a court of law, how would one prove 'misogyny' as opposed to a more generic misanthropy? This is not, sadly, a rhetorical question, and has led to some genuine and some (perhaps) deliberate misunderstandings of the distinctions.

In a rather depressing misreading, or simply an extremely ill-informed over-literalisation of this theoretical framework, a recent Statistics South Africa report on 'Crime against Women in South Africa'[16] repeated Russell's definition of femicide, namely 'the killing of females by males because they are females', before going on to assert that by this 'narrow definition', the brutal rape and murder of lesbian soccer player Eudy Simelane, killed in Kwa-Thema in 2008, would somehow 'not count as femicide'.

This is a patently absurd statement. Simelane was targeted for rape and murder precisely because she was a woman, and because she was a lesbian. This points to a massive gap in the very understanding of violence against women by the statisticians' office, which is repeated in multiple subsequent statements in the report, which states, for example, that the central problem of femicide is 'the level of crime in the country rather than crime against women' and that 'men have been victimised more than women'. While the latter is statistically correct, it completely misrepresents the nature of gender-based violence and violence against women from a societal and criminological perspective.

The authors of the paper conclude their thoughts on femicide by deducing that 'femicide is a term that is often misused by activists and the media' and that the 'killing of females simply because they are females is a rare phenomenon in South Africa'. The report adds that the alleged 'misuse' of the term femicide occurs 'while the incidence of female homicide resulting from domestic violence or violence emanating from broken relationships is unacceptably high'. This implies that, in the view of the statistician's office, the murder of a woman as a result of domestic or intimate-partner violence is also somehow not gender-related and therefore not a femicide. It is quite frankly bizarre, incoherent and damaging.

Another casualty of Russell's definition can be seen within the police services. When I first requested 'femicide' data from the South African Police Service, I was politely informed that they could not assist me because their Crime Administration System allowed them to register either murder, murder of a police official or farm murder, but that their system could not tell me whether a female victim 'was murdered on account of being a woman'.[17] To get the information I required, I eventually had to request data on all female homicides for my research period, and manually remove the murders of infants and children to determine the total reported [adult] femicide cases.

Later, I discovered that even in this instance I was quite fortunate in that, in South Africa, most of these killings were reported to the police. In India, women often died in 'accidents' involving cooking stoves and kerosene fuel or exploding gas cylinders – but which were actually deliberate murders, mostly related to dowry disputes (even though dowries have been illegal in the country since the 1960s) and which are so ubiquitous that they are even known as 'bride burnings'. The spectrum of 'dowry harassment' also sometimes involves pressuring the bride to commit suicide, which might also be overlooked as a murder. In 2015, it was estimated that in India nearly 21 women *a day* were killed due to dowry demands – and those were just the reported or known cases.

While Russell's definition of femicide was important for its time and was essential in defining the murder of women as a *feature* (not a bug) of patriarchal societies, I believe that its narrow terms have become not just redundant but actually obstructive in the study of violence against women. This is because we do not always know who the perpetrator is of a female homicide; and because, even when the perpetrator is known, the issue of a priori motive is extremely complex; and it is also most certainly because indicators of gender-based violence are equally complex, and differ vastly across cultures, communities and countries. Dowry killings, honour killings and killings resulting from female genital mutilation are common in certain areas and cultures (India, Pakistan and Somalia, for example) and uncommon in others. In South Africa, too, there are sub-types of femicides that, while not exclusive to the region, have specific features and statistical prominence different to the profile/s of all other regions. These include, for example, family killings (where a female and her children are murdered by her intimate partner – who then often commits suicide following the murders) or the 'corrective' rape and murder of black lesbians.

There is no single universal version of what constitutes hate crimes against women, nor do most countries even include femicide as a category of crime other than possibly murder. This means that, for the most part, there is very little data on femicide – mostly this is because this information is simply not collected, but it is also because femicide is not recognised as a specific crime category, and because there is no consensus on its definition. Even when data is available, the type of data may differ greatly between regions and sources because each may have slightly different criteria. So, one country might capture all female homicides; another might only list females who are killed by their intimate partners. The South African Police Service provides data for the numbers of women aged eighteen years and older who are murdered – but the South African Medical Research Council's definition of femicide (which is also the one used in this book) includes victims aged fourteen years and older, because public health data clearly indicates that once females start engaging in or having the potential to engage in 'romantic'-type relationships with adult men (and I don't necessarily mean relationships that are reciprocal), their risk profile changes.

Definitions of femicide don't just affect research and comparisons. They also impact how police and criminal justice systems might handle prospective femicide cases, from how a police investigation is conducted, to how a court case is prosecuted. If unnatural female deaths referred to inquest were treated as potential femicides, would the police look for different types of evidence more quickly rather than taking sometimes months, at which time important forensic evidence is lost or degraded – and would this help to decrease the number of cases with missing or incomplete data?

For these reasons and more, I strongly believe that a more pragmatic approach and a broad but specific definition of femicide is required – to include the homicides of all adult females, by any perpetrator and for any reason, and to include victims from the age of fourteen years and older because of their risk profile while, at the same time, excluding victims aged thirteen years and younger because of their distinct epidemiological risk profiles.

As I mentioned above, the definitions that I use are in line with those used by the South African Medical Research Council in its second national femicide study conducted in 2009,[18] in which 'femicide' is equivalent to 'female homicide', and where 'women' include females aged fourteen years and older because very few dating or sexually intimate relationships occur before this age.[19]

> **Definition of terms**[20]
> **Female homicide:** Killing of women
> **Femicide:** Killing of women

Gender-based homicide: Homicide with distinct gendered circumstances, such as intimate-partner femicide and suspected rape homicide

Intimate femicide/intimate-partner femicide: Killing of women by intimate partners (i.e. a current or former husband/boyfriend, same-sex partner, or rejected would-be lover)

Non-intimate femicide: Killing of women by someone other than an intimate partner (stranger, family member, acquaintance, etc.)

Suspected rape homicide: Homicide occurring with a sexual component identified during investigation.

What this book aims to do is explore and explain these different categories or types of femicides through real stories – the stories we know about, in any event, which means the stories that have been reported in the media – and through a discussion of some of the many detailed research papers on homicide and femicide that have been produced over the last 25 years and which give us probably the most detailed national picture of femicide that exists in any country in the world. While we should be proud of our genuinely ground-breaking and world-class research, of course we also have to acknowledge that the reason we are experts in this completely shitty sub-set of violence studies is because too many people are dying.

In this book I refer to several key studies that provide a baseline for understanding the phenomenon of femicide in South Africa. These include two autopsy- and [police] docket-based national studies on femicide conducted by the South African Medical Research Council, for the years 1999 and 2009 (a third study is being planned for the 2019 calendar year – the studies are performed retrospectively), and studies using data from the Medical Research Council's National Injury Mortality Surveillance System (NIMSS). Many of the papers based on these studies are available freely online, and in various formats (from summarised policy briefs to more detailed academic papers). In an attempt not to bog down the discussion with too many numbers and tables I have not, for the most part, replicated this data – but I would encourage you to read them for yourself. The book includes extensive references, and I hope you will consider them as a recommended reading list.

Where I refer to my own research, this is primarily based on my doctoral thesis looking at South African media coverage of femicide, which is also available to read from the University of the Witwatersrand's website. What my thesis looks at (and this book is hopefully proof of) is how media coverage of murder can be integrated with other data to create a broader and deeper understanding of violent crime – but, at the same time, acknowledging how the media's coverage of femicide has tended to create a typically narrow and shallow understanding of the phenomenon instead.

3. Urban legends

In late 2018 there was a sudden spike in news reports of children being abducted in South Africa. Several of the stories quoted data from the NGO Missing Children South Africa, repeating claims that a child went missing in South Africa every five hours – even though this statement had been corrected two years earlier by fact-checking organisation Africa Check, which found that missing children under the age of eighteen were only reported every ten hours, on average, and that many of these missing kids, including children who had gotten lost in a mall, or had gone to a friend's house without telling their parents, were safely found within a few hours.[1] (Disclosure: I used to work at Africa Check, but was not involved in this particular report.)

Sometime in August 2018, someone on one of the (way too many) WhatsApp groups I was in shared a video of what they claimed was an attempted student abduction in an unnamed South African suburb. I didn't pay much attention until, a few days later, another community WhatsApp group put out a formal alert about an increased risk for child abductions, warning parents that they should be extra vigilant.

When I read the alert, something about its content didn't ring true. Partly this was because it claimed that kidnappings and child trafficking were both on the increase in South Africa, and I had a strong suspicion that at the very least the latter – the claim about child trafficking – wasn't true, because of another Africa Check report. A few years earlier, I had been peripherally involved in several meetings where we had discussed the issue of child trafficking with a representative from members of the travel industry.

25

This was around the time when then Minister of Home Affairs Malusi Gigaba introduced new legislation forcing parents with minors travelling to and from South Africa to produce their children's unabridged birth certificates together with their passports, allegedly in a bid to reduce cross-border child trafficking – which, the department claimed, was as high as 30 000 victims a year (although their own data showed that only 23 victims had been reported in the preceding three-year period). Africa Check had gone on to publish several reports which found that most claims about the topic grossly exaggerated the available data.

At the time, I also understood that the majority of what we would consider child trafficking was domestic in nature – South African children being trafficked from one city to another, from rural to urban areas, either for work, or other worse things, including sex trafficking. Because there was no border control involved, this kind of trafficking was not well documented and tended to include a high number of poor black victims, certainly not middle-class suburban toddlers and youth who were the subjects of the WhatsApp panic.

Still, as I had been spending most of my time of late researching violence against women, not children, I reasoned that there might have been some changes I had not been aware of. I contacted colleagues who worked with security and crime data and asked if they had heard anything about increases in child kidnappings or trafficking. My queries revealed that there had been an increase in kidnappings overall, but that this included both adult and child kidnappings. (Abduction, in South African law, has a different meaning, which is basically unlawfully taking a minor child from his or her custodian, with the intention of 'enabling someone to marry or have sexual intercourse with that minor'. Kidnapping is 'unlawfully and intentionally depriving a person of his or her freedom of movement and/or, if such person is a child, the custodians of their control over the child'.[2])

Although the breakdown of kidnapping data wasn't entirely

clear, it did seem like there had been a specific increase in adult kidnappings, a number of which were linked to foreign nationals in South Africa who were kidnapped either for ransom, or to force repayment of debts. Child kidnappings, my colleagues explained, were mostly linked to domestic disputes – divorced parents taking a child without the other's permission, or returning a child late after a weekend in contravention of a custody agreement.

But nobody had or knew of any new data that suggested there was an increase in stranger abductions or kidnappings of children, or in child trafficking for that matter. Eventually I contacted the community organisation that had issued the alert and asked where they had sourced their data. I was told that it came from child trafficking NGOs, and from 'the media'.

For different reasons, both of these were a red flag for me. The NGO part because, as important as non-governmental agencies are, I had encountered a number of misleading claims made by NGOs in a misguided attempt to draw attention to their causes. The Missing Children example I mentioned at the beginning was just one; Africa Check had also fact-checked various other organisations that had overstated data on everything from rape statistics to suicide figures to hearing loss.

A bigger concern, though, was using media reports as a reliable original source about crime in particular.

I have worked as a journalist, editor and publisher for well over 20 years, and as much as I have worked with many fantastic, incredible, devoted journalists and editors, I also know that newspapers only cover a fraction of the crime stories that take place. Even in the best work environments there are also multiple processes of selection or rejection and reporter and editor bias when it comes to which stories will or won't be given space on the page – and sometimes it's not even deliberate; it's just because the pages are already filled with other stories. This is coupled with the inevitable errors that occur, sometimes due to negligence or apathy, but often just because reporters are overworked and underpaid and have fewer and fewer resources and support structures.

Research into media coverage of crime – including my own work on South African media – has consistently found that media reports of crime usually have little resemblance to the reality of crime itself, although, at the same time, news media is ironically where most people learn about crime, particularly violent crime, and how to understand it.

So when I heard that the 'source' of the panic about child abductions was based on media reports rather than, say, police information (I'd also contacted the South African Police Service to ask about the alert), I expressed my concern. A few days later, SAPS issued a statement asking families and communities not to share unverified viral video footage, suggesting that the videos might have been re-enactments or even hoaxes and adding that none of them had been reported to the police – and that there was some doubt as to whether the events had even taken place in South Africa, or were legitimate crimes.

But, once it's out there, false information is a bit like a zombie. It refuses to die completely.

About a month later I came across a post on social media from a Cape Town-based mother who claimed to have reliable information about a three-year-old child who had nearly been abducted at a popular Winelands family destination. She wrote that the child had been found, drugged and passed out in the bathroom, after a three-hour lockdown of the venue. In a separate tweet, she added that the kidnappers had used earplugs so the toddler wasn't able to hear his parents calling for him.

It didn't just sound like every parent's worst nightmare. It sounded like an urban legend (I highly recommend reading or following Snopes.com for these kind of debunks) and, like any good urban legend, it was spreading fast – with hundreds of likes and re-posts.

My fact-checker mode kicked in again. I Googled the name of the venue to see if anything had been reported in the news. Nothing. I also checked on social media to see if anyone had tweeted about the place being 'locked down' (generally people don't like being forcibly locked into public places, or even being stuck in a traffic jam without complaining on Twitter). Again there was nothing. Eventually I called the venue and spoke to the manager. She was polite and helpful, and very emphatic that there had been no attempted child abduction or missing child discovered in the bathroom.

Back on Twitter, I engaged with the original poster and told her the venue said there had been no such incident. I added that the story she'd heard sounded suspiciously like a series of American child abduction hoaxes (Snopes had covered a number of them, over several years), all of which had involved a young child being allegedly abducted in a public place and either being drugged and fitted with earplugs, sometimes having their appearance changed, in order to stop parents from finding them, and which ended miraculously with the child being found after a lockdown.

Sad to say, my self-righteous rightness didn't go down well, and the mother wasn't persuaded. She insisted that she'd had the information from her 'friend's sister-in-law's best friend' (you honestly couldn't make it up, could you?). She then suggested that perhaps the winelands venue *and* the police were participating in a cover-up.

Dear reader, it was not a cover-up. It was a hoax or an urban legend, whichever one you like. And we all fall for them, at one time or another.

Well-meaning or not, the problem with scares and hoaxes like this is that they often wind up creating very real fear and panic – in addition to taking up real people's time, or using up already scarce police and other resources. They also perpetuate myths around who is vulnerable, who poses a threat, and (this is the really important bit) they detract from the real stories that take place every single day.

A few weeks before the fake winelands incident, nine-year-old

Previledge Mabvongwe from Bloekombos in Kraaifontein, a mere 20 minutes away from the luxury wine farm, was found dead on a dump site after going missing three days earlier. Although the young girl's murder was reported in multiple news stories, news of her abduction garnered little reaction on social media. This is because, bluntly, a missing black child from a lower-income area will always attract less interest than a story about a missing middle-class child. And it's the former children who are most at risk of daily violence.

When I scratched a little deeper, I also discovered some irregularities in the newspaper reports that had been circulating about child abductions at the time – which, themselves, had provoked the kind of fear that had made an otherwise well-meaning suburban mom post a fake abduction scare online.

A month earlier, the office of the premier of the Eastern Cape had told newspapers that there had been four 'child abductions' in the area of Whittlesea, south-west of Queenstown. This information was reported in the leading local paper and then almost immediately picked up in news stories across the country, reported as part of what was allegedly a spate of child abductions.

Except, two days after the original statement, the Eastern Cape police said that the alleged abductions had taken place *three years earlier*, and had involved the abduction of one teenager (not four) and three adults. The premier's office doubled down and insisted that, according to the Department of Social Services, there had been four child abductions in the area, and they did not want to jeopardise a 'sensitive' investigation.

Re-reading the news coverage it was apparent that, with the exception of the newspaper that reported on its own error, many of the newspapers and even radio stations covering the alleged incident hadn't bothered to confirm the information for themselves; they'd just taken it from other news reports and repeated it verbatim. I noticed belatedly that some news features about the (non-existent) Whittlesea abductions even embellished the story, adding that the four imaginary abductees had been taken to a place of safety.

Almost none of the other papers or pages that had included the Whittlesea abductions in earlier reports carried anything about the subsequent correction. This is something that is common across media, and social media. Researcher Craig Silverman once described it as a 'Law of Incorrect Tweets', that initial, inaccurate information will be [shared] more than any subsequent correction.[3]

One of the things that this book will show you is that the media is a very fallible and often quite flawed source of information about violent crime. Even when media does its job well, the crime news that gets published usually only provides a very narrow (and highly curated) slice of a much bigger picture.

Having said this, that slice can still be useful.

When used correctly, media reports can be a very rich source of information about the crimes themselves, and about the society in which these crimes takes place – because newspapers are full of indicators that let us know who or what was considered valuable and important or what was considered a threat, not just in a physical place, but even at a particular point in time.

Forty years ago, it was socially and professionally acceptable, by and large, to make disparaging or belittling comments about women, about homosexuals, about sex workers, and so on. Forty years ago in South Africa it was not only acceptable but encouraged for most English and Afrikaans newspapers to write stories in terms and tones that sanctioned the apartheid regime and its policies of separate development. All of these societal biases impacted on the stories that the mainly white- and male-owned media chose to report on.

Today, while racism, sexism, homophobia and other bigotries are still very much part of our societal make-up, the language and content of commercial media increasingly (but not always) reflects a more progressive and inclusive environment, where racism is both proscribed and taboo,[4] where pejorative words for LGBTI individuals or for sex workers are avoided. Over time, this has also meant that the media has consciously attempted to become more inclusive in the types of stories and subjects it covers, although this often still skews along racial lines and along class lines – by which I mean that a suburban crime story will almost always have more 'news value' than a crime story in an informal settlement.

As a media researcher and a crime/violence researcher, I use media archives in part to understand how these narratives around crime and violence are constructed and perpetuated over time, and how (or if) or when these narratives change. By matching this with other contextual and historical data – such as when new laws were introduced, or other important national or global events took place – I can build up a fairly rich and multi-dimensional picture of the past, a bit like using the dinosaur blood trapped in an amber-clad mosquito in Michael Crichton's *Jurassic Park*.

Also, crime reporting *does* have value as a record of crime, just so long as you don't mistake it for an accurate, comprehensive or impartial record.

Digital archives and digitally enabled search functionality have made it possible to select and build quite large sets of media-based data, cross-referenced to thousands of news articles[5] (this is not 'big data'; if anything it's small- to medium-sized, and micro-sized compared to the world of data; but it is incrementally bigger than many traditional media studies, which are often based on quite small samples).

The data in these articles can provide us with information that is not available in the police's annual crime statistics, or in mortuary-based studies, and that is information about the victim, who she was, and more details about how she died (which may also be important when it comes to analysis of how violent crime happens). News stories also sometimes tell us about perpetrators – not only their relationship to the victim, but their alleged motives – and about the justice system: were there any arrests, was there a court case, was anyone convicted, what was the sentence?

As long as you understand that the data provided by news stories has limitations, it can provide added perspective and a context that statistics and epidemiological studies alone cannot, and which may help us more fully understand what violence is, why it happens, and why it happens in certain ways at certain times and in certain places.

Media coverage of crime can also supplement (or even stand in for) sparse or non-existent statistics, for example, in regions where there is insufficient bureaucratic infrastructure to collect reliable crime data (which is a reality in many parts of the Global South) – or where there is bureaucratic or societal obstruction to providing transparent data about crime and violence (ditto). As I explained earlier, even data around murders are not necessarily consistent or consistently collected across the globe, and it is possible that using media reports as one type of source might help to make data about violence and crime easier to gather and compare. Because most media stories are 'public' information (I'm not talking about paywalls here), there are also fewer ethical challenges in gathering this kind of data, which makes it more accessible to a broader range of researchers.

What do we really (think we) know about crime?

My early research on media coverage of femicide tried to answer a fairly broad question: why did people think the way they did about violent crime in general? In particular, I wanted to try and understand why certain groups of people (in my case, many white South Africans) had fixed and often false ideas of how women died and who was killing them. This had been shown quite starkly when myself, Lisa Vetten, Africa Check and the Medical Research Council were charged with alleged hate speech against white men for, respectively, statements and peer-reviewed studies in which we had variously noted that white women (and all South African women) were at greater risk of fatal violence from their intimate partners than from strangers (this is discussed in more detail later on).

I suspected that one of the reasons why these groups, in particular sections of right-wing Afrikaans-speaking white South Africans, subscribed to certain, often racist, worldviews wasn't only because they held on to their bigotry like a child with a safety blanket, but also because the news coverage they were exposed to somehow encouraged this narrative about femicide. My data would later show that I was correct, and that Afrikaans-language media in particular almost exclusively covered white victims of fatal violence. But, back in 2013, I only had hunches about the role media played in creating a particular version of the South African 'crime story'.

Over many years as a journalist, and particularly during the years I worked at Africa Check, I had regularly encountered myths, urban legends and hoaxes, like the child abduction stories I discussed earlier.

What my work at Africa Check taught me in particular was that false information (whether it was shared with good intentions or not) almost always had negative consequences. It was what was preventing parents from immunising their children against preventable, potentially fatal childhood illnesses like measles and polio. It was what drove ongoing violence against foreigners (a combination of misinformation and prejudice). It was what was stopping people from realising that man-made climate change was a reality, and a threat.

Misinformation about crime had two primary negative outcomes: one was that it often re-enforced stereotypes (usually linked to race) about who was to blame for crime and who was most at risk, and this perpetuated existing biases and created or entrenched suspicion and division within communities. These elements frequently congealed into messy mobs (kangaroo courts or vigilante justice), or group panics. Misinformation also taught people to hate their neighbours instead of building stronger communities.

A second outcome was that, because people made choices based on faulty if not entirely false information, the solutions that were put in place to combat or prevent crime were flawed – because they were based on the wrong data, and because they were based on people's biases which had been propped up by the same questionable information. As my former Africa Check boss Peter Cunliffe-Jones used to say, poor information can only contribute to poor decision-making.

In the nineteenth century Victorian physicians believed that cholera outbreaks and various other epidemics were caused by a 'miasma', noxious and dirty air produced by anything from rotting vegetables to decaying corpses and sewage, or indeed a combination of any of these. When a London anaesthetist named John Snow (who, it appears, *did* know something) suggested that cholera was somehow linked with water, so strong was the belief in the miasmatic theory – which, its exponents said, could only be remedied by *fresh air* – that Snow's hypothesis was rejected by the English parliament's Committee for Scientific Enquiry.[6] Italian anatomist Filippo Pacini and German microbiologist Robert Koch would separately go on to discover the waterborne bacteria *Vibrio cholerae*, which was responsible for the disease. But even then, it would take many years before the miasma believers would concede their theories and remedies were (a) wrong and (b) useless. During this period, of course, many people died because the 'experts' were prescribing clean air instead of clean water.

Don't think for a moment that some of our contemporary theories about crime aren't as foolish. I still regularly encounter neighbours and community members who believe criminals use colour-coded rubbish (or sometimes chalk signals) to leave 'crime' signals about potential targets. So, red litter means something like 'beware', while green rubbish allegedly means the house is an easy target.

Firstly, there is no evidence of this actually happening anywhere (in the world). Secondly, most thieves tend *not* to advertise their prospects to other criminals. Also, they generally use cellphones to communicate with each other, not an old Fanta bottle. Not that I would discourage anyone from cleaning up litter outside their house, but as a crime prevention strategy it's pretty ineffective. (Ditto CCTV cameras, and hundreds of other high-tech and expensive gadgets that do a great job making private security companies even more profitable but do little for our actual safety.)

The other thing is that making up stories to make sense of the world is part of human nature. We come up with theories and share anecdotes about crime, and about who commits crime, because this is how we are able to function as a society – we need to find meaning, we want to believe in some sense of order instead of chaos, accidents or just random bad luck.

But we are also sometimes mischievous, malicious and deceitful. We are titillated by scary stories, real or not. We say bad things (whether they are true or not) knowing they will cause pain for other people. We lie about events, to gain attention, to make ourselves sound better, or to cover up our own mistakes. We don't like violence to be too close. It should be something that *other* people do, not us. And, ideally, it should happen to other people – to *those types* of people – not to us. We use falsehood and fiction to deflect. We enjoy monster stories because these stories tell us that the Bad Things lurk *outside* our communities, not within our walls. And to be fair, this form of denial is also a necessary coping mechanism without which we might be overwhelmed, particularly in a country like South Africa where violence does stalk us, every day, at home and in the streets, in fields, in parking lots, in post offices . . .

These are some of the reasons that help explain *why* people may think the way they think about crime.

What I was interested in examining was how media played a role in that eco-system. Most people don't get their knowledge of crime from reading police statistics or going to court. They get it from the newspapers, or the radio, or TV, and they get it from friends and neighbours and co-workers who got it from other newspapers, TV shows etc. Even the gossip and anecdotes we share are usually informed by or contextualised within what we have read or seen in the news. Newspapers or news sites tell us not only what crimes have been happening, but they also tell us which crimes matter – this is a reciprocal relationship, because newspapers also choose to focus on stories or crimes that they think will matter to their readers.

To study how media told the story of femicide in South Africa, I spent five years building a database of South African news coverage of one year's worth of femicides. All of the murders took place between 1 April 2012 and 31 March 2013 (the police reporting year); the news coverage was from any time after the murder, until August 2017, when I stopped adding to my database. In this way, I identified 408[7] femicides and cross-referenced them to 5 778 media articles (this included duplications, for example, when one article mentioned two or more victims – the article would be entered again under each victim's name; if these are excluded there were 3 278 unique stories).

That same year, some 2 587 female homicides were reported to the police (where the victims were aged fourteen years or older). This meant that less than 20 per cent of the actual female homicide cases that had taken place during that period were ever mentioned in the press.

When I started to analyse the profiles of the victims and incidents that were covered in the media, it also became clear that the media constructed a very particular narrative about femicide in South Africa, which often deviated from the epidemiological profile of these murders. News reporting tended to over-emphasise white victims and elderly victims, and under-reported intimate partner violence and coloured victims. Possibly because Gauteng and the Western Cape have the largest number of media outlets, murders in these regions were also more reported than in other provinces. There were many other differences, some of which I will discuss in the later chapters of this book.

I'd like to add a note on how I built my database, because while this isn't necessarily everyone's area of interest, I have always emphasised that, in research, how you collect and build data influences the type of data you create. I still get frustrated with studies – of media samples, or murder cases – where there is no transparency and no discussion around how or where the data was selected. I read papers that say 'we used a computer programme to search for stories mentioning female homicides in [this part of America]', but don't say which newspapers were included in or excluded from the search, or which words the computer programme used, or how they tested whether or not the programme was accurate. I saw the importance of this myself when I tested my own results, which had primarily used one media archive/clippings service (Sabinet, discussed below), and compared this with a similar survey using a completely different media archive (LexisNexis).

The Sabinet SA Media news clippings service was started in 1977 at the University of the Free State and was purchased by the South African Bibliographic and Information Network or Sabinet, a commercial library, cataloguing and information management service, in 2014. The titles included in the press clippings service 'represent influential media voices in South Africa'.[8] The current South African media database includes 39 print titles, of which 31 are English and 8 in Afrikaans, and the archive extends to 156 titles (88 in English, 65 in Afrikaans, 1 dual medium, and 1 in Dutch). For the older news archive material in this book, I have primarily used the Sabinet service, which is also why I usually only go back as far as 1977.

Sabinet receives newspapers/publications in print and digital format (previously these would have all been hard copies). These copies are manually reviewed by a team at Sabinet, who identify articles for inclusion using a rubric based on subject or theme and content type. Suitable articles will be flagged to be added to the database. For example, under the subject of 'Justice, Safety and Security', the Sabinet team will look for articles that include content on:

> Safety; crime; murders; rape; police; coverage of well-known court cases, e.g. Oscar Pistorius, Panayiotou; Krejcir; cover reported cases as complete as possible especially where names are mentioned; farm murders; hate speech cases; rescues from mountains, oceans, rivers; earthquakes; assisted death case; smuggling; drugs; shootings; bribes; children's rights; NSRI; illegal immigrants[9]

Currently, print articles are scanned and the text is captured using the Abbyy FineReader Optical Character Recognition engine. Articles are uploaded to the South African media database six weeks after the date of publication.

Sabinet's SA media archive represents the most comprehensive news clippings archive and service in South Africa, and, unlike the LexisNexis media service, features media articles in both English and Afrikaans. But it should be evident that 39 titles is not a comprehensive database of South African news media. Sabinet's representation of 'influential media voices' by definition excludes the majority of smaller news titles, particularly local and community news publications that are available across South Africa (many of these titles are centralised under the ownership of big media groups such as Caxton and Media24, but there are also a number of independent publishers of local/community news, which are also members of print or news media organisations). The Sabinet clippings service also does not include digital/online-only content platforms, like News24, nor any online-only content posted by either print or broadcast media (radio stations, the SABC, and so on).

When I built my media coverage database I tried to develop an approach that was systematic but which could also cover or include the largest possible number of sources. Most large commercial news archives (for example, the archives owned by large media companies such as Independent Media, Tiso Blackstar – formerly Times Media Limited and many other names – or Caxton Media) were and are, sadly, quite useless for any serious systemic archive research. Between the time I started my work in 2013 and when I submitted my thesis in 2019, hundreds of archive links I had previously used no longer existed. This wasn't about paywalls (although those, too, posed a number of problems), but because, in the interim, many of the publishers had updated the front ends of their websites and, in the process, had simply removed and even possibly deleted all their older records. Even for those that did have some version of an online archive, the back end was usually not suitably structured for systemic archive searches – by this I mean, I could search for stories that came up with a match for 'murder', but I couldn't separate these by year, even when I entered specific years into the search bar. This is a longer discussion for another time, but the complete lack of investment in digital archiving of news is going to be a major headache for future researchers.

Anyway, because the commercial news sites were so difficult to search for specific dates, I started my archive research on the Sabinet media clippings website, where I could delimit my search not only by year but by month. My first exercise was to search through Sabinet news clippings from 01 April 2012 to the end of May 2013, to try and identify news reports of female homicides that had taken place during my study period (I extended my search to May, reasoning that this would allow a buffer for murders that may not have been reported immediately).

I didn't obviously search or read every single story in the clippings archive, but used the Sabinet search function to select stories that had a positive match (word or tag) for 'murder' or 'moord'. Reading the various murder stories, I would exclude reports that were male homicides or child murders and excluded murders that took place outside of my specified time frame. To break my search into manageable sections, I completed this exercise month by month for the research period. This was a fairly painstaking process (there were 600 news stories that included a match for 'murder' in April 2012 alone), but it was a necessarily broad approach because almost none of the stories referred to 'femicide' or even 'female homicide', even when there was a female victim. Most of them didn't even use the word 'female', but rather one of multiple synonyms – mother, wife, sister, daughter, aunt, niece, grandmother, gogo, granny, girlfriend, widow, and so on.

When I did find matching reports, I would log details about the victim and the incident, which I used later to search for additional stories and information. After I had completed this process on Sabinet, I tried as best I could to follow similar processes on commercial news sites (that is, searching 'murder' and 'April 2012'); for smaller publications like local/community newspapers, I would read through an entire year's worth of issues, and search for the phrase 'murder' or 'moord' in each file.

Once I had collected a list of victims' names and/or incident details, I went back and searched again through both the Sabinet archives and online news platforms (mostly using Google) to identify further matches. In many instances I would find a story about the victim or the murder, in which another murder would be referenced. For example, there would be a concluding paragraph saying, 'Last week another pensioner was murdered in her flat on the other side of town' – which would give me an additional incident to log.

In the end, my media survey included articles from 177 different publications – all considered to be formal or commercial news publications. I defined 'commercial' media as content that was produced by formal or professional news media organisations, either at local, regional or national level, including professional community news media organisations. This included publications or platforms that fell under the Press Council of South Africa, such as the members of umbrella organisations like Print and Digital Media South Africa. The reason for selecting 'commercial' or 'professional' outlets was, first, to limit the number of eligible titles; but it was also, deliberately, to distinguish news media content – which falls under a clear Press Code – from other content which does not. Although the lines between who is and who is not 'a journalist' are increasingly ambiguous, there is still recognition of differences between news media and non-news media, and the criteria above, while not necessarily perfect, offer some form of replicable delineation.

This definition of 'commercial media' excluded:

- publication in books;
- publication in non-news media (for example, academic publications, educational publications, governmental publications, press releases);
- publication on social media (including Facebook and Twitter);
- publication on a private blog or web page;
- publication on a public or commercial web page that was not considered a formal/commercial news media outlet (for example, content which was published by lobby or activist groups or by institutions);
- non-South African media.

Social media was specifically excluded because, firstly, it was not news media as I defined it – although news media often post information on social media, it is not typically a primary news platform in itself – and, secondly, given the sheer volume of social media posts versus news media articles, it would have been impossible for 'social media' to be studied in any comparably meaningful way in this study. (Most studies of social media content are either so small that there is a question as to whether their sample sizes can be seen as representative of any larger group, and are extremely vulnerable to selection bias; or they are so large as to disallow for any in-depth textual analysis.)

Anecdotally, social media conversations around femicide in South Africa also tend to be strongly based around rhetoric – we must 'do something' – and offer little information compared to what is usually contained in news reports. This is not to say there is no potential future value in studying social media content, particularly for sentiment, but this content is markedly different from formal 'news'.

In the final year of my research, I tested my own initial survey results by performing the same search process but using a different media archive service, LexisNexis, which had a much smaller sample of news titles but which utilised a different search platform and archiving process. The two databases had 170 victims in common; 238 femicide victims were in my (Sabinet-based) media survey that did not appear in the LexisNexis results; but there were 48 victims that I found in the LexisNexis archives which I had not previously identified in my other searches. What this showed me was that individual media clippings or archive services could have unknown or unidentified limitations, and that the best way to accommodate this and to strengthen media-derived data in future was to simply include multiple such sets or services, rather than only rely on one.

For this book I've used a slightly different approach, based on my original academic research, but looking back at over 40 years of crime reporting on female murders in South Africa. Although I started almost the same way – searching for stories that were a match for 'murder' – the results that I found were remarkably different in some aspects and surprisingly similar in others. Some of these convergences and divergences were things I had expected to find but I was still pleasantly surprised that my media search showed them up so clearly. Others were unanticipated but, when I went over other historical data and media stories, made odd 'sense' (not to be confused with rightness or justice, because there is a lot of injustice in this book).

What I have tried to do is use case studies drawn from these media files to illustrate and explain a sort of history and, where possible, to give an overview of femicide in modern South Africa. Where other data such as crime statistics or studies on particular types of crimes are available, I have tried to include these too, and used multiple and mixed sources to build up a mosaic of information that show us the bigger picture of femicide without blurring out the smaller details. Because it is important to keep in mind that those smaller details were once a life.

PART ONE

Intimate femicide

4. 'A love story gone wrong': Finding the words

One morning in June 1977, in the upmarket Johannesburg suburb of Houghton, a 37-year-old attorney named Hadley Kavin 'erupted into a psychotic rage' and shot dead his 32-year-old wife Denise together with two of their children, 11-year-old Adele and 6-year-old Lance. He also shot a third child, a 10-year-old daughter, but the bullet entered her head and blinded her for life instead of killing her.[1]

Newspaper reports at the time commented that Kavin had been 'in a state of depression'.[2] He was rumoured to have had mounting debts exacerbated by a recent gambling spree. Stories recounted how Kavin felt like an under-performer compared to an over-achieving twin brother, and that he had never fully recovered from the humiliation of failing Standard Three. All of this, the writers speculated, had turned the husband and father into a 'walking time bomb'.

After Hadley was arrested, he was admitted to a mental institution as a patient of the State President. He was tried for murder in October that same year. The case was heard in the Rand Supreme Court under Justice Irving Steyn, a judge who handed down death sentences in a third of all the eligible cases he heard[3] before the death sentence was suspended in the early 1990s. Justice Steyn found that Kavin had been mentally ill at the time of the killings and was therefore not criminally culpable for his actions. The judge publicly stated that Kavin had killed his family 'for love – albeit misguided' and acquitted him of murder.[4]

In South Africa in the late 1970s, as in many other parts of the world, there was still very little acknowledgement of the inter-personal violence that took place in 'private' spaces, particularly in the home. In fact, 'domestic violence' implied something completely different than what it does today[5]. In apartheid South Africa in particular, the term implied civil unrest or political violence, specifically the threat of domestic terrorism.

Just one year after the student uprisings of June 1976, white suburban South Africa remained on a particularly narrow-minded knife's edge. In 1977 there were a spate of bombings across the central Transvaal, including at the Carlton Centre, and at the Germiston and Benoni police stations. A week after Denise Kavin and her children were murdered, two civilians working at a John Orr warehouse near Goch Street were shot and killed by MK cadres Monty Motloung and Solomon Mahlangu, who had opened fire on them while attempting to escape the police. In September of that year Steve Biko would be found dead in a Pretoria prison cell, his torture and murder subsequently whitewashed by the regime. Two months later, in November 1977, National Party member and parliamentary candidate Robert Smit would be shot and killed with his wife Jean-Cora the night before the country's general elections in what was later believed to be a state-sanctioned hit designed to prevent Smit from revealing information about the apartheid government's illicit finance deals. A few weeks after that, in January 1978, banned[6] political activist and academic Dr Rick Turner was assassinated at his home in Durban.

The media narrated this 'terror within' as a kind of duet, and the South African press was full of equally menacing stories about the lurking danger on our immediate and near borders. There were trade tensions with the newly independent (and, worse, socialist!) Mozambique led by FRELIMO's Samora Machel. In Rhodesia an embattled Ian Smith was attempting to hold on to white minority rule through the end of a protracted bush war. In South-West Africa[7] and its northern Ovamboland border with Angola, South African security forces battled with Namibian freedom fighters from SWAPO and Angola's Cuban- and Soviet-backed MPLA.[8] On South Africa's other border, with Botswana, four South African Defence Force soldiers were accused of swimming across the Limpopo River and gang-raping a seven-month-pregnant woman.[9]

Newspaper stories mentioning terrorism outnumbered stories about murder and crime by ten to one, essentially framing the country's entire understanding of violence through the lens of a country at war. Which, in many senses, it was.

It was also this type of violence that contextualised (and enabled) violence in the home.

One report in *The Citizen*[10] from August 1977 describes how a Mrs Lida Marx, wife of one Major Nico Marx, had become proficient with firearms while spending time with her husband at the Madimbo military training base near the border between South Africa and (now) Zimbabwe and Mozambique. It was there that Mrs Marx, 'for the first time, realised the dangers threatening our country and that women must be able to take action in a crisis situation as well'.[11] On their return to Germiston, the Marxes established the Germiston Civil Defence Shooting Club for housewives.

But a few months later, the same newspaper published a gun story with a rather less cheerful angle – asking whether South Africans were 'gun crazy'[12] and reporting that, in the eight-week period between December 1977 and January 1978, at least 33 people had died in what were described as 'family and lover quarrel' shooting incidents in the Witwatersrand, Vaal Triangle and Pretoria areas. At least five of the victims, it said, were the female intimate partners of the killers. Fourteen of the deaths were suicides (by the perpetrators).

Sam Bloomberg, a psychologist from Suicides Anonymous, told *The Citizen* that a large part of the blame could be attributed to the 'military preparedness' of the offenders. Bloomberg mentioned a recent report which had found that one in four white

South Africans owned a firearm. This, he said, was a concern because people armed themselves with ease, but subsequently exhibited a 'low tolerance level to problems'.[13]

What could be done about this threat? Well, at the time, experts suggested that the responsibility for defusing the 'walking time bomb' of an armed and deadly spouse would best lie with the woman he was potentially going to kill.

In a separate article, a 'Johannesburg psychiatrist' (who was not identified by name) told the *Sunday Express* that the Kavin tragedy could have been avoided if Denise had only 'had the capacity of mind to note [her husband's] changes of behaviour and moods in the months leading up to her death, and had the presence of mind to do something about it'.[14] Bloomberg, the psychologist again (an exceedingly popular commentator, as we shall later see), added that, in his view sexual inadequacy was one of the biggest factors leading to family violence. He cautioned that wives often exacerbated the problem by goading or teasing their husbands or withdrawing from them. What should a woman do when confronted by a partner who was in 'a muddle' or was a 'bad loser'? Bloomberg suggested that women must 'bend backwards to prevent a flare-up even if she is very angry herself.'[15]

The director of the Pretoria Marriage Council, Mrs Bea Conroy, gave similar advice in a later story in the *Pretoria News*[16] on the problem of husbands who beat their wives. 'The husband is automatically cast as the villain of the piece but often the woman has so provoked him that he feels his only retaliation is with his fists,' she said.

'Retaliation' also sometimes took the form of gassing, hacking and, of course, shooting family members, often before the perpetrator killed or attempted to kill himself. Over the next few years, newspapers would begin to single out the growing problem of what they started to describe as 'family murders' in South Africa.

Even there, the stories were often written as if no one in particular was to blame.

For example, in August 1983 *The Star* described how a young woman, her baby daughter and the woman's estranged husband had been killed outside an East Rand house. 'Mrs Lorraine Serfontein (22) was shot in the head, 18-month-old Natasha was shot through the heart and Mr Jan Serfontein (28) shot in the head,' the journalist wrote. It was only in the second half of the paragraph that the reporter included the important information that Mr Serfontein, whose body was 'crumpled to the ground near the body of his daughter', *was the shooter*, and had died with his gun in his hand, shooting himself in the head after shooting his estranged wife and infant child, and severely wounding another child.[17]

Or another example, again in *The Star*, from five years earlier: In a round-up of the year's worst crimes, the paper's East Rand bureau wrote that '[t]wo teenagers playing pinball in an Alberton café' had seen the proprietor and his wife shot dead. The article belatedly went on to explain that the shocked teenagers had seen 'Mrs Lorraine Pappas (30)' fall to the floor, before her husband, Peter, turned his gun on himself.[18]

By the early 1980s, most murders involving white victims were described as being 'domestic' in nature. Experts claimed that the rise in family violence was because of stress, and because men 'felt threatened by the various changes in society and also by the social changes in the status of women'.[19]

In 1984, *The Citizen* claimed that 16 of the 24 white murder victims reported in Pretoria that year had been murdered in 'family slayings'.

During the same year there were an additional 225 murders reported 'in townships surrounding the capital [Pretoria]',[20] about which little further information was provided other than that 60 per cent of these murders were stabbings and that the brigadier in charge of the then-Northern Transvaal believed that the higher murder rate in black townships was as a result of alcohol abuse.

Reading through hundreds of news reports from that time it

is clear that, while the murders of white women by their partners was reported on poorly, often in the bare minimum of words and usually in a way that either blamed the victim or excused the perpetrator, they still created or implied a level of empathy and complexity that was completely absent from the media's coverage of homicides in black communities.

In fact, news stories about black women and violence in the late 1970s and early 1980s followed a notably different arc – one which was centred almost entirely around rape.

Reliable data on sexual assault and rape is hard to obtain, then even more so than now, firstly because so many of these kinds of incidents go unreported, and also because the apartheid government was not generally interested in policing or recording violence within black communities. So it is impossible to say if the township 'rape crisis' that began to dominate newspaper headlines in the late 1970s was something new, or just a new version of an old problem (also, how many rapes do we need before we consider it a crisis?).

What news reports from the late 1970s and early 1980s do suggest is that around that time there was a shift or escalation in the way sexual violence in particular became weaponised against women in township areas, and that rape was increasingly used as both a performative and even competitive means of establishing a very twisted and violent form of masculinity and masculine power, which in turn was set within a broader environment of gradually and then rapidly increasing political violence primarily involving black men.

In the early 1970s Stanley Cohen, a South African-born criminologist working in the United Kingdom, had coined the phrase 'moral panic' to describe how societies responded or reacted to certain perceived threats. Cohen's original work looked at the phenomenon of 'mods and rockers' in 1960s Britain – knife-wielding groups who allegedly went about trashing seaside towns and fighting with each other. Cohen was interested not in the events themselves, but in how society (and, as part of that, the media) stereotyped and responded to them. Moral panics defined a 'condition, episode, person or groups of persons'[21] that represented a threat to societal *values*. The threat would be narrated, stylised and dramatised by the mass media, and mediated in turn by moral 'experts' – politicians, church officials, editors – who were also used to suggest solutions. Both the threat and the solution were often framed in ways that bolstered pre-existing power structures and relationships rather than actually resolve the (real or perceived) problem, and which did so in a way which excluded any other narratives and allowed for little in the way of nuance.

In the case of South Africa, the rape crisis was almost certainly genuine on one level, but it was narrated in deliberately hyperbolic language that entrenched stereotypes around crime, gender and race, and which played into already fragmented security hierarchies between police in the townships, local or community justice structures (the neighbourhood makgotlas), and the eroded or fractured family units that persisted as a result of apartheid's spatial planning and migrant labour policies.

The 'township rape crisis' was seemingly rooted in the events following the school boycotts that had started after June 1976. Widespread resistance and protest actions had continued long after June, mobilised by student organisations across the country, and extended well into the following year. Between September and December 1977, high schools in Soweto were closed and end-of-year exams were cancelled. As a result, tens of thousands of teenagers were left at home, instead of being in class, while their parents went to work each day. Newspapers reported that, unsupervised and bored, children were turning to drugs and booze, and participating in 'indiscriminate sex'. A representative from the South African National Council on Alcoholism told the *Weekend Post* that he estimated a third of children in Soweto were on alcohol or drugs.[22]

These behaviours, in turn, were seen to contribute to not just violence in general but rape[23] in particular. The *Daily News* reported that, between 1976 and 1977, more than three rapes a day were reported in Soweto,[24] and it was believed that the number of unreported rapes meant the true figure was even higher. An enquiry by the Human Sciences Research Council in 1977 had found that in Soweto as few as one in four serious crimes were even reported to the police. There was little trust in or affection for the apartheid force, and the police reciprocated by showing seemingly little interest in solving the growing numbers of crimes against black victims.

In lieu of effective policing, neighbourhood makgotlas tried in vain to implement crackdowns in their own areas. Shebeens were urged to close after 10 pm, and teenagers were told to be off the streets before 8 pm or risk being punished. Women, again, were made to be the responsible parties. The Naledi makgotla warned that it would sjambok (whip) all girls under eighteen who were not indoors by 8 pm.[25]

In this telling, not just rape but even consensual sex became shorthand for the 'moral decay' that was allegedly affecting black communities. Nowhere was this more apparent than in one of the most high-profile black serial murder cases of the late 1970s, that of Joseph Mahlangu, the so-called 'Lover's Lane' killer and rapist, who targeted 'courting' couples while they were parked in secluded spaces around Orlando East and Baragwanath Hospital. Mahlangu was caught and charged with 27 killings and convicted on ten counts of murder. He was sentenced to death and hanged in 1982.

Within this narrative of violence against women, though, the concept of individual violence between men and women – and, in particular, between intimate or romantic partners – only existed in a very narrow and almost exclusively white space. Black female victims of intimate partner murders were almost non-existent in the press. Where names of murdered black women did feature in newspaper stories, they were often victims of the same unspecified 'acts of violence' that were killing black men, implying that black violence was somehow communal, and only white victims experienced individual acts of killing.

In 1979, the same year as the Lover's Lane killings, an elderly woman in Dobsonville was stoned to death by a mob after her son had allegedly killed and raped his neighbour, a schoolgirl named Julia Mabuza. In August 1980 a 26-year-old woman named Constance Jabela was shot three times in the chest and killed, together with two unidentified men, in what police described as suspected faction fighting on the East Rand. (The same article briefly mentions the fatal stabbing of a Ms Shirley Moeketsi of Tembisa, by an 'alleged boyfriend'.)[26]

To be fair, because murder rates were so high in many black townships, black women did make up a relatively small proportion of black murder victims – in Soweto at least, where there is relatively much richer reported data about homicide than in many other black areas under apartheid. Information gathered by the *Rand Daily Mail,* obtained from daily crime conferences held at the Soweto police headquarters in Protea, found that in the first six months of 1980 there were 500 murders committed in the Soweto area, of which only 23 victims were women – so, less than five per cent of black murders; but, still, nearly one woman killed a week. (By comparison, there were only 25 white murder victims in *total* in greater Johannesburg during this same period.)

And, yet, there is other (admittedly slightly later) data which clearly indicates black women were experiencing substantial rates of domestic violence.

Between 1989 and 1990, researchers from the University of South Africa and the Medical Research Council[27] conducted a series of studies on non-fatal injuries resulting from inter-personal violence (as opposed to injuries from road accidents, for example). To do this, the researchers looked at hospital admissions in the casualty departments and inpatient wards at several state and private hospitals serving the Johannesburg and Soweto regions. Although the study was relatively small, it was significant because there was little other detailed demographic or epidemiological information about victims of violence at the time (particularly black victims), and it revealed perhaps the extent of the disconnect between narratives of violence as portrayed in the media, and violence as seen first-hand by nurses and doctors patching wounds.

While the study found that men made up nearly 84 per cent of injury admissions,[28] which was not particularly surprising (men are the primary perpetrators of physical violence, and also its chief victims), it also found that political violence was responsible for just ten per cent of incidents – even though political violence made up *more than half of all news coverage at the time*.[29] Although female victims made up a much smaller proportion of admissions, there was also a clear trend here: unlike male victims of violence, who were typically attacked on the street, the majority of women were 'attacked at home by a spouse or lover'.[30] More than half of the female victims included in this study were black.

If this kind of violence against women was so prevalent, why was it so invisible?

To understand this, we need to return to the issue of rape for a second. Until the early 1990s, the act of rape in South Africa was legally held to mean the 'forceable perpetration of an act of sexual intercourse on the body of a woman *not one's wife*'[31] (emphasis mine). This meant that the concept of 'rape' did not exist where the act took place between a husband and wife. In cases where a husband was charged with having sexual intercourse with his wife without her consent (that is, when he raped her), the husband would sometimes be charged with the lesser crime of assault. Even then, some legal practitioners (particularly counsel acting for men who had raped their wives) argued that a husband was entitled to use 'reasonable means, including violence, to exercise his conjugal rights'[32], in which case, they suggested, even the charge of abuse should be dropped – although it was not clear exactly how much violence was acceptable, in law, to compel a woman to have intercourse with her husband.

This interpretation was not necessarily always supported by the courts, but it was commonly invoked and argued, and the idea of prosecuting marital rape was subject to heated debate in South Africa for many years. Even by the mid-1980s, opponents argued that allowing married women any form of bodily integrity and permitting them to charge their husbands with rape would inhibit any chance of reconciliation between the parties and would contribute to South Africa's already high divorce rate (which was another regularly invoked 'moral panic' of the time).

What is important to understand from this is that, in the 1970s and 1980s in South Africa, there were very few legal protections for women who experienced violence within the context of a formal intimate partner relationship – in fact, in many cases the courts did not even see the use of force by a husband against his wife as being a criminal act. Not only did we not have strong laws against the physical abuse of women by their spouses, at the time, we didn't even have words for it. This was about to change.

In the mid- to late-1970s, the issue of abused women had become a focal issue for activists and feminist organisations, particularly in the United States and Great Britain. By the end of the decade there were a growing number of studies, journal papers and even books (including works by Del Martin, Lenore Walker[33], and Maria Roy) that had begun to use the specific phrase 'battered woman' (or wife battering).

Early headlines mentioning 'battered wives' appear in the *Pretoria News*, in April 1978[34] (in the 'Women's Trend' section), and in Durban's *Daily News*, in July 1979[35] – again in the women's section, as if it was a fashion item. But it wasn't until May the following year that the phrase properly entered into the public lexicon, with the broadcast of a television insert on battered wives that was produced by well-known local journalist and producer

Carole Charlewood, and shown on the TV show *Spectrum*. One of the people watching the broadcast was MP Helen Suzman, who went on to raise the matter of battered wives in parliament that same week. Suddenly, there was a flurry of news stories (six stories were published within two weeks of the TV broadcast) – all using the phrase 'battered women' or 'battered wives' and discussing the problem of women abuse.

In case it needs to be emphasised, up until that moment there was very little formal acknowledgement of women as victims of domestic abuse, or even an understanding of or terminology for domestic abuse. And this was a global phenomenon, not just something restricted to parochial and conservative South Africa. At the United Nations' Second World Conference on Women held in Copenhagen in July 1980, a resolution was adopted on 'battered women and violence in the family', which marked the first time that violence in the home was specifically acknowledged by the organisation.

The resolution that was adopted was one part of a much bigger shift that was taking place, amidst a groundswell of activism around violence against women which had begun to grow from the late 1970s onward, and which was linked to global events, including the UN's First World Conference on Women which was held in Mexico City in 1975, and an International Tribunal on Crimes Against Women that was held in Belgium in 1976. Although South Africa was no longer a member of the United Nations by that time, these events had directly contributed to the formation of independent organisation Rape Crisis in Cape Town, in 1976, and, three years later (in 1979), People Opposing Women Abuse (POWA) in Johannesburg. POWA set up South Africa's very first shelter for abused women in 1984.

But because of apartheid Group Area laws, both Rape Crisis and POWA initially only offered services for white women.[36] This meant that, at the early stages at least, the focus on women's rights and safety within the home environment were, again, skewed along racial lines and focused largely on white, suburban women.

This became and even persisted as a feature of the broader understanding of violence against women. A paper published by the Centre for the Study of Violence and Reconciliation in 1991 commented how women's organisations in South Africa were either 'dominated by a political conservatism [and] government-supporting', or, if they were liberal, tended to be 'white, middle-class dominated'. Black women's organisations, they said, were primarily linked to organisations such as the African National Congress, the Pan Africanist Congress or the United Democratic Front, and their focus was largely political, aimed at empowering women 'as a constituency that needs to be mobilised and organised against apartheid and around community issues, e.g. rent boycotts, rather than in relation to issues specifically related to women's oppression, e.g. violence and abuse'.[37]

So, even in well-meaning NGOs, civil society organisations and activist movements, there was a distortion that continued to only really acknowledge inter-personal (non-criminal, non-political) violence as something that happened to white or middle-class South Africans, while discourse on black violence was dominated by politics, political and 'collective' violence.

The emphasis on political violence meant that black murder victims who were named in the press were usually male, their deaths reported in terrifying bullet-pointed lists together with the names of other black male victims. Sometimes these lists would include the street name and house number of the deceased, or the name of the hostel where they lived (at the time all hostels were exclusively single sex, so by mentioning a hostel it emphasised the maleness of the crime, and also implied that the violence was related to cultural or factional causes). Little other information was provided about how or why these men died, or who had killed them. News reports also occasionally mentioned black male police officers who had been killed, either for interfering in some form of alleged criminal activity or as retribution for their role in supporting the state.

Just like the white English- and Afrikaans-language newspapers cultivated a narrative of political violence, guns and fear, reports on black violence, including reports in newspapers targeted at black readers, cultivated the perception that, in black townships, the crime of homicide was directly connected with maleness (this is not entirely untrue, but it is also not the whole truth), that it probably had something to do with politics or faction fighting, and which was almost always represented as a collective act against a largely faceless individual.

But the structures and strictures of the apartheid state also hid other forms of violence, including intimate violence against black women, sometimes in plain sight.

Buried in between 'ordinary' stories of violence against black women – like the murder of a fifteen-year-old black housemaid who was sjambokked to death by her white employers who suspected her of stealing; or that of a fifteen-year-old black female who was assaulted, stripped naked and run over, twice, by a 22 year old named Stephanus Jooste who had gone out on a drinking spree and spent the day assaulting black people – there were also stories which deceived, even as they told the truth. In 1982, a white farmer named Gabriel Ernst Kriel was sentenced to death for poisoning a black female servant with strychnine. His wife, Magdalena Julia Kriel, was convicted as an accomplice. It was only later that the media reported that the motive for the killing was that the deceased black employee had been pregnant with Kriel's child (which was also a crime in terms of the country's Immorality laws prohibiting intimate relations across the colour bar).

These are some of the myriad reasons why it is so difficult to construct an accurate historical picture of intimate-partner femicide in South Africa. Not because it wasn't happening, but because so much of what was happening was obscured – through the acquittal of white perpetrators and euphemisms around white victims; through the sheer absence of language and laws to describe fatal violence against women; through the absurdities of apartheid laws and justice structures that literally enumerated murders and murderers by their race in relation to each other. And because the state deliberately tried to hide or downplay any violence other than what could be assigned political motives or which could be relegated to a generic catch-all of 'black-on-black' violence – for which the state, obviously, could not be held responsible.

By controlling the capture and release of crime statistics[38] and related information, and by overtly controlling the media (including the public broadcaster, and through state-mouthpiece newspapers like *The Citizen*), the apartheid state directly and deliberately emphasised notions of a '"deep-rooted tribal animosity" among black people in South Africa' which drew on racist stereotypes and promoted theories of 'ethnicity' in which ethnic conflict was not only inevitable but natural, 'based on the "atavistic tendencies of blacks"'.[39]

In the mid-1980s, there was a notable escalation in violent conflict overall, including violent crime, which would persist for another two decades. The spikes in violence were punctuated and provoked by the declaration of successive States of Emergency[40], which heightened the powers of both the police and military, and restricted reporting of political activities, including independent reporting on violence and unrest (during this period news coverage of all violent crime dropped significantly). And it was this volatile state that pushed researchers and activists to try and not only expose, but also understand what they understood as political violence. Organisations such as the Centre for the Study of Violence and Reconciliation (originally launched in 1989 as the Project for the Study of Violence) emerged within this context.

At the same time, there was a growing awareness among researchers about the problem of violence against women, and there was a strong suggestion that the narrative focus on political violence was potentially masking many other forms of violence, in particular domestic violence. These questions would only start to be addressed in the early 1990s.

Femicide and democracy?

Even within the broad area of 'women's rights', institutional acknowledgement of the issue of violence against women was, globally, a relative latecomer. At the very first United Nations World Conference on Women, held in Mexico in 1975, the agenda focused on improving gender equality and ending gender discrimination. This led to the drafting of what became the United Nations Convention on the Elimination of All Forms of Discrimination against Women (CEDAW), which was adopted by the UN in 1979. Violence, however, was specifically *not* included, as many still considered violence against women to be a private matter rather than a concern of the state.[41]

By the second UN Conference on Women, held in Copenhagen in 1980, delegates had begun to identify that there were discrepancies between the rights accorded to women in the convention, and women's ability to actually exercise these rights.[42] Among the inhibiting factors were a lack of political will, not enough involvement from men and insufficient support, such as financial support and day-care centres, for women. In addition, at the Copenhagen conference a resolution was adopted on 'battered women and violence in the family', the first time that violence in the home was specifically acknowledged by the organisation – the Mexico conference had alluded rather to the need for 'dignity', 'equality', and 'security' in the home.

It was only at the third UN Conference on Women, held in Nairobi in 1985, that violence against women, in those specific terms, was recognised as an obstacle to achieving the stated objectives of 'equality, development, and peace'. Within the context of broader discussions held in Nairobi, the organisation recommended developing a set of measures to combat violence against women, culminating in the Declaration on the Elimination of Violence Against Women which was adopted in 1993 at the World Conference on Human Rights. In 1994, the United Nations established the formal post of a Special Rapporteur on Violence against Women, who was tasked with seeking out information on such violence, its causes and its consequences, and who would also make recommendations as to measures to eliminate violence and remedy its effects.

The fourth UN World Conference on Women took place in Beijing in 1995. The Beijing conference was important for a number of reasons: it formalised the transition from 'women's rights' to 'women's rights as human rights' and, within that, shifted the focus from 'women' to the concept of gender, within which societal structures and the relationships and hierarchies between men and women had to be seen and understood in order to understand the issue of women's rights. Twelve 'platforms for action' emerged from Beijing, two of which specifically looked at violence against women: one was general violence against women and the other was women in armed conflict. In the former, the platform for action determined three strategic objectives: to prevent and eliminate violence against women; to study the causes and consequences of violence against women; and to eliminate trafficking of women and provide assistance to victims of violence caused by prostitution and human trafficking.

The Beijing conference would also mark the newly democratic South Africa's first participation in any of the World Conferences on Women (South Africa had been expelled from the United Nations in 1974 and was only readmitted in 1994). Ahead of the event, the Southern African region of Women and Law in South Africa decided to focus on femicide, and research was initiated in six southern African countries – including a pilot study on intimate femicide conducted by researcher Lisa Vetten, which was commissioned by POWA and funded by the South African

NGO Secretariat for Beijing; it was later presented at the World Conference. At the conference, South Africa also signed the Beijing Declaration and Platform for Action and ratified the terms of the Convention on the Elimination of All Forms of Discrimination Against Women.

It was through this project that the word 'femicide' made its very first appearance in South African media, appearing in an article published in *The Star* in May 1995, about the work of the NGO Secretariat for Beijing and the importance of the upcoming conference.[43]

The events of Beijing were, of course, part of a much bigger shift that was taking place in South Africa, as the country moved out of apartheid and into a democracy, which, by 1996, included a Constitution with a Bill of Rights. During the same time, the legal rights and protections, and the very framework within which we could understand and name violence against women, began to change.

One of the earliest changes was the introduction of the Prevention of Family Violence Act (Act No. 133 of 1993), which was the first piece of legislation to specifically deal with domestic violence – although the act still referred to 'family violence', which was not defined, and only extended to couples who were married under civil or customary law or in common-law marriages.

What the Act did, in theory, was allow victims of family violence access to simple and fast interdicts against perpetrators, prohibiting respondents from, among other things, threatening or assaulting the applicant, and preventing the respondent from entering the applicant's home (or part of the home). The Act also finally made marital rape a crime for which husbands could be prosecuted. But because of the Act's wording, many vulnerable women (such as sex workers, or women who were in 'dating' relationships) were excluded from accessing its protections, as were children. In addition, abusive partners still regularly prevented spouses from going to the courts; magistrates, too, were not always aware of how to apply the Act's new provisions.[44]

After 1994, a number of smaller and larger amendments and new acts were introduced that aimed to improve this. These included various amendments to the Criminal Procedure Act of 1977 (the Criminal Procedure Second Amendment Act No. 75 of 1995, the Criminal Procedure Act No. 51 of 1997, and the Criminal Procedure Second Amendment Act No. 85 of 1997) which tightened bail guidelines and explicitly defined certain forms of violence against women and children, particularly rape, as serious offences, under which bail was regulated.

The first study (in 1995) to specifically look at intimate femicide in South Africa took place around this time, and was based on court inquest records from the Johannesburg magistrate's court, together with a content analysis of three English-language newspapers – *The Star*, *The Citizen* and *The Sowetan* – which served the same region. The study's author, Lisa Vetten, identified 29 female victims from court inquest records and 45 female homicide cases from the media sample.

The following year (1996), Vetten authored a second report, using the same newspaper titles but extending the coverage period to include 1993 and 1994, yielding a total of 118 results for intimate femicide (the total media sample was actually larger but included 11 cases that had occurred prior to 1993).

In the first study, Vetten found that 55 per cent of the sample of murder victims drawn from the inquest had been killed by men known to them. Within the media samples, motives could not be determined for as much as a third of the stories on female homicides, but 'at least a quarter' of the murders appeared to have been motivated by the victim's decision to terminate her relationship with the murderer. Others, Vetten wrote, were motivated by sexual jealousy and arguments of indeterminate cause.

Vetten noted that 'eighty-three per cent of the female murder victims were African, yet the amount of newspaper coverage given to their murders was disproportionately low in comparison to the coverage given to white female murder victims'[45]. She also found that just under one-third of the perpetrators mentioned in the media sample were policemen.

In her second paper, Vetten (1996) found that only a quarter of identified inquest cases were covered in the news media (a figure that would tally with the findings of my own research more than two decades later). Vetten identified a number of other recurring trends in the media cases. One was that nearly 20 per cent of the murders reported in the media were said to have been prompted by the perpetrator's inability to deal with the ending of a relationship. Vetten also found that ten per cent of the victims in the newspaper sample were aged 20 years or younger, with the youngest being fourteen. This was (and is) quite significant, as she noted, the 'youth of these women is cause for concern, as it suggests that young women may become involved in abusive relationships while still adolescents.' She added a recommendation that research into violence within relationships should be expanded beyond 'only long-term or marital relationships' and should consider that 'young women start dating fairly early, often going out with men quite a few years their senior'.[46]

Effectively, what she had correctly noticed and highlighted was that entering into (romantic-type) relationships with men was in itself a risk factor for violence against women.

Based on her data, Vetten found, in Gauteng, a woman was killed by her intimate partner every six days – although she cautioned that the figure needed to be treated as an underestimate.

The following year the Centre for the Study of Violence and Reconciliation began a campaign called 'Justice for Women' which sought to compile data on conviction and sentencing patterns in cases of spousal homicides. The campaign was provoked by the killing of a woman by her husband over a maintenance dispute. The Centre gathered data from between 1994 and 1998 about both male and female perpetrators of spousal murders heard in the then Transvaal province, eventually identifying 164 cases, of which

39 involved female perpetrators. Their research found that the 'greatest proportion of men killed their female partners over their sexual choices and behaviour', while most women 'killed their male partners in response to ongoing abuse [at the hands of their partner]'.[47] Of the male perpetrators, fifteen per cent killed additional victims, including children, the woman's mother or sister, or the woman's new partner. This, together with Vetten's previous studies, began to construct, for the first time, an idea of what femicide meant in the South African context.

The Centre for the Study of Violence and Reconciliation's presentation on the campaign to the Parliamentary Monitoring Group also discussed the female perpetrators' actions in the context of what was seen as the state's failure effectively to implement supposedly new and improved domestic violence policies such as the Domestic Violence Act, which had been introduced in 1998.

The Domestic Violence Act No. 116 of 1998 broadened the scope of what was considered domestic violence and expanded the definition of abuse against women to include emotional, verbal and psychological abuse, sexual abuse, economic abuse, damage to property, harassment, stalking and entering the complainant's residence without consent (where the parties did not share the same residence).

The same year also saw the promulgation of the Recognition of Customary Marriages Act No. 120 of 1998, which recognised women in customary marriages and/or polygamous unions, and the Maintenance Act No. 99 of 1998, which made it an offence not to pay court-ordered maintenance, and allowed the courts to access the defaulting partner's salary, if needed.

But, as many activists would discover after the Acts they had campaigned so hard for had been promulgated, legislative reform did not necessarily translate into social change.

In a memo called 'More haste less speed? The South African Domestic Violence Act', women's rights organisation Gender Links commented that, in hindsight, attempts to fast-track new legislation before the 1999 elections had possibly backfired as the changes had not been properly costed or resourced, and departments were not necessarily able to provide the extent of services the new laws promised.

Gender Links noted how applications for protection orders at the Alberton court had more than quadrupled, from 374 applications in 1999 to 1 696 applications in 2000, and that the courts were not able to cope with the massively increased demand. In addition to resourcing the courts and justice system, the Joint Monitoring Committee on the Improvement of the Quality of Life and Status of Women also found that there would need to be extensive public education and awareness campaigns around the new provisions, as few South African women were aware of the changes.

Even in isolation these were not insignificant challenges. But they also took place within the context of a much larger violence problem.

Graeme Simpson, one of the founders of the Centre for the Study of Violence and Reconciliation, once described violence against women and children as a barometer of the 'culture of violence' in society. And in newly democratic South Africa, a violent state to begin with, violence was rising.

Violent crime had, in fact, been increasing consistently for the better part of a decade, since 1985. Murder, specifically, had more than doubled, increasing by 119 per cent between 1975 and 1995.[48] Violence researchers Brett Hamber and Sharon Lewis commented that 'the experience of being violently victimised in South Africa has become a statistically normal feature of everyday life in the urban and rural setting'.[49]

Reading crime reports in the news from around time – in particular from 1994, the start date of our imaginary Rainbow Nation – is quite a jarring experience, even when you are used to reading crime. Reports from the Centre for the Study of Violence and Reconciliation indicated that there was a surge in reported crimes in 1993/94, but that this was mostly because of a 'statistical quirk', specifically the re-incorporation of the ten black homeland states and their eighteen million residents into South Africa. There was also a quite subtle but fundamental change under the Government of National Unity, which saw the 'problem' of violence shift from being defined as a political issue to being immediately reframed as a criminal one.[50] This influenced how newspapers chose to report on violence, and also what the government's policies would be in response to this. And, so, political unrest and tension, never really fully seen or documented in the restricted press of apartheid, segued almost seamlessly into a crime wave that never really ended, and no one could determine when or where it had begun.

It appeared that, in line with general crime trends, during this time violence against women was on the rise, too. POWA told reporters that between 1994 and 1995 the number of cases of abused women they received reached an all-time high.[51] In another article, a column written by Amma Ogan in December 1995, the headline captured an entire story in itself: 'A woman dies while an overburdened system struggles to get to grips with domestic violence'.[52]

Ogan wrote about a woman in Yeoville who was stabbed to death by her estranged husband when she tried to move out of their shared apartment. The man was already on probation for assaulting his spouse. The police accompanied the woman to her flat so she could remove her belongings, but the escort left before she was finished. After the cops left, the man stabbed his wife. A friend who witnessed the attack called the Flying Squad on 10111, but nobody came. It took more than an hour for an ambulance to arrive and even longer for the police to get there. The 36-year-old woman was declared dead at the scene.

Ogan had changed the names of everyone involved in the story, for reasons that are unclear. Later, while I was reading through court reports from 1996, I realised that victim in question would have been Australian-born Susan Hamilton, a women's activist. She was stabbed six times with a kitchen knife by her husband, Sam Sithole.[53]

The word 'femicide' began to appear more frequently in news reports – although at this early stage it almost always directly referred to Vetten's pilot studies, often repeating her finding that one woman was killed by an intimate partner every six days.

One of the murders cited in Vetten's research was the fatal shooting of Italian artist Francesca Gobbi by her ex-husband Guiseppe di Blasi in Cape Town in 1992. After Gobbi had filed for divorce, Di Blasi had flown to South Africa from London, had followed Gobbi to her home in Hout Bay, and had proceeded to gun her down in the street. He told the court it was an 'act of mercy' and that he did not feel any guilt, adding: 'the guilt was hers alone'. Di Blasi even boasted in court about how he had killed her:

> She tried to run away across the road. I chased her and shot her in the back while she was still running. She fell to the ground. I walked to her and pointed the gun at her head because I was determined to kill her. I shot three times. I closed my eyes. I believe I missed once. She died of the injuries I caused her.[54]

Di Blasi pleaded guilty, but the judge presiding over the trial made the finding that Di Blasi had not been full in control of himself at the time of the shooting, and sentenced him to just four years in prison, describing Gobbi's murder as 'a story of heartache and obsessive love which evokes much compassion'. (Yes, that was the *judge* who said that – femicide déjà vu a full 20 years after Denise Kavin's murder.)

But – a sign of perhaps changing times – the Western Cape Attorney General took the judge's decision on appeal and four years later the Supreme Court overturned the original judgement and sentenced Di Blasi to fifteen years in prison instead. The appeal decision included a critique of the original trial judge's 'insufficient regard to the respondent's moral blameworthiness as well as the interests of society and the crime'.[55] Di Blasi served a little over six years of his sentence before being released early on parole. Three years later he was arrested by the Italian authorities at his house in Sicily and was once again tried for the murder of his wife. In 2002 he was convicted of her murder for a third time and sentenced to ten years in jail.

Another case that made headlines was the court case connected with the 1991 killing of 35-year-old Janine Bellingan, who had been bludgeoned and strangled to death in her house in Gallo Manor, Sandton, by her husband, former security police member Michael Bellingan. The investigation into Janine's death initially dragged out for months, as the victim's family accused the then Attorney General of deliberately delaying the case, and even included the accused of trying to flee the country to New Zealand together with his two children and a new wife in tow.[56]

The details of the Bellingan murder were like something out of a Hollywood thriller. On the night of Janine's death, in September 1991, Michael had a seemingly perfect alibi: he was in Durban, nearly 600 km away, attending a conference. Michael had finished work in Pietermaritzburg at 6 pm the night of the murder and claimed to have gone to bed at around 11 pm. The following morning, he had taken his sister in Durban for breakfast at around 9 am. By his version, it would have been impossible for him to have committed the crime in Joburg that same night.

But Michael Bellingan was lying.

What the ex-security police member had done in reality, as soon as he had finished consulting in Pietermaritzburg, was climb into his car and race to Johannesburg. He had then crept through his neighbour's garden and jumped over the wall into his own property before entering his house, bludgeoning his wife to death, and leaving, repeating the insanely fast return trip in order to be back in Durban for his breakfast.

The only reason the police were able to catch the perpetrator out in his lie was because the Bellingan's domestic worker had noticed that Michael's expensive blue Salvatore Ferragamo shoes – which he had taken with him on his trip – were in the sitting room on the morning when she found Janine's body. There were shoe prints in the neighbour's garden, and scuff marks and paint on the shoes from where he had jumped the wall. Once inside, Michael had taken off his shoes so that he would not wake his wife before he killed her by beating her with a spanner wrench, then strangling her with the cord from a hairdryer.

In an attempt to cover up his mistake, Michael went and bought an identical blue pair of Ferragamos which, he claimed, were the ones he had worn to Durban. But, using the serial number inside the designer shoes, police investigators were able to prove that the new pair had only been purchased five days *after* the murder.

As a footnote, in 1999 Michael Bellingan applied for amnesty for the murder of Janine, claiming that he had killed her because she was threatening to expose 'sensitive security police information' that had come into her possession (at the time of the trial, Michael Bellingan was also rumoured to have been involved in a fraud against the National Union of Metalworkers). In June 2000 the Truth and Reconciliation Commission rejected his plea of a political motive, and he was denied amnesty for Janine's murder. He did, however, receive amnesty for his role in other politically motivated crimes, including the 1988 bombing of Khotso House, in which nineteen people had been injured.

In February 1996, less than a year after Bellingan's conviction, 30-year-old Zahida Sabadia, a medical student and mother of three, was killed by three hitmen who had been hired by her husband, 44-year-old psychiatrist Dr Omar Sabadia. Omar Sabadia had arranged for the murder so that he could cash in on a R2.9 million insurance policy he had taken on his wife, and he had instructed the three men to fake a hijacking. Zahida's body was found 22 days later, tied to a tree in GaRankuwa. Despite opposition from Zahida's family and her children, Omar Sabadia was released on parole in 2019 after serving less than half his 50-year sentence.

A month before Zahida Sabadia's death, another murder had taken place, this time inside the premises of the Johannesburg Maintenance Court where a woman named Yvonne Ramontoedi had gone in an attempt to get her husband, prison warder Sandy Ramontoedi, to pay maintenance for the couple's child. It was this case in particular that had inspired the establishment of the Femicide/Justice for Women Working Group mentioned earlier.

On the day of her maintenance hearing, Yvonne Ramontoedi had gone to Johannesburg Central police station and asked for protection against her husband. She had previously reported to the police that her husband had fired shots at her and threatened to kill her. Because of Sandy Ramontoedi's job, however, his gun was never taken away from him. At some point during the maintenance hearing the prosecutor left the room, leaving the couple alone, at which stage Sandy pulled out his firearm and shot Yvonne in the back of the head while she was kneeling. For this, Sandy was sentenced to just three years correctional supervision, to be served in 20-hour instalments over weekends. During sentencing, the court noted that the lighter sentence was because of its view that the guilty party had been 'provoked over a long period of time', by which it was understood that Sandy had suspected his wife of having an affair, and that he was not the father of the child.[57]

What made Sandy Ramontoedi's sentence even more shocking was that, in two other cases where women had been found guilty of murdering their abusive husbands, the female perpetrators had received much harsher sentences, including one of the women being sentenced to death.

It was these gaps – the failure of protection orders, the failure of the police, the failure of the judiciary consistently to impose appropriate sentences (and the persistence of the judiciary in looking for 'justification' that male perpetrators had somehow been provoked) – that, in theory, were supposed to be addressed by the Domestic Violence Act.

But, even as the new law was passed, a senior police superintendent named Dave Schwarz was sentenced to just five years for hacking to death his police captain wife Sonia in front of their young child, after apparently suspecting Sonia of having an affair with another officer. Just after the murder had taken place, the usually upright *Mail & Guardian* described the case as a 'crime of passion' and included it in its annual round-up of sex scandals, an article which also featured jokey puns about Bill Clinton's penis.[58]

It is almost certainly a waste of time to get angry over how these kinds of stories were covered in the past (although readers of news will note that probably not all that much has changed). Outside of the 'big' cases though, whether or not the press coverage or court proceedings used questionable language, there were also tens of smaller murder stories that seeped through, many meriting only a single mention.

'Every six hours'

In 2002, a team of researchers from the Gender and Health Group at the Medical Research Council began to work on what would be the first national female homicide study in South Africa. The retrospective study compiled data on female homicide victims over the age of fourteen years, whose bodies were presented at a representative sample of 25 medico-legal laboratories between 1 January 1999 and 31 December 1999.[59] Data was 'collected from the mortuary file, autopsy report, police record, and during interviews with the police', which took place between March 2002 and December 2003.[60] The delay between the date of the murders and the date of data collection ensured that sufficient time had elapsed for the cases to have been reported and processed. The findings from the study were then weighted to create a nationally representative sample. Data from this study was used in a number of related retrospective studies published between 2004 and 2012 which examined specific aspects of the findings, such as rape-homicide, intimate-femicide-suicide and the role of guns in gender-based violence (these are discussed later in subsequent chapters in this book).

The total number of weighted cases in the study was 3 793 murders. Dockets were missing in 6.4 per cent of the cases and no cases could be traced in 6.9 per cent of the reports, leaving a remaining weighted sample of 3 296 cases for which data was collected. It is perhaps worth pointing out that in a later paper on this data[61], the researchers suggested that missing dockets might be 'more common with cases of murder where there was more police sympathy with the perpetrator, as is common with [intimate-partner violence]'. In cases where there was no suspect, the authors further noted that it was their perception that 'the deaths of African women were often not thoroughly investigated, nor were known perpetrators pursued. This reflects both historically based inequalities in public service resources in historically African areas, as well as the low status of African women in the national race and gender hierarchy'.[62]

Based on the information that was obtained from the dockets, 40.5 per cent of the cases in this study were designated as non-intimate femicides, 41 per cent as intimate femicides, and in 18.6 per cent of cases the relationship between the perpetrator and victim was unknown. The authors noted that intimate femicide was most likely under-represented; but that, in cases where the victim-perpetrator relationship was known, the majority of killings were committed by the female victim's intimate partner. According to these findings, the study found that approximately every six hours a woman was murdered by her intimate partner – that's four intimate-partner femicides, with an additional four women killed each day by non-intimate or unknown perpetrators.

The study's authors calculated a rate of female homicide per 100 000 female population in South Africa at 24.7 (by comparison, the 2016 Small Arms Survey report on 'A Gendered Analysis of Violent Deaths' estimated that in Syria in 2015 this figure was 25.7 per 100 000), while that of intimate-partner femicide was 8.8/100 000 – at the time, the highest femicide figure(s) reported in research anywhere in the world.

The initial paper, published in 2004, suggested it would be useful to establish a centralised crime register for female murders and 'highlighted a number of weaknesses in the management of female homicides ... by the police and judicial system', which included the need to build the 'capacity of [police] officers to investigate female homicides'.[63]

The special case of femicide

Why would police need special training to investigate female homicides? Because, with weighted data for several thousand murders now available, the hypothesis suggested earlier – of femicide as it exists within a violent, patriarchal and misogynistic society – was literally embodied and enumerated. In fact, those very attributes had been identified as playing critical roles in predicting the risks of female homicide and aiding the search for and collection of evidence post mortem (for example, forensic evidence) that might assist the effective prosecution of a homicide or attempted homicide. As the study's authors concluded, 'female homicide is different from other crimes'.

This is not a uniquely South African distinction. The 2014 Latin American Model Protocol notes that while femicide has 'diverse manifestations', it is a global phenomenon – adding that 'available reports reveal that gender-related killings of women show signs of disproportional violence before, during or following the criminal act. This indicates a particular brutality and ruthlessness against the body of the woman. In many cases the killing is the final act on a continuum of violence.'[64] (The Latin American

Model Protocol discusses femicide or female homicide as a type of aggravated homicide, which has specific criminal, legal and penal implications.)

Many of the initial results discussed in the first Medical Research Council Policy Brief issued in 2004 focused on intimate femicides. The study found that, by race, coloured women were at the highest risk of intimate femicide (18.3/100 000), followed by African women (8.9/100 000) and Indian women (7.5/100 000), and that white women were at the lowest risk of intimate femicide (2.8/100 000).

According to the study, victims of intimate femicide were more likely than victims of non-intimate femicides to: be killed in their home; be younger; work as domestic workers; be killed by a legal firearm; be killed by blunt force; or be killed by perpetrators who have a problem with alcohol.

The perpetrators of intimate femicide by race (with the % of population in 1999 in brackets) were given as 76.4% African [76.6%], 17.7% coloured [8.8%], 3.9% white [10.9%], and 2% Indian [2.6%]. The study also found that 'perpetrators of intimate femicides were more likely to be blue collar workers, farm workers and security workers, while perpetrators of non-intimate femicides were more likely to be unemployed, students, self-employed or their occupation was unknown.'[65]

According to the 1999 study, 37% of the recorded female homicide cases ended in a conviction. This figure appears to be significantly higher than convictions obtained for general homicides during the same time period. A report published by the South African Law Commission looking at a random sample of reported murders during 1997/1998 found that just over 10.5% of murder cases resulted in convictions within two years of the murder – but more than 60% of murder cases did not even go to court during that time.

Blaming the victim, excusing the perpetrator

Four months before Shanaaz Mathews, Naeemah Abrahams, Lorna Martin, Lisa Vetten, Lize van der Merwe and Rachel Jewkes published the findings of the first South African femicide study, a man named William Beeton was sentenced to an effective six-year imprisonment for shooting and killing his wife Brenda Beeton at a pub in Midrand in 2000. During the same incident William Beeton had also shot and wounded Brenda's lover, Braam Pretorius, who survived the attack.

When William Beeton was found guilty of murder and attempted murder, the *Pretoria News* ran the story together with the headline, 'Man sorry he killed cheating wife'.[66] The next day the *The Citizen* followed suit, with a story about the '"Pain" of a man who shot cheating wife'.[67]

Even the judge seemed to agree with the newspapers' sentiments and commented that Brenda Beeton had led William 'up the garden path', and that her infidelity was a mitigating factor in her murder.

Except, even in the same news reports at the time, it was quite evident that Brenda and William Beeton were estranged. And that Brenda Beeton had been living apart from her husband in an apartment above her business (a bar) in Midrand, which was where William had found her and where he had killed her. William believed that he and Brenda – they had been married for nineteen years before separating – were on the verge of reconciling. The night before the murder Brenda had invited William to her pub for dinner. He told the court he believed this invitation was a sign that all was well and that their relationship was about to resume. In spite of this, William hadn't managed to make the dinner (and decided instead to pop over and 'surprise' his wife at breakfast the next morning). Brenda's lover, however, testified that the reason they had decided to invite William over was to 'clear the air', and to finally acknowledge that Brenda and Braam were in a relationship together (William had previously caught Brenda and Braam together, and suspected she had been unfaithful; Braam, who was also married, had not told his wife about his relationship with Brenda).

William Beeton himself could not remember much of what he had done, his memory 'becoming vague' after he had discovered his wife in bed with Pretorius. Beeton had then apparently gone to his car, retrieved his firearm, fired several shots in the bedroom, and left. He spent one day at Carnival City and two nights at a Holiday Inn before handing himself over to the police, knowing only that he had done something 'terribly wrong'.[68]

This book is not an attempt to take the place of a court of law but, having read through several hundred femicide cases from not just South Africa but around the world, and not from just this decade but even dating back several centuries, I do find myself wondering, at which point during or after the end of a relationship – if ever – does it stop being considered 'acceptable' for a male to murder his female partner because she left him and has moved on?

This is actually a historical question, because men being allowed to kill their wives for infidelity is so old it's literally in the oldest rule books we know of. The 4 000-year-old Sumerian legal codes of Ur-Nammu (which are even older than the Ten Commandments) stipulate that if the wife of one man used her charms to entice another man to sleep with her, she should be slain, but the other male party should be set free.[69]

Until the introduction of the *lex Iulia de adulteriis coercendis* in around 17 BCE, it was still considered quite acceptable under Roman law for a husband to kill his wife if she was caught being unfaithful (the law also allowed a husband to kill the male party to the adultery, but only under certain circumstances). In fact, the husband's right to kill his wife for adultery – there was no reciprocal right – was considered so important that it was eventually reinstated by the Emperor Constantine in 331 CE, five years after he had executed his own wife, Fausta, for infidelity.[70]

Fathers were also legally permitted to kill adulterous daughters, not just under Roman law or in the expansive Roman Empire, but in many other regions. And not just for adultery; often, daughters could legally be killed for any type of sexual immorality or even for a perceived slight to the father's name or good standing. These so-called 'honour killings' of women have long histories and can still be found in almost every region of the world, from South America to Europe, in Africa, the Middle and Far East, and across the Asian subcontinent.[71] In many countries, such killings are still considered to be private or family matters rather than a matter for the state, and may even go unreported to the authorities.

While such killings of women typically fall under these countries' laws dealing with murder, so-called 'crimes of honour' are often considered to have extenuating circumstances (for the male perpetrators, not the female victims) and may provide for significant reductions of penalties for the murderers, if they are prosecuted at all.[72]

Another lethal euphemism is the so-called 'crime of passion', which has been and continues to be treated as having special or extenuating circumstances, in which the (usually male) perpetrator is at least partially excused from culpability for his murderous act because of the perceived extreme provocation of a sexual infidelity (see Exhibit A, above). In fact, under some jurisdictional laws, infidelity is considered equivalent provocation to that of mutual combat or assault[73] – or, indeed, any sort of romantic or sexual betrayal, which might include the termination or simply the rejection of a romantic or sexual relationship. In her work *Life and Death* (1997), Andrea Dworkin describes the 'interesting and eloquent assertion of gender, implying as it does that it is natural for a man to use massive, grotesque violence against a woman, any woman, when he is upset'.

When researchers began to study news coverage of the murder of women (which, kind of like the timing on the arrival of the word 'femicide' into our lexicon also only really started happening in the 1990s – in particular with works like Marian Meyers' *News Coverage of Violence Against Women*), they also started noticing that many of the news stories written about women who had been killed tended to use language that somehow blamed the women for participating in their own deaths and, at the same time, sought to excuse or mitigate the actions of the perpetrator. This could be anything from calling the murdered woman a 'love cheat' and describing her killer as a 'devoted father' to implying much simpler culpabilities, like women who forgot to lock their doors or close their windows.

It was this kind of language – the persistent euphemism of victim blaming – that prompted Australian journalist Jane Gilmore to start her #FixedIt campaign, correcting the headlines of news stories that blamed victims and not only minimised but even praised perpetrators of violence against women. In one example, from August 2018, the BBC posted about an 'amazing father' – who had just killed his pregnant wife and their two children, and placed their bodies in a fuel tank (the website later changed its headline to read 'US husband held after missing family "found dead in fuel tanks"').[74]

Another common trend Gilmore identifies in her work is that of the 'invisible perpetrator' – the culprit behind stories like 'Woman has throat cut' and 'Woman beaten on beach'. As Gilmore quite rightly points out, these stories should more truthfully be headlined 'Man cuts woman's throat' and 'Man beats woman on beach'. Although there is also an eerie resonance with accounts given by perpetrators themselves like Beeton, particularly in court testimony, where there are common memory lapses or temporary amnesia at around the exact time they killed their current or former intimate partner.

In 2018 British feminist organisation Level Up published a set of media guidelines, under the heading 'Dignity for dead women',[75] for reporting on domestic violence deaths. The paper makes the case that victims of domestic violence experience very undignified deaths, and that reporting on these murders should attempt not to perpetuate this. In addition, the paper notes that inaccurate reporting on domestic violence has a lasting traumatic impact on the families, and represents a failed opportunity to prevent future domestic violence deaths.

Among their recommendations, the Level Up paper suggests the following: that responsibility for intimate partner killings should be placed solely on the perpetrator, without framing the killer as a sympathetic figure (a 'jilted lover'); that the killing should be called what it is: domestic violence – rather than a family 'tragedy'; that sensationalised and graphic language should be avoided; and that stories should avoid using stock images suggesting domestic violence is only physical in nature. The guide also includes recommendations around the use of sources in media reporting, for example, including only the perpetrator's version of events when the victim is no longer able to speak for herself.

These guidelines would all apply equally to reporting on intimate partner violence in the South African context. Even though we do have words – many of them – for violence against women, there is often a strange but also understandable reluctance when it comes to acknowledging this. In South Africa, although intimate femicides make up the majority of female homicides, they make up only 30 per cent of femicide stories in the news.

5. 'Two die in tragedy': Femicide-suicide and family killings

When I started researching news coverage of femicide, I tried to develop a method that I could repeat, so I was able to follow the same steps each time I came across a new murder case in the press archives. I would start by logging all the forensic information I could determine from the first article I came across about each particular incident – sometimes this would be the victim's name, but often it was just a date and a place of death; or it might include snippets of information like that the victim was elderly, or that she had been stabbed. I would then use these specific details to search again through the archives, looking for additional matches so I could mark any other stories that were about or which mentioned the same victim.

It turned out that this was an important practice because, firstly, not all articles use the murder victim's name. Sometimes a headline might just say 'Nurse found in bathroom'. Also, personal details about victims would often be incorrect or inconsistent. Names would be misspelled, or spelled three different ways in as many different stories. I understand it's hard to check the correct spelling of a subject who has been killed, but the lack of attention to detail always bugged me. Victims' ages would also be wrong, although that was perhaps more understandable as an oversight.

Searching for information about the incident rather than just the person meant that I was able to find and use a broader number of sources, including ones I might otherwise have missed. As part of this exercise, I would also search for news stories that mentioned not just the victim but also the accused – if there had been arrests or court cases associated with the killing. Sometimes this exercise would reveal a whole other story of its own.

One of the cases I read, and which really stuck with me, was a murder-suicide and an attempted family killing that had taken place in Bronkhorstspruit in early January 2013. The father, a 51-year-old man named Eugene Marais, had stabbed his 39-year-old wife Tania to death in front of their three children. He then forced his children – aged 11, 5 and 4 – to swallow sleeping pills. His eldest daughter, who reportedly tried to stop her father from killing her mother, palmed the pill and pretended to fall asleep with her siblings. A little while later she slipped out of the house and, covered in her mother's blood, ran five kilometres in the dark to the nearest police station to get help. Eugene Marais shot himself in the head with a handgun shortly after the cops arrived, but the girl's quick thinking saved the lives of her younger brother and sister – who were rushed off to hospital and had their stomachs pumped.

As if this wasn't already enough to take in, in the days after Tania Marais' murder it emerged that Eugene was actually a mass murderer.

In October 1990 Eugene Marais together with two other men, David Botha and Adriaan Smuts, all members of the right-wing Afrikaner Weerstandsbeweging (AWB) and the Orde Boerevolk, had opened fire on a commuter bus in KwaMashu near Durban, killing seven people and wounding 27 others. At his trial Marais was sentenced to death seven times, but his sentence was later commuted to 25 years. Marais and the others subsequently applied for amnesty at the Truth and Reconciliation Commission – claiming that they considered the bus massacre to be an 'act of war', and that the killings were in retaliation for an earlier attack (on white people) by Pan African Congress members, which had taken place on the Durban beachfront that morning. Marais, who had previously been married, had met Tania while he was in jail (she was visiting another inmate), and they married after he was granted amnesty in 1997.

I still think about this case sometimes. About the daughter running in the dark, so much responsibility resting on her shoulders. I also think about what it must be like to knowingly marry a mass murderer. Not that it in any way makes Tania Marais culpable even in the slightest for her own murder. Just that I wonder how it is possible to un-see a person's violence when you know it is there. I have since watched a video of Marais and his co-attackers giving testimony at the Truth and Reconciliation Commission, and I have seen photographs and heard testimony from some of the survivors of the bus attack. In his final appeal to the Commission, Marais quoted from Nelson Mandela's inauguration speech, that we should forget the past. That what was past was past.

*

Around ten per cent of all femicides and nearly 20 per cent of intimate femicides involve the suicide of the perpetrator – this is what is referred to as a femicide-suicide or a homicide-suicide, where the perpetrator takes his or her own life within a short time frame after the murder (usually within a week).[1] The time between the murder and the suicide is important, because it 'demonstrates that neither act is incidental to the other'.[2]

Professor Shanaaz Mathews, one of the authors of the two Medical Research Council studies into femicide, produced a series of additional works based on the 1999 study looking specifically at intimate femicide-suicide. She found that South Africa had the highest reported rate of intimate femicide-suicide in the world. Mathews' research also showed that, when compared to non-suicide femicide cases, intimate femicide-suicides were more strongly associated with perpetrators who were white (and male), who were employed as professional or white-collar workers, and who owned a legal firearm.

Mathews' research and the data from the Medical Research Council studies appeared to confirm a fairly well-established narrative about white males – and particularly white Afrikaans-speaking males – as the primary perpetrators of this kind of violence. Research into suicide rates in South Africa had consistently shown that around 80 per cent of suicides in South Africa were males[3]; that, proportionally, mortality from suicide was statistically much higher among white South Africans; and that the rate of white male suicides had been steadily increasing since the 1960s.[4]

In South Africa, homicide-suicides are also associated with what are known as 'family murders' (in Afrikaans, 'gesinsmoord'). In the South African context, the phrase 'family murders' specifically describes homicides where the perpetrator – usually a parent and commonly but not always the male parent – kills one or more of his or her own children and, in the case of male perpetrators, also frequently kills or attempts to kill his spouse, before committing or attempting suicide. Female homicide-suicides rarely involve another adult, and usually involve a mother killing her children and then herself.[5]

Research into murder-suicides suggests that female perpetrators may have more altruistic motives for their killings; in other words, mothers kill their children because they believe that nobody else will care for them after their death.[6] Male perpetrators' motives tend to be described as more narcissistic. Femicide-suicides and family killings with male perpetrators occur most commonly when couples are separated or going through separation or divorce proceedings. Male perpetrators may exhibit extreme jealousy and/or rage about the termination of a relationship, and may attempt to kill their partners either in retribution (punishment for ending the relationship), or because they claim to love their former partner 'too much to let her go', or because they can't bear the thought of their partner with anyone else ('if I can't have you, then nobody else can').

In family murders, male perpetrators might also kill minor children as a means of 'punishing' the mother – for leaving or ending the relationship, for suspected infidelity, for failing to keep the family together; or they might kill the children for appearing to take the mother's 'side', thus betraying the father. In an inverse of female (maternal) suicide-filicide, male perpetrators of family killings often cannot imagine the family unit as being able to continue without *them* and, even as they claim that they love their children too much to live without them[7], what they really mean is that, if they die then their children should die too.

There are additional iterations of femicide-suicide that include the killing of other family members and which perhaps require further distinction. These are homicide-suicide cases, where the male perpetrator murders his current or former female intimate partner (the primary victim) and, during the course of this killing, also murders another close female relative such as his primary victim's mother, sister, and so on, before taking or attempting to take his own life. This kind of family killing usually occurs when the primary victim has ended her relationship with the perpetrator and has left or is attempting to leave a shared home and has sought safety or temporary accommodation with her own mother or grandmother, or another female relative (sometimes also a friend). When I was working through the SA Police Service data on female homicide statistics (which was anonymised except for the date of death, the police station, and the age and gender of the victim), I would often come across entries where there were two female homicides reported on exactly the same day at exactly the same police station and the only difference between the cases would be the victims' ages, 20-odd years apart (the data supplied by the SA Police Service obviously doesn't show confidential information such as names or case numbers). This was often a clear indication of the kind of family killing I describe above.

Finally, there are also femicide-suicides with more than one victim, where the additional victim/s are not necessarily considered 'family', and are also not always female – for example, when a jealous male kills his former female partner together with a new (or a suspected) male partner, before killing himself.

If we assume that more than half of all femicides are intimate partner murders, and that 20 per cent of these are femicide-suicides, that would suggest that in South Africa, currently, between 300 and 315 men[8] each year commit suicide after killing their female partners.

Even this rather staggering number represents only five to six per cent of the annual suicides for South African males of all ages[9] (although the number of femicide-suicide perpetrators would be higher if we were able to take into account *unsuccessful* femicide-suicides, that is, where the perpetrator killed himself but, for one reason or another, was not successful in his attempt to kill his partner, which could be because the perpetrator was prevented from or interrupted during his attempt; or because his attack was not fatal and the female victim somehow survived).

Although suicide is one of the top causes of non-natural deaths in South Africa not related to disease (after inter-personal violence and road deaths), epidemiological data about suicide in South Africa is relatively limited. In part, this is because suicides are historically under-reported on death certificates, which is a global issue and is almost certainly because of the negative connotations associated with suicide, including but not limited to religious prohibitions and even penalties against self-harm (this might include anything from the denial of burial rites to refutations of insurance claims related to suicide deaths). An Africa Check report noted that in the Medical Research Council's 2012 Burden of Disease study[10], the number of suicide deaths was put at over 6 100, using modelled estimates – compared to just 500 suicides recorded on death certificates for that same year.

In South Africa there are additional limitations. One primary issue is that, for most of the country's history, data on black mortality (including suicide) was almost non-existent, and black demographic information was, in turn, equally narrow. A longitudinal study on suicide rates in South Africa between 1968 and 1990 commented that its data on black subjects was so compromised that it precluded making any definitive conclusions about suicide trends among black South Africans.

This is a widespread problem. It impacts on how we understand mortality (including deaths as a result of crime) not just in the past, but also in the present.

Professor Keith Breckenridge, who has written extensively about the 'Biometric State'[11] and the associated 'politics of identification and surveillance' in South Africa, explains how, ironically, colonial and apartheid states' desire to define and control its subjects instead introduced and perpetuated paradoxes and blindspots about almost everyone except their white citizens.

In the 1950s, for example, after the passing of the apartheid Population Registration Act, white, coloured and Indian citizens of South Africa were recorded on one database managed by the Census Bureau, and black Africans were recorded on another, under a separate Central Reference Bureau. When the homeland states were declared in 1970, these, too, began to undertake their own population registrations. Breckenridge notes that by the end of apartheid, 'over a dozen discrete yet overlapping and duplicated population registers were in place'[12], all of which were expected to somehow be integrated into a newly deracialised national register after 1994.

This biometric bureaucracy presented equal challenges for establishing the number of lives *or* the number of deaths. A study that attempted to estimate mortality rates between 1985 and 1990[13] showed that, in mid-1980s South Africa, 'only 56% of male and 44% of female deaths were recorded for the Black population group', and even the estimates for 'White, Coloured and Asian population groups' were suspect.

In 1992 the Births and Deaths Registration Act was introduced, in part to implement changes which were supposed to address these problems. However, there were still statistical gaps between deaths due to violence (documented by the police) and fatalities due to transport accidents, which were recorded, and other non-natural deaths (suicides, undetermined causes), which were not. Between 1992 and 1998, mortality statistics also didn't include information on race.[14] This means that we have decades of information deserts, where the best researchers can do is cobble together different smaller data sets, and hope to make some sort of sense out of the whole.

Demographic data is also highly political. It is no coincidence that such information vacuums fall at a time when AIDS-related deaths were climbing, and South Africa's violent crime rate was starting to peak. In 2000, South Africa's Police Minister Steve Tshwete declared a moratorium on crime statistics, which lasted until the following year (I should note here that Tshwete was not the first minister to do so; in the early 1980s, Louis le Grange withheld similar crime data about the Cape Peninsula, which was already one of the country's 'murder capitals').

In 1999, the Medical Research Council established a National Injury Mortality Surveillance System (NIMSS), which collected data from medico-legal laboratories and state forensic laboratories, so that it could provide more detailed information about fatal injuries in South Africa. Data from the NIMSS reports were also included in subsequent Global Burden of Disease studies for South Africa. NIMSS reports were initially provided for most of South Africa's major urban centres but after 2005, coverage of this system became more limited. (Statistics South Africa still produces annual reports on mortality and causes of death, but these rely on data from death notification forms and tend to exponentially under-count suicides, as above.)

This combination of bureaucracy, oversight, ignorance and bigotry is patently visible in archive news reports around either suicide and/or homicide-suicide (including femicides and family killings); and, like newspaper coverage of femicide itself, is deeply skewed along racial lines.

In the late 1970s, although stories of white husbands shooting their wives (and sometimes their children) before killing themselves were fairly common, as I have noted before these were almost always reported as if the killer had been a victim of some terrifying unnamed gunman rather than having died at his own hand. In news stories at the time, the term 'suicide' was used predominantly to refer to deaths in detention, primarily of black victims, although there were also a few prominent white figures who died under suspicious circumstances.

The other frequent appearance of the term 'suicide' was in connection with editorial pieces expressing concern about what was apparently the growing rate of suicide in South Africa, usually featuring quotes or insight from our very own Sam Bloomberg in the earlier chapter. Bloomberg was a former police reservist and one-time National Party MP for Bezuidenhout Valley, and had been the head of the South African chapter of Suicides Anonymous since the late 1960s. He had all sorts of insights and observations about the causes and profile of suicide in apartheid South Africa, and he appeared in literally hundreds of articles between the late 1970s and early 1990s.

Bloomberg's theories around suicide were quite varied, and tended to be both oddly unsympathetic while still expressing care for potential victims. He frequently blamed white South African males for not being resilient enough, and having a poor ability to deal with hardship. He once described (white and black) South African men as 'bad lovers and bad losers'. At the same time, though, he was extremely vocal about the negative role that South African women played in this dynamic, and regularly blamed female partners of homicidal and suicidal men for 'triggering' their partners into killing them, most frequently through withholding sexual favours, or taunts about their partner's sexual inadequacies. Bloomberg's views on race and suicide were also quite stark. At a presentation at the 5th International Conference for Suicide Prevention, held in London in 1969[15], he commented that the suicide rate among black South Africans was minimal because black subjects, even when urbanised, were inherently closer to 'the rhythm of nature' (including their communities and culture) – as opposed to the competitive city environment of the white man – and that as a result black expression of stress and aggression was 'extrapunitive', whereas whites' reactions were more 'intrapunitive'. This, Bloomberg said, was why black men tended toward homicidal rather than suicidal behaviour.

This statement in itself points to a remarkable hypocrisy in terms of how suicide was narrated in this particular period of apartheid South Africa – because most of the stories reported in the news, about a white South African male taking his own life, *did* involve homicide too, usually the wife or girlfriend of the perpetrator. Reading countless news stories from the late 1970s and early 1980s, of white men who killed their wives and then themselves, usually with a firearm, it is apparent that, in many cases, the deaths of the women weren't really considered as *'murder'* murders. These were family problems, marriage problems. Not problems that the state could or should or would intervene in.

What was becoming a problem, though, was when these murders included children. Even if a husband killing his wife could be tolerated (possibly even expected, certainly understood in certain circumstances), a white man killing his entire family represented a different threat to the status quo.

By early 1978 at least[16], 'gesinsmoord' was generating concerned editorials in the conservative Afrikaans-language press[17], including three full pages in one of the year's final editions of the popular magazine *Huisgenoot* in which journalist Petrovna Metelerkamp asked what drove parents to murder their children.[18] The *Huisgenoot* article cited five recent cases of family killings: one in Bethlehem, where a Sasolburg man had killed his five-year-old son and two-year-old daughter with an R1 rifle before killing himself; an Ogies father who gassed himself and his two- and four-year-old children in his car somewhere near

Witbank; a father in Muldersdrift who wrote a letter about how much he loved his family shortly before shooting and killing his eleven-year-old son, and then shooting himself. There were also two separate instances where young mothers killed themselves and their children – a gassing near Rustenburg which killed the mother and a five-year-old daughter, leaving a four-year-old child alive (and a seven-year-old son who was at school); and a Wellington mother who shot three of her children and herself in the head. Her seven-year-old son survived and was found alive by passers-by. The journalist added that in the previous two decades at least 70 white children had been murdered by their parents[19] – a rate of 3.5 child killings a year – but this was quite evidently, and starkly, exceeded by the nine children's deaths reported in the article alone.

What the magazine's headlines and pull-quotes didn't reference (although it was discussed in the text) was that, in both the Bethlehem and Muldersdrift incidents, the perpetrator had also murdered his wife. In fact, in the latter incident, the perpetrator had killed his son *while* the eleven-year-old was trying with his bare hands to stop his father from murdering his mother with a gun.

The newspapers, consulting experts like Sam Bloomberg, and various other unnamed psychiatrists, suggested a number of possible causes for the spate of white family violence. Men, in particular, were under a lot of stress, they said. There was political uncertainty. The economy was doing problematic things. Unemployment was rising. Women were taking over roles previously held by men. Divorce rates were rising. South Africa also had one of the highest rates of private gun ownership in the world, owned by a generation of men who had undergone compulsory military service. And violence was very much a part of everyday life in South Africa – it was a common language, easily understood. This is partly what is meant when we refer to a 'culture of violence', as a space or place where violence is accepted and even endorsed as an 'acceptable and legitimate means to resolve problems and achieve goals'.[20]

In her works on 'Whiteness and family murder', Professor Nicky Falkof explains that one of the reasons white family killings became so prominent in news stories was because the acts themselves 'struck at the organised relations of the family, on which apartheid's political mythology depended', adding that there was a 'sense in which family murder can be understood as a failure of whiteness'.[21] White family murders, and particularly white *Afrikaner* family murders, were not just failures of the patriarchal father but of the patriarchal state itself.

At the same time, Falkof points out that the media's near obsession with white Afrikaans family murders was also a device through which white Afrikaans-speaking South Africans could safely raise, discuss and critique their own pathologies – relative to each other, rather than through potentially problematic comparisons with those of people of other races.

For the next decade and more, a fairly singular narrative of white family killings would dominate news stories of family homicides. In 1980, *Huisgenoot* journalist Petra Pieterse asked if such family killings were 'contagious'.[22] In July 1984, English-language paper *The Star* wrote about the 'horror' in South African homes, in which 32 white victims had died in family murders and suicides in less than seven months. In 1985 *Die Vaderland* wrote an editorial describing it as the 'year of family murder'. In 1988, Jacques Pauw wrote a profile of a family killer, asking, 'Hoe lyk die man wat so iets beplan?'[23] (What does the man who plans such a thing look like?]. He described the average family murderer as being between 30 and 40 years old, in any occupation from a lawyer to a handyman, as being neurotic, uncertain, prone to insomnia and depression, and convinced he was committing an 'act of love' (perhaps the killers simply listened to the sentences judges passed on family killers?). A psychiatrist who worked at Weskoppies psychiatric hospital explained to Pauw that, in the mind of such killers, they didn't see their killings as acts of murder but rather as 'extended suicides'.

There are two issues that need to be understood here: one is that, although the police do not specifically record data on what was counted as a 'family murder' (the definition itself is widely debated, and varies between researchers), based on tallies published in news reports it does appear that from the late 1970s onwards there was (a) an increased number of intra-familial homicide-suicides among white South Africans; and (b) there was a similar or even greater increase in news coverage of the issue of family murder-suicides as a coherent social problem.

The problem with this, though, is that – not unlike how newspapers both did and did not report on the murders of women, and invisibilised black women – there is no indication that what South African newspapers reported on family murder-suicides had any correlation to the actual number, or modes, of killings within families. In particular, the almost exclusive focus on white, Afrikaans-speaking males and families as the primary locus of this kind of murder meant that all other groups were simultaneously excluded from consideration.

As early as 1978, however, medical officers' reports were indicating that – contrary to what Sam Bloomberg suggested about black South Africans having a different and more natural 'rhythm' – suicide *was* becoming a significant cause of death among urban black populations[24]; or, more simply: even though suicide was considerably less common in black populations than white populations, it was still a significant cause of non-natural deaths. And, in a country where black people made up (then) some 75 per cent of the population, it meant that the actual numbers of black suicides were possibly nearly equal to those of white victims, even though the *rate* of black suicides (per population size) was nearly half that of whites.

This data, although reported, was largely overlooked by the press which, as a rule, didn't cover black suicides or family killings or really any form of violence that individualised black victims, instead reducing them to a collective casualty of 'black-on-black' violence (white family murders were never referred to as 'white-on-white' violence, of course). One exception was a report in the *Rand Daily Mail*, from October 1980, which briefly mentioned that a man named Henry Chaba had thrown himself down a mine pit after killing his children.[25]

The suggestion that black men were possibly suicidal was also widely rejected by many black men themselves, who accepted that the homicide rate was high but told reporters that they only knew of a handful of suicide cases in their own communities.[26]

One of the permitted exceptions to this (aside from black men allegedly committing suicide in detention) were black policemen. In the mid-1980s, the *Sowetan* reported on what was apparently a recent spate of (black) police suicides, at least one of which included a femicide-suicide, when Soweto Constable SP Mothobi shot and killed his partner Elizabeth Maduna before killing himself, all while Elizabeth's fifteen-year-old son was in the next room. The newspaper reflected that black policemen felt they were 'torn between the force' and their communities.[27]

Other media stories from the time corroborate the fraught position black policemen – who, by 1985, made up nearly half of the police force – found themselves in. Between the end of 1984 and the first half of 1985, more than 100 black policemen's homes were firebombed[28], and many community members saw them as traitors and puppets, propping up the apartheid state rather than instilling law and order. As rates of violence increased, from the end of apartheid and through the transition to democracy, this faultline would fracture entirely, but it would largely be subsumed by the similar explosion in other murders.

A note on police killings

The trend of black femicide-suicides was set to continue well into the next decade, which also (perhaps not coincidentally) coincided with a spike in police suicides, which more than doubled between 1991 and 1994, jumping from 65 deaths in 1991 to over 150 suicides a year by 1994.

Reading news reports of homicide-suicides involving policemen (perpetrators, and sometimes as victims) is, quite frankly, unrelenting. A never-ending playbook of police reservists, constables, sergeants, detective sergeants, even a superintendent, taking the lives of their current or former or estranged wives and partners (I realised in reading that this is almost the only place I ever see the term 'estranged' being used, when it's referring to a man who has killed a woman who has left him). They shot their wives in Parow, in Kenilworth, in Kleinvlei, in Kensington, in Dobsonville, in Atlantis, in Dobsonville again, and once again, in Kagiso, in Actonville, in Heidelberg, in Stilfontein, in Kimberley. In Kokstad, a policeman named Innocent killed his ex-girlfriend Buhle Jojo, his wife Doreen Mngadi and their five-year old daughter, before shooting himself, *all at the police barracks.*[29]

Jennifer Nix's 1998 study[30] into domestic abuse experienced by intimate partners of policemen showed that such behaviour was not unusual, particularly at police barracks where the 'brotherhood' of the male officers and 'sisterhood' of their wives and partners created an environment that frequently tolerated abnormal behaviour, and closed ranks on outsiders. Nix documented how one of her interviewees recalled a police officer picking up and shooting a dog, after having a public fight with his wife.

Without trying to analyse the multiple reasons for the extreme violence and hair-trigger volatility demonstrated by South African (and other) police officers, what is important to note is how these systems effectively enabled the continuation of violence against police members' intimate partners and, at the same time, disabled the systems that were supposed to help them. Nix commented that there was a:

brotherhood and loyalty among police which is difficult to break through to lay a charge. Police culture is sexist and traditional in its views towards women. The survivors may be too scared of their partner or of his friends in the police service and may be convinced that nothing will happen if she complains or lays a charge. Sadly, this is often true. (Nix J. 1988)

A decade later, when the then Independent Complaints Directorate (now the Independent Police Investigative Directorate or IPID, which is responsible for investigating complaints against SAPS and municipal police services) published a report[31] on femicide within the South African Police Service, it appeared that little, if anything, had changed. The study, which showed that cases of femicide committed by SAPS members had increased each year between 2004 and 2007, also showed that in many of the cases the women had attempted to lay charges of domestic violence against their partners, or had begged for their partners' service pistols to be taken away from them (the study showed that the majority of policemen killed their female partners with their service weapons). At the time, the minister of Safety and Security was being sued by a widow, Mrs N Hlomza, whose late husband (described in the report as being 'trigger happy', 'suicidal', and with a 'drinking problem') had been allowed to keep his service weapon despite his wife's repeated requests that it be taken away from him. The police officer subsequently committed suicide after shooting Mrs Hlomza in the neck and jaw. She survived, he did not.

Although the Independent Complaints Directorate report was not quite complete – remarkably, for a police document, only 30 of the 49 dockets were available – it also revealed another feature of the femicides, which was that 80% of the victims and the perpetrators were black, and only 3% were white (around this time, blacks made up 64% of sworn police officers and whites just over

22%, with coloured and Indian officers making up 10% and 4% respectively[32]).

Killing the rainbow

Between 1983 and 1986, the Centre for the Study of Violence and Reconciliation stated that only two out of 126 reported family killings that had taken place involved black families (and that 90 per cent of the cases involved Afrikaans-speaking families). By the end of 1990, however, there were reports of thirteen black family murders in just six months.[33]

This marked a shift in the profile of family murders in South Africa – or at least the reporting of it. After this time, an increasing number of black family murders and femicide-suicides would be reported in the press.

When viewed against the admittedly patchy data on suicide and homicide-suicide that is available around this period, what emerges is a picture that, while not entirely overturning the narrative that whites experienced the highest rate of suicide and therefore also homicide-suicide, certainly challenged the idea that it was a 'disease' that was exclusive to whites.

A study by Jena, Mountany and Muller (2008) on homicide-suicides presenting at the Pretoria medico-legal laboratory between January 1997 and October 2001[34] identified 46 cases during that time, of which 45 perpetrators were male and one was female. There were 50 victims associated with these incidents, 45 female and five male (the victims also included children); 78% of the perpetrators were black and 22% were white (there were no homicide-suicide cases from other race groups).

A later study on suicide only in Pretoria (Engelbrecht et al., 2017[35]), looking at deaths between 2007 and 2010, found that whites made up slightly more victims overall – 477 or 50% of victims in the study, compared to 447 (47%) black victims, where the population of Pretoria was around 75% black and 22% white. While this demonstrates a significant over-representation of white suicides in Pretoria, it would also not be correct to say that, because of the comparison relative to population size, black suicides were unimportant or non-existent.

In a separate study on homicide-suicide in the city of Durban, Roberts et al. (2010) looked at homicide-suicide cases that presented at the Durban central mortuary between January 2000 and December 2001. The authors found that 91% of perpetrators and 87% of victims were black, that the perpetrators were mostly male, and that 75% of perpetrators were the intimate partners of the victim (other victims, including children, would obviously not count as intimate partners). The study found that 10% of perpetrators were Indian, and there were no white or coloured perpetrators reported at that mortuary during the study period. At that time, Durban's population was estimated to be 68% black, 20% Indian, and 9% white.[36]

In my own study of femicide-suicides that took place in 2012/13, and which were reported in the press, there were a total of 36 perpetrators associated with 40 femicide victims (plus at least six child victims). All but four of the adult victims were intimate partners, and all of the non-intimate victims were immediate family members (a mother, a mother-in-law and a sister-in-law), except for one victim who was the female best friend of the primary (intimate partner) victim. Of the killers, only four were white, two were coloured, and the race of four of the perpetrators could not be determined based on news reports. This means that 72 per cent of femicide-suicide perpetrators covered in news stories were black men, while white perpetrators were only responsible for ten per cent of the femicides. A quarter of all the perpetrators were policemen or former cops.

As many suicide studies have previously commented, what these data show is that we need more information and better information about suicide in South Africa. But, even incomplete, they also make a strong case that the 'missing' data on black family killings (and, as part of this, black femicide-suicides) – which was suggested by researchers for decades – deserves much closer attention and was not necessarily a scheme cooked up by apartheid propagandists to somehow draw attention away from the murderous habits of white Afrikaans families.

Either something quite radical happened in South Africa around 1990, which completely and entirely upturned the profile of family killings and suicides in the black community (it's unlikely the release of Nelson Mandela made black men suddenly more murderous towards their wives); or these incidents existed long before that time, and just weren't recorded or weren't considered important enough to record. Having spent a fair amount of time reading other South African crime data, and how it was recorded and reported, there is a fairly strong case for the latter – although it might also be a case where both statements are true. Because there is one other factor that I believe may have played a role in the profile of inter-personal violence, including family and intimate partner killings by black perpetrators. This is the availability of firearms (which will be discussed in the next chapter). Because of apartheid laws, black men were only really able to purchase personal firearms after the early to mid-1980s, which is also the same time we start to see an uptick in firearm femicides and femicide-suicides in black communities.

Current news coverage of femicide-suicides also raises a further question for me: if the data from the 1999 Medical Research Council study shows that the largest category of perpetrators of intimate femicide-suicides are white men, and historically the news used to focus a lot of resources on covering white family killings and couple killings, where are these deaths now? It seems improbable to me that, after centuries of successful misogyny, white South African males have suddenly become more peaceful under democracy, and have stopped murdering their wives and killing themselves. In which case, it suggests that for one reason or the other, the media is simply no longer reporting on these cases.

6. 'Man Shoots Woman': Firearms and femicide in South Africa

'Man shoots wife himself, after roadside argument' – *Pretoria News*, 6 September 2001

'Man kills woman and himself on PE street' – *EP Herald*, 29 January 2002

'Man shoots wife then kills himself' – *The Citizen*, 28 October 2002

'Man shoots wife in city, then kills himself' – *Pretoria News*, 19 December 2003

'Cop jailed for shooting wife' – *The Citizen*, 26 February 2004

'Man shoots wife, cop, himself' – *The Star*, 9 June 2004

'Man shoots family' – *Daily News*, 9 August 2004

'Girlfriend gunned down in shop' – *The Star*, 27 January 2005

'Man shoots wife as he hands gun to police' – *Pretoria News*, 8 April 2005

'Husband shoots wife and two young sons dead' – *Sunday Times*, 12 March 2006

'Man shoots ex-wife on arrival at church' – *Cape Argus*, 22 January 2007

'Man kills pregnant woman, then shoots himself in EL store' – *Daily Dispatch*, 13 June 2007

'Man shoots wife, kills son' – *Witness*, 2 January 2008

'Man kills wife, shoots self' – *City Press*, 17 February 2008

'Man fatally shoots wife, misses kids, kills himself' – *The Star*, 4 March 2009

'Warder shoots wife at prison' – *Cape Times*, 24 August 2009

'Man shoots wife and then kills himself' – *The Star*, 18 April 2012

'Man kills ex-wife, shoots himself' – *The New Age*, 2 January 2013

'Traffic cop held for shooting wife' – *Daily Dispatch*, 15 February 2013

'Police officer allegedly shoots wife in head' – *The Star*, 9 June 2017

'Man shoots woman and then himself' – *Cape Argus*, 1 November 2017

*

Before you read the rest of this chapter, think on this: the majority of women who are murdered in South Africa are killed by their intimate partners. More than 80 per cent of intimate femicide victims are killed by a firearm injury, mostly from a single gunshot to the head or face. Most of them are killed in their own homes. In three-quarters of these cases, the perpetrator is a legal firearm owner using a licensed weapon.

*

Whenever there is another mini 'femicide crisis' in the news (the crisis is happening every day, but it's only at certain times that the public and media pays attention), I am almost guaranteed of coming across a message on social media that goes something along the lines of 'If only more women had more guns, we wouldn't have such a femicide problem.'

This is not only untrue, it's dishonest. Because we have decades' worth of data showing exactly the opposite. But this doesn't stop the misleading rhetoric that more gun ownership is somehow the key to reducing violence. In 2015, the lobby group Gun Owners of South Africa even created a campaign to encourage women to arm themselves. They called it 'Girls on Fire' and the logo included a 'sexy' silhouette of a woman holding an M-16 rifle. The campaign hashtag is #VictimNoLonger and it states that women should be 'equipped with the appropriate tools to protect themselves and their families' (that is, guns), apparently oblivious to the fact that most women are murdered by intimate partners or close family members. In photographs on the organisation's website, the Girls on Fire women (who are not actually girls, it seems) can be seen wearing black golf shirts with what I assume is an image of actual fire printed on the fabric. This has the unfortunate effect of making the women look like they are being braaied. Which, in my view, is possibly more accurate than claims that guns will help defeat gender-based violence.

Let's go back to what we know about femicide for a moment: that most women are killed by their intimate partners, and that many of these women are killed by a gun legally owned by their murderer. It has never really been clear to me how arming women would improve this, the most likely potentially fatal situation women would find themselves in – unless the gun owner lobby is recommending a family-style six-gun shootout in the living room and whichever parent draws first, wins. I'm being deliberately flippant here, because it's a grotesque scenario.

But what about if the male perpetrator isn't armed, you ask? If we imagine a scenario where a male perpetrator is about to stab, beat or strangle his intimate partner to death – surely there, you suggest, an armed woman at least now has a fighting chance. Guns are the great equalisers and might allow a woman to defeat an almost certainly physically stronger opponent, right? The problem with this scenario is that it relies on a host of other problematic assumptions, long before we get to the Julia Roberts Hollywood ending where she magically finds, draws and fires her weapon at the last minute. First, a reminder that women in abusive relationships sometimes aren't even allowed to bathe or shower without their partner's knowledge or approval. It's hard to see how a woman in this kind of situation, where her every move is closely monitored and controlled, would go and secretly get a gun, and hide it from her partner. Then there is the even bigger question as to whether, even if she did get a gun, she would be able to get to its (secret?) hiding place in time and actually be able to use it before she was killed. This is not just conjecture. Every year there are multiple femicide cases involving female police officers who are killed by their partners. Port Shepstone Constable Nandipha 'Carol' Zibi was shot and killed with her own service pistol by an ex-boyfriend who attacked her at her home. Constable Nonhlanhla Martha Masia was shot at six times by her police captain husband – who came back to shoot her in the head when he saw her stand up again after the first volley. He later claimed he had shot her in self-defence. Warrant Officer Tessa Steyn was lying on a couch in her home when she was shot in the head by her estranged ex-cop husband, while their twelve-year-old daughter was asleep in the room next door. Constable Mbali Nxumalo was shot and killed by her boyfriend, a Metro Police officer. And these are just some of the policewomen deaths that took place between 2012 and 2013.

The point is that if a trained police officer isn't able to get to her service weapon to use it in her own defence, what are the odds that most other women – with less proficiency and quite probably a weapon that is not conveniently ready on a hip or leg or concealed holster but in a handbag or in a safe – would fare any better in the same situation?

'But what if a gun saved even one woman?' you ask.

Well, that is something to consider. But this is not what the data shows us.

Research into murder, violence and mortality in South Africa repeatedly and consistently shows that guns have entirely the opposite effect when it comes to the safety and lives of women (and men, for that matter; men, after all, make up nearly 90 per cent of gun deaths in South Africa). And that having a firearm in the home is a major risk factor in intimate femicide.

Not only do we have longitudinal data that tells us how and how many people die from gunshot injuries, we also have data that shows us what happens when tighter controls are imposed on gun ownership (murders go down) *and* what happens when access to firearms increases again after that (murders go up).

The people who have produced, analysed and published this data are, as a rule, highly qualified academics and researchers, with decades of expertise in studying the demography and epidemiology of violence and mortality in particular. They (like me) study violence because they hope that better information can help us develop better solutions to reducing violence. And, trust me, if a single one of us thought more guns were a good solution, you can be sure we would say so.

The gun lobby repeatedly accuses these researchers of being partisan, but it's not clear what kind of partisanship is involved in wanting fewer people to die in brutal ways – as opposed to the quite obvious agenda of the gun lobby which, over the past few years in particular, has increasingly adopted the mindless rhetoric of the heavily funded American pro-gun faction. Not coincidentally, this narrative corresponds with Donald Trump's presidency and gun manufacturers' attempts to expand their global markets outside of the United States (in much the same way as the tobacco lobby has now targeted Africa and Asia for death sticks).

Which brings us back to the ridiculousness of the assertion that the only way to stop a bad man with a gun is to have a good woman (or is it a girl?) with her own gun. This makes some additional problematic assumptions about who is supposedly a 'good' person (or a 'good girl'). But it's a myth. One that has been fact-checked and debunked quite thoroughly.

Naeemah Abrahams, Rachel Jewkes and Shanaaz Mathews' 2010 study on guns and gender-based violence in South Africa (using data from the Medical Research Council's 1999 femicide study) looked at the role of firearms in all female homicides, not just intimate-partner shootings. They found that, of teenage and adult women murdered in South Africa in 1999, a third of the victims had died from gunshot injuries, and more than 60 per cent of these injuries had occurred at home. For the women who were victims of intimate partner gun homicide, '67.4% were killed with a single shot, most often to the head and face (63.7%)'.[1]

Another chilling statistic stood out from the study: nearly three-quarters of the guns used in these murders were licensed and legally owned, with unlicensed firearms used only in a quarter of gun femicides. Legal gun ownership was also linked with higher rates of suicide after the murder, increasing suicide risk seven times (or 700%) even after the researchers had adjusted the data for other social and demographic factors.

Another common argument I see online is that guns don't kill people, people kill people, and that even if we took people's guns away, they would find other ways of killing each other.

This is partly true but in this case it's not the entire truth. Taking guns away wouldn't stop murder as a whole. It would just stop a lot of it. One of the reasons for this is because guns are so efficient at doing what they are designed to do (kill people, fast) that it's hard to change the outcome once a firearm has been drawn and used. Guns are extremely easy to fire, and gunshot wounds are more likely to be fatal than other injuries. Also, Stephen King movies notwithstanding, it is quite difficult to stab someone to death through a locked door.

South Africa is quite an important country for studies of gun violence, because we have a fairly large population (we're more than double the size of Australia's population, for example), and also because we have quite a lot of guns – useful when studying gun violence, but not so great for other things. Related to this fact, we also have quite a lot of violence.

Another reason why South Africa is an important case study for gun violence, though, is because about 20 years ago we changed our gun laws; and, as soon as these changes were rolled out, we also saw a corresponding change in the profile and proportion of gun deaths.

The Firearms Control Act

In 2000, new legislation on gun control was introduced in South Africa. The Firearms Control Act No. 60 of 2000 was drafted to replace the outdated Arms and Ammunition Act of 1969 and created measures to prevent the proliferation of illegal firearms, improve controls over legal firearms and provide for the disposal of illegal firearms, among other things.

The Act, broadly, introduced much stricter requirements for private and business owners, including that each gun had to be licensed individually (and licences had to be renewed every five to ten years); individual owners were limited to a single firearm for self-defence and a total of four firearms for self-defence and other uses (such as sports shooting and hunting); and gun owners had to complete competency certificates, which must be renewed every five years. Fully automatic firearms and certain types of modified firearms (sawn-off shotguns, for example) were prohibited.[2]

The new Act was assented to in April 2001 but was only fully implemented as late as 2004.[3] As Matzopoulos et al. explain in a study on firearm vs non-firearm deaths:

> The stricter licensing conditions under the Firearms Control Act No. 60 of 2000 were part of a broader strategy to reduce the number of guns in circulation, and there was a firearm-access gradient between the FCA being passed in 2000 and its full implementation in 2004. The period was characterised by firearm amnesties and hand-ins, in which legal and illegal guns were recovered by the authorities, more rigorous application of existing licensing conditions, and the destruction of surplus and illegal weapons. The South African Defence Force destroyed an estimated 270,000 weapons between January 1998 and May 2001, and the police destroyed 30,000 in 2001 (Meek & Stott, 2003). It was also notable that there was a 75% increase in the number of firearms recov-

ered by the police in 2003 compared with the previous year (i.e. from 20,000 weapons confiscated and recovered in 2002 to 35,000 in 2003) (Mthembu-Salter & Lamb, 2008). This coincides with the period in which the decline in firearm homicide became evident. After full implementation of the FCA in 2004, this effort was redoubled and a further 100,000 firearms were collected in the first six months of 2005.[4]

The implementation of the Firearms Control Act had a significant influence on South African firearm homicide rates in particular, which had increased at an annual rate of thirteen per cent between 1994 and 2000 but declined by fifteen per cent from 2003 to 2006.[5]

Because these increases and later decreases had taken place during periods when the overall homicide rate was rising and decreasing in South Africa, when researchers began to study the change in gun homicides they specifically investigated whether, within the context of generally declining homicide rates in South Africa between 2001 and 2005, the decrease was specific to gun homicides and whether it could be specifically attributed to the stricter gun controls that had come into place during the phased implementation of the Firearms Control Act.[6]

To do this, the researchers conducted a retrospective study of 37 067 homicide cases presented to mortuaries in Cape Town, Durban (eThekwini), Johannesburg, Port Elizabeth (Nelson Mandela Bay), and Pretoria (Tshwane) during the five-year period from 2001 to 2005. The data was acquired through the National Injury Mortality Surveillance System, with the authors noting that there was 'erratic coverage' for this data after 2005.[7]

To work out homicide *rates* (that is, frequency of murders relative to different population sizes over time), the homicide data was used together with population estimates from municipal demarcation boards and the 2001 national census. The study only covered the large urban areas mentioned and did not include data from the Free State, Northern Cape, Mpumalanga, North West and Limpopo, but it did refer to a number of other mortuary-based and similar studies which appeared to confirm the general hypothesis. (This study, like most of the other large mortuary- or autopsy-based studies I cite in this book, is freely available to read online.)

What the researchers found was that, during the study period, firearm homicides had declined at a faster rate than all non-firearm homicides, altering the ratio to the extent that by 2005, firearms were (marginally) no longer the leading means of murder in South Africa. The study estimated that during the study period alone more than 4 500 lives had been saved by the implementation of the Firearms Control Act.[8]

This was borne out by the results from the Medical Research Council's second national femicide study, which looked at deaths that occurred in 2009 (again the data was based on post mortems and police dockets). Here, the researchers found that femicide rates overall had decreased compared to 1999 – dropping by nearly 38 per cent (although homicide had declined by an even greater rate during that time). Equally important, they found that gun-related homicides across both intimate and non-intimate femicides had nearly halved, a factor the authors suggested was specifically due to the introduction of the gun control legislation.

These findings were quite controversial among gun-owning circles who, like their brethren in 1977, felt rather strongly about their need to own firearms (the Firearms Control Act did not prevent gun ownership, of course, it just introduced more controls), and the pro-gun lobby made a number of attempts to query or challenge the research. They published incensed op-eds on local media platforms, in which they questioned data about firearm deaths – in particular, they used figures from a Statistics South Africa report, in which the state statistical agency said that death by 'other and unspecified firearm discharge' made up just 1.7 per cent of the 5 019 'assault deaths'[9] – a far cry from the majority and near majority of violent deaths the studies had claimed.

Richard Matzopoulos, Pamela Groenewald, Naeemah Abrahams and Debbie Bradshaw subsequently published a paper in the *South African Medical Journal* that asked, 'Where Have All the Gun Deaths Gone?', addressing this seeming contradiction.

The authors identified 105 694 gunshot-injury-related deaths over a seventeen-year period (from 1997 to 2013) and discussed these together with the findings of several other national and regional studies into injury mortality profiles. After a review of the data, the authors explained that the apparent absence of (homicidal) gun deaths in statistical records was largely due to 'extensive misclassification' of the cause of death in assault cases. They added that prior to 2006, 'most gunshot-related injury deaths (between 76% and 94% annually) were recorded as due to undetermined intent' rather than being classified as 'intentional, assault' (as opposed to 'intentional, self-harm' or 'unintentional').[10] The authors again concluded that the introduction of the Firearms Control Act was the cause of the decrease in gunshot deaths from 2000 until 2010.

Although it rather proved Matzopoulos et al.'s argument, there was an unhappy footnote to the study. The paper noted that from 2011 onwards there had been an increase in firearm homicides, which corresponded with 'the police fast-tracking the finalisation of more than a million firearm-related applications for firearm licences, licence renewals for individuals, and competency certificates between November 2010 and July 2011',[11] together with an increase in the trafficking of illegal firearms in several high-profile cases.

In some of those cases, it was policemen themselves who were responsible for the trafficking and sale of illegal weapons. In one case, a (now former) police colonel sold an estimated 2 000 firearms that were meant to be destroyed, and which ultimately wound up in the hands of Cape Flats gang members. News reports state that an estimated 1 066 murders were carried out with 888 of these guns between 2010 and 2014.[12]

According to Gun Free South Africa, there is no accurate data on the number of illegal guns in the country. In April 2019 more than 30 000 firearms were destroyed at the ArcelorMittal plant in Vereeniging; another 20 000 illegal weapons were scheduled for destruction in November the same year. But these are a drop in the ocean compared to the 4.5 million legal guns in South Africa (licensed to 1.8 million gun owners; and yes, that is more than two guns per owner). Gun Free South Africa reports that more than 90 per cent of gun owners are civilians and the overwhelming majority of licensed gun owners – around 81 per cent – are men. In 2017/2018, civilian gun owners reported the loss or theft of 8 867 guns (during the same period the police lost only 358 guns). Despite the perception that illegal handguns are smuggled into South Africa, researchers say that there are indications these types of weapons are more likely to be smuggled *from* South Africa to neighbouring countries.[13]

This is at the heart of the pro-gun lobby argument: that to counter illegal guns, we need more people with legal firearms. And, extending the same logic, to counter these men with legal guns, we now need more women with guns. It's not quite a circle, it's just vicious, and only seeks to escalate rather than de-escalate violence. (Perhaps it won't come as a complete surprise that Paul and Lynette Oxley, the couple behind Gun Owners of South Africa, own a weapons business.)

History also tells us the same story in South Africa – how guns escalate violence, not the other way around (not ever, actually).

The first firearms in South Africa were brought in by colonisers. When Jan van Riebeeck arrived in 1652, his men brought with them long matchlock muskets. A report in the *South African Journal of Military Studies*[14] says that these guns – which were up to 1.5 metres long and weighed over six kilograms – were so heavy the barrel had to be rested on a forked stick when they were fired. Soldiers also quickly discovered that the fuses and powder were difficult to light in windy conditions, or when they got wet, and so they were replaced with flintlock muskets, which were used with potent effect against indigenous Khoekhoen and San people, and, later, against amaXhosa and other Bantu groups on the Eastern 'frontier'.

Various iterations and improvements on these firearms were introduced over the years, and guns were used as both a means of taking the land and controlling it, as well as transactional items. There are records of BaPedi men being paid in guns to come and work at the diamond fields in Kimberley in the late 1800s. Less than a century later South Africa would boast a world-renowned arms industry, bolstered by a strong domestic market which was attempting to fight off the growing threats of both internal and external liberation movements in the southern African region. Later, as international sanctions took effect, the importance of the domestic arms industry strengthened as the apartheid government was no longer able to import weapons or components.

After the uprisings of 1976, moves to arm white South Africans individually were also ramped up – the East Rand Bantu Affairs Board reportedly set up a fund to pay for guns for its employees, while the South African Railways apparently sold rifles to its staff for just R7 a gun.[15] It may or may not be coincidence that this is exactly the period where we start to see a marked increase in at least the reporting of family killings in the white community. Under the Arms and Ammunition Act No. 75 of 1969, black South Africans were prohibited from owning personal firearms[16] before 1983. But, at the same time, the South African government was busy providing arms to security forces in the Bantustans, to anti-communism movements in other African states, and even to political parties within South Africa that were seen as a means of assisting the apartheid state's agenda against freedom fighters. Hit squad commander and counter-insurgency policeman Eugene de Kock supplied 64 tonnes of weapons to Inkatha Freedom Party (IFP) warlords, calculated to feed the feud between the IFP and the African National Congress. In response to and because of the increased and widespread trade in weapons, the ANC began to smuggle weapons into South Africa to arm its own cadres, and an increased black-market demand for firearms grew in the townships.[17] In this environment, parallel hierarchies of militarism (one state, one liberation) became entrenched and, with them, cultures of violence, which moved almost seamlessly between the violence of politics, the violence of crime and violence in the home.

If we read our previous chapters against this historical backdrop, a new correlation becomes much more prominent, more probable: that the emergence of Pretoria as the (white) 'murder capital of the world', from the late 1970s to the early 1990s, and the subsequent surge of black male suicides, homicide-suicides and family killings from the mid-1980s onward were directly tied not just to political tension and a growing 'culture of violence', but were directly and undeniably linked to increased access to *legal* firearms.

If we are truly interested in protecting women's lives, all the data points consistently to the same solution, which is: we need to disarm more men, not arm more women.

PART TWO

Non-intimate femicide

7. 'A fate worse than death': Rape and femicide

In late 2019 I travelled to Delhi[1] to present research which looked at the connections between media coverage of two prominent rape-homicides in two different countries: the murder of Jyoti Singh, in Delhi in December 2012; and the killing of Anene Booysen, in Bredasdorp in February 2013.[2]

At times it felt surreal discussing 'academic' work just ten, maybe fifteen kilometres from where Jyoti Singh had been so brutally attacked. Her death – and the many other violent rapes and homicides that have since been featured in the Indian press – formed a constant background noise throughout the trip, an unmistakable klaxon of warning every time I walked down a street on my own, every time I caught an Uber . . . I think that all women know this feeling in one form or another, but it is one that women in India and in South Africa perhaps know in particular.

A few days before the Delhi workshop I had been in the smaller city of Jaipur. My hosts had warned me not to attempt to walk one particular stretch of road by myself, even in the middle of the day. There was no real explanation given, only that it was too empty for a woman to safely be alone. Twenty years ago, perhaps I would have laughed and said, 'Don't worry, I'm from South Africa', and pressed on regardless. But I am no longer fearless, if indeed I ever really was. I am cynical and sometimes overly cautious. And I am quite frequently afraid, although some might just say it's pragmatic. I am also angry. We should not have to live like this. But we have always lived like this.

There are many reasons why strong narrative ties exist between the cases of Jyoti Singh and Anene Booysen, and between violence against women in India and in South Africa. Our two countries have some of the highest rates of gender-based violence in the world, and (even though, as Africa Check argues[3], we don't have enough data to award a title for 'worst' offender when it comes to sexual violence) newspapers and politicians frequently like to name each country as the leading contenders in a truly terrible contest for who can be called the world's 'Rape Capital'.

It was coverage of Jyoti's death (or, more precisely, coverage of the protests after her rape and subsequent death) that provided the frame within which the initial coverage of Anene's killing was reported. A number of research papers have identified this relationship but have not necessarily explored how it played out, or why it did so almost exclusively for Anene and not for other women (which is the subject of my own research).

Some writers attribute the narrative overlap to the similarities between the two deaths – both women were raped and later died from internal injuries as a result of the attacks; both women lived just long enough to describe their attack or their attackers.

But the truth is there was little in common between Jyoti Singh and Anene Booysen other than what they came to represent.

Jyoti Singh was a middle-class physiotherapy student attending university in Delhi. Her parents were married, and her father had sold off family land to pay for his daughter's education. Jyoti had been out with a male friend and was abducted, beaten and raped by a group of strangers – including the driver – on a bus.

Anene Booysen was a foster child who had dropped out of school at the end of Grade 7 to get a job. At the time of her death, she had been working on a construction site for low-income (RDP) houses in the town of Bredasdorp. Anene had been drinking at a tavern a few blocks from her home and had been raped and beaten by men who were known to her.

There were, of course, parallels in the injuries inflicted on both women – Jyoti Singh and Anene Booysen suffered massive, ultimately fatal, internal injuries as a direct result of their rapes. In the Delhi attack an iron bar was used during the assault and had torn out the victim's intestines; when Anene was found, still alive, at the construction site where she worked, witnesses described her intestines as hanging out between her legs.

But even these details were sadly not unique in South Africa's femicide files. Within weeks of Anene's death, at least two other South African women were raped and beaten so badly that they were left mutilated. In Grahamstown a woman named Thandiswa Qubuda was left brain-damaged after a gang rape in January, which had left her so badly disfigured that she was initially admitted to hospital as a victim of a suspected motor vehicle accident. Later that same month, a fourteen-year-old high school student named Thandeka Madonsela was raped and disembowelled by two teenage assailants, her body left in the veld near Naturena. Neither of these cases received particularly prominent media coverage (just thirteen and sixteen news reports, respectively). But Anene Booysen's death went on to become the second most-highly covered femicide of the entire year, after the killing of model Reeva Steenkamp, mentioned in at least 679 news reports. Sometimes, this is just how the media works. There is no clever answer or reason, it just is what it is. Later in this book I talk about what the media gets wrong in its coverage of femicide, and why we 'choose' some victims but cannot choose all of them.

While I was reading about Jyoti Singh's case, many years after I had first read the horrific news accounts of the fatal attack, I observed something else. That, in most reports, to this day, even in the Wikipedia entry about the attack, it is still referred to as the 'Delhi gang rape' – as if the victim's death was somehow the lesser of the crimes that resulted from that night. As if being raped was somehow a fate worse than death.

This was not a unique example. Similar effects are recorded and compounded across thousands of other media reports on femicide, what UK researchers Paul Mason and Jane Monckton-Smith describe as a conflation of the offences of the rape and murder of women.[4]

This widespread practice has meant that there is frequently a tendency to sexualise reports on the murder of women (for example, mentioning the victim's state of undress, or even that she was fully clothed – as a pre-emptive narrative – whether or not there was any evidence of sexual assault during her murder); and, also, that sexual assaults of women are often framed within a broader discourse of lethal violence – that is, that the act of rape, or sexual assault, is always positioned 'potentially fatal'. While the latter may be true in some instances, in many it is patently not; and, as Mason and Monckton-Smith point out, the repeated narration of rape as 'deadly' has the net effect of casting doubt over less-violent sexual assaults, perpetuating the misconception that only a rape that threatens the victim's life can be considered a 'real rape'.[5]

This is an important point if we want to understand what media reporting about rape-homicide reveals about our own perceptions of sexual assault and about violence. In order for an adult woman's rape to be taken seriously – for her rape to be credible beyond any doubt – she has to have died (or very nearly died) as a result of the attack. The moment a woman survives, she is immediately considered complicit in her own rape.

These same factors also contribute to sensationalised reporting of femicides with possible or alleged 'sexual' motives, and also to an under-reporting (in the press) of rape-homicides committed by intimate partners compared to rape-homicides perpetrated by strangers. We become afraid of the men under the bridge, the man driving an Uber, but not the friend at a bar, or the man who shares a bed with us.

As with femicide, the term 'rape-homicide' is not recognised as a specific forensic category by pathologists, and such data is not routinely collected outside of studies.[6] Rape also cannot be verified through autopsy alone (that is, even evidence of sexual intercourse, penetration of genitals, genital injury etc. is not in itself conclusive of a rape). For this reason, many studies refer to 'suspected' rape homicides, or may describe the category of rape-homicide as 'homicides occurring with a sexual component (not limited to the penetration of the genitalia by a penis)'. The definitions of rape and sexual assault in South Africa also changed after 2007[7], and this should be taken into account when reading data on rape and homicide that were published at different times.

Nearly 30 years ago, Professor Lorna Martin – now the head of Forensic Medicine and Toxicology at the University of Cape Town, then a district surgeon in Hillbrow – published a groundbreaking study on rape in Johannesburg in 1992. A few years later she followed up with a study on rape-homicide in the Cape Town metropolitan area. This research in part informed the subsequent Medical Research Council national studies on femicide, which Martin co-authored, and which, together with other information, provided us with national data on the phenomenon of rape and female homicide in South Africa in 1999 and 2009.

A few years after the first (1999) femicide findings were published in 2004, the study's authors released an additional paper looking specifically at suspected rape homicides within the data.[8]

Data from this study found that rape-homicides were suspected in a little over sixteen per cent of femicides, and that rape-homicides were 'more likely . . . than other female homicides to be crimes where the perpetrator and victim were strangers, where the crime happened in public spaces and the victim [was] older than the perpetrator'.[9] The researchers added that they 'did not differentiate between the intent to rape with death as an outcome and the intent to murder with rape as a component'. (If this part doesn't yet make sense to you, it might in a moment.)

Data from the 2009 autopsy-based femicide study[10] found suspected rape-homicides in nearly 20 per cent of the sample – it was questioned whether this increase may have been due to an improvement of artefacts such as rape kits rather than an increase in the incidence of rape as part of female homicide, but researchers said they did not believe this was the case.

Although the perpetrator was unknown in a third of sexual homicide cases, where this information was available the data found again that there was a higher proportion of rape-homicides within the non-intimate femicide set – 28.5% of non-intimate femicides involved a suspected sexual component, compared with 13.2% in 1999. But (and this is important), although only 11% of intimate partner femicides had a sexual component, intimate partners were still responsible for 22.5% of sexual homicides. The Medical Research Council data also found that there was a much higher proportion of sexual homicides among victims who were pregnant – more than a quarter of adult women and nearly a fifth of pregnant child victims (which is an abhorrent phrase in itself) showed features of sexual assault as part of the murder. In addition, nearly 28% of sexual homicides were committed by acquaintances. This serves as a reminder that women's greatest threats are, consistently, the people closest to them. Family members also made up a little over 4% of perpetrators of alleged rape homicide for adult victims, and more than 27% of perpetrators of sexual homicides of child victims.

This speaks to a complex and quite uncomfortable theatre of horror around the reality of sexual homicides – the kind that won't make it to Hollywood movies. In October 2012, for example, a man named Morena Petrus Mofokeng broke into his aunt Betty Mofokeng's house and raped and murdered her. DNA evidence from the crime scene later linked him back to the rape and murder of an earlier victim: his 85-year-old grandmother, who he had killed in October 2010. Mofokeng's grandmother had died shortly after the attack and the case had been provisionally withdrawn as there was no other evidence, until the perpetrator raped and killed again.

Both the 1999 and 2009 femicide studies revealed other information: strangulation was the most common cause of death in suspected rape-homicides, although it was only the fourth most-common cause of death for all adult female homicides. This was important because – this takes us back to that earlier point of motive and murder – as Abrahams et al. (2017) noted, the prominence of strangulation as a cause of death pointed to the 'possibility that the primary motive [for many of the murders] may have been rape'. Strangulation is a consistent feature in non-fatal rape cases, as it is used to subdue the victim or induce unconsciousness. The researchers also added that this knowledge could be important 'for investigative purposes as it can guide forensic and police inquiry' – a point that is made earlier on in this book, and which bears repeating probably more than once: that femicides often have specific features, which need to be investigated properly in order to improve police and justice responses to these crimes. For example, what this might suggest is that strangulation could be considered a proxy for potential sexual assault, that is, if a victim is strangled to death, this might pre-emptively prescribe the use of a sexual evidence collection kit during the investigation, before the evidence is lost or degraded.

What the studies also found was that, consistent with higher proportions of non-intimate perpetrators, there were much higher levels of unidentified perpetrators among sexual homicide than in non-sexual homicides, and that there was a low rate of convictions for sexual homicide cases (only 28 per cent of sexual homicides of adult women resulted in convictions), which pointed further to cases that were 'not always well investigated'. In a 2017 paper, the authors noted that they had previously 'suggested protocols be developed to ensure routine screening and investigation of all female homicides for sexual crimes, and proposed the inclusion of a prescribed proforma document' and that, to their knowledge, this had not been done. They repeated a call for 'all female and child murders to have focused investigations by the police and the forensic pathologist for evidence of a sexual crime'.[11]

The reason for this goes beyond forensic and epidemiological queries. It impacts on the outcome of the justice process – if indeed a case ever crosses the threshold from police docket to court case.

Over the last few years, the South African government has repeatedly made loud-noise promises that perpetrators of gender-based violence should 'be warned' they could face 'lengthy prison sentences'[12]. In principle, the Criminal Law (Sexual Offences and Related Matters) Amendment Act allows for much harsher sentences for aggravating factors – if a rape is particularly brutal, and so on. The idea being that longer sentences supposedly act as a deterrent to other offenders.

But that requires reaching the end-game stage of a usually long and frequently ambivalent justice process which, at its inception, requires a foundation of solid police and forensic work in order to even make a case that can be prosecuted in the courts.

In an article discussing labelling and the definition of the crime of murder, criminal law professor Louise Jordaan explains that when 'convicting a person of murder' there is no difference between a 'ruthless killer who intentionally kills his victim to conceal a crime such as rape or purely for his own gratification and, for instance, a person who kills as a result of triggering factors such as fear of abuse, emotional stress or severe provocation'.[13] The circumstances of the killing and the 'degree of moral blameworthiness', she continues, only become relevant during sentencing. And a perpetrator only gets sentenced if he is convicted.

So, in order to achieve harsher sentences for sexual homicides, we would need first to ensure more convictions. Which would require not only a functional and relatively well-resourced and productive prosecuting authority, but which would also rely on good quality investigative work being done and documented by a functional and well-resourced police force. (And this is not even taking into account the vast number of rapes and sexual assaults which don't get reported, often *because* women and other victims have no faith that they will be taken seriously.) There is little functional purpose in having legislation that allows for longer sentencing, if we can't even get past the much earlier policing and prosecution hurdles.

During apartheid, rape was considered a capital crime (which is not to say all rape convictions ended in death sentences, only that they could). South Africa abolished capital punishment in 1995[14]; but every time there is another big rape case in the media there are usually renewed calls for the death penalty to be reinstated. This is a problematic call for many reasons. There is no evidence (anywhere) that such measures would achieve anything except assuage the public's bloodlust. Also, if you read my paragraph above, again, you might note that the police and justice systems are not currently in what you might describe as the optimal state, which is kind of the worst situation to implement an irreversible, fatal 'solution' that relies entirely on the supposedly undeniable guilt of the perpetrator. Or, in simpler terms: if we are only able to convict perpetrators in less than a third of all rape-homicide cases – and this figure is even lower for rape cases, where less than 20 per cent make it to court and less than ten per cent result in convictions[15] – on what basis do we imagine we would somehow effectively sentence men to death for rape, when the vast majority of the men who commit rape and rape-homicides are never even prosecuted?

But the death penalty remains a popular political gambit – an easy sop for politicians looking to sound like they take violence against women seriously, but without them having to really do anything about it. Nowhere is this more evident than in present-day India.

In the wake of the murder of Jyoti Singh, India's government passed the 2013 Criminal Law Amendment Act which allowed for a death sentence to be given (the death penalty still exists in India, but is rarely implemented) when a rape results in the death or the persistent vegetative state of the victim. In 2018, additional laws regarding the Protection of Children from Sexual Offences were amended to allow the death penalty for 'aggravated penetrative sexual assault' where the victim was a child under the age of twelve years, even where the victim did not die. This, too, came in the wake of another high-profile rape-homicide case, this time the killing of an eight-year-old Muslim girl who was abducted, drugged, held in a Hindu temple and raped multiple times by different men over a period of days before being strangled and hit over the head. Two of the men convicted of her death were police officers. Another two police officers were arrested and convicted of attempting to destroy evidence. More recently, in December 2019, four men accused of raping and killing a veterinary student in Hyderabad in India were shot and killed during a 'police encounter'. This took place when the accused and police were allegedly recreating the scene of the crime and, according to police accounts, the four accused stole weapons and fired on the police in an attempt to escape. The police returned fire and the accused were all shot dead. In many quarters this was hailed as a quick and satisfying means of justice. (Yet again, the Hyderabad killing has been used to introduce yet another bill[16], this time proposing the fast-tracking of the trials and death sentences for criminals found guilty of gang rape and murder.)

You might imagine that, after researching and writing about the awful and violent ways in which women die, I might also think that fast-tracking death sentences for rapists is 'justice'. I don't. I just have more questions about what 'justice' really means; and a growing awareness that, even though in South Africa we have tried to create a system which, on paper, situates us as equals, there remains tremendous inequality before the law. This inequality is why women are often not fully seen and heard, and certainly not respected or believed. But it is also why calls for things like the death penalty are not just ridiculous but ultimately malicious, because history has taught us that famous men, white men, wealthy men will have more access to 'justice' and less chance of a capital sentence than poor brown men, whether they are in India or in South Africa. (The same applies to repeated calls for a public sex offender registry in South Africa.)

However, I also believe that the law is also the very same area where this inequality must be challenged, and where nuance must be continually described and reclaimed. And indeed it is.

In December 2019, the South African Constitutional Court found that the doctrine of common purpose applied to the crime of rape – common purpose holds that when a group of people commit a crime together they share liability for the crime, even if they did not all individually commit the criminal act.

The case in question was linked to a series of attacks and rapes that had been committed by a criminal gang in Tembisa on the East Rand in the late 1990s. During a spate of robberies and housebreakings, several members of the gang had participated in raping eight different women. During some of the attacks, other gang members were posted outside to keep a lookout. Two of these men, Jabulane Tshabalala and Annanius Ntuli, had been convicted of rape under common purpose but argued that it should not apply in their case as the crime of rape specifically 'required the unlawful insertion of the male genitalia into the female genitalia' (the assaults had been committed prior to the new definition of rape), that is, that rape is an instrumentality offence and 'can only be committed by a male using his own genitalia'[17] – that is, through the instrumentality of his own body and not the instrumentality of another person's body.

When the Constitutional Court dismissed the applicants' appeal, in a majority judgement, the justices carefully spelled out why they had done so, describing the 'instrumentality' objection as obsolete and patriarchal, and explaining that it was 'necessary that the relationship between rape and power [be] considered [...] To characterise it simply as an act of a man inserting his genitalia into a female's genitalia without her consent is unsustainable. In instances of group rape, as in this case, the mere presence of a group of men results in power and dominance being exerted over women victims.'

The judgement goes on to say that '... rape can be committed by more than one person for as long as the others have the intention of exerting power and dominance over the women, just by their presence in the room'.[18]

This implies a participation and a culpability well beyond the imagination or comprehension of most men – certainly beyond the ken of the 'not all men' cadres – and even of many women. It is a harsh but accurate iteration of what feminists in the 1970s and 1980s meant when they first described the concept of a 'rape culture'.

In her book *Rape: A South African Nightmare,* Professor Pumla Gqola describes reaching the painful realisation that she 'no longer think[s] a small minority of men are holding us hostage'. Like the Constitutional Court judges, women are still learning how acts of violence against women are not committed only by the body or the actions of individual perpetrators, but that this violence is directly enabled by all the other men who are 'in the room', so to speak.

Sexual violence is, of course, not directly analogous to murder, but, in addition to being associated with fatal violence against women, it is, as Helen Moffett writes, primarily 'an instrument of gender domination'[19] – as is femicide. Both rape and femicide need be seen and understood as parts of a continuum or a continuity of violence against women, where killing is the final act, and rape is one of many weapons.

8. 'We only write about them when they are dead': Hate killings of black lesbians in South Africa

A few years ago, I ran a series of workshops for the editorial department of a large daily newspaper. In one of our sessions we were discussing the impact of prejudice and bias on reporting – how our own individual or societal value systems grooved us into often unsubstantiated or even irrational positive or negative associations with individuals and groups who were either like or unlike us.

This isn't a South African phenomenon, of course, but a human one. We rely on shared social meanings to make sense of the world around us, and to cue us as to how to respond to that world. Depending on our circumstances, we might be taught to trust (or fear) teachers, police officers, nurses, doctors, and so on. When we see a smiling granny with cookies, we usually think of being comforted and not the witch who baked a gingerbread house to trap children for her supper.

These shared social or cultural meanings reflect certain communal and societal values and, because of that, they are often an inherent part of how the media chooses and narrates stories about women who are victims of violence. Teenage girls are either innocent or wayward, depending on the girl (if she has a boyfriend, she is probably the latter). A woman drinking at a bar or going to or from a shebeen or a party is complicit in what happens to her afterward. Elderly women are blameless and passive – so much so that they are 'ideal' victims, by which I mean society is most likely to give them the status of a being a 'legitimate' victim.

The nature of media is also that it deals much better in stereotypes than in nuances, and sometimes this means that news stories take on characteristics of old-fashioned folktales, where the monsters are Very Big and Very Bad, and Dark Strangers offering you sweeties from their car bear little resemblance to the uncle who is statistically more likely to molest you.

While I was teaching this group of journalists and editors about diversity and prejudice and bias, and how these related to issues of fear and trust, and how those in turn affected accuracy and credibility, one of the editors made the observation that the only time their newspaper ever wrote about lesbians was when they had been killed.

And indeed, in the pages of their newspaper there were never any lesbian grannies sharing cooking recipes, or lesbian policewomen, or lesbian business owners, or lesbian mothers, or lesbian beauty salon owners sharing skincare tips. With few (predictable) exceptions, the only time black lesbians made it into print was when they had been raped and killed. This was important because, from a media theory perspective, it meant that black lesbians never got to occupy any sort of conventional or 'normal' part of the stories that were told about society, an absence which, in itself, had the effect of 'othering' these women – that is, they were not included in the everyday; they were only ever part of something monstrous, and gruesome.

When I started looking through archival news coverage in South Africa I noticed that, for the most part, this was historically true of most media platforms. Stories that mentioned lesbians were few and far between, and almost always sensational. In the white newspapers[1], they were usually tragicomic stories about the failures of lesbian relationships which had started with one woman cheating on her husband with another woman, punctuated by occasional children (providing the opportunity to mock the other lesbian partner for proudly exclaiming she was now 'a father'), which often involved 'lesbian love triangles' (in Afrikaans the prurient-sounding 'lesbies driehoek'), and which sometimes ended in a dramatic attempted or even successful murder of one partner by the other.

The only other times that lesbianism was mentioned in the press – barring a few risqué book and film reviews – was usually when one or other church leader was counselling against same-sex relationships as being an abomination before God, although apartheid South Africa's immorality laws did not actually prohibit sexual relations between women (sodomy, on the other hand, was a crime, and there was apparently even provision in the Criminal Procedure Act of 1977 which allowed a member of the public to carry out a citizen's arrest if they suspected an act of sodomy was in progress[2]).

In 1990, the year that Nelson Mandela was released, Johannesburg held the very first Gay and Lesbian Pride march, at which Simon Nkoli, Beverly Ditsie and Justice Edwin Cameron were among the speakers. The marchers chanted, 'Out of the closet and into the streets.'

It was a significant moment, but it would take several more years before gay, lesbian, bisexual, transsexual and intersex individuals would be granted similar rights and protections as hetero- and cissexual South Africans, first under an interim and then a final Constitution, which prohibited discrimination on the basis of sexual orientation and gender.

Between 1994 and 2005 a number of legal amendments were made and new laws introduced, which formalised rights of LGBTI individuals. In due course, the criminalisation of sodomy was declared unconstitutional. Same-sex partners were granted similar rights in terms of immigration and financial benefits as those granted to different-sex spouses or partners. Trans and intersex individuals were allowed to change their legally recognised sex. Same-sex couples were allowed to jointly adopt children or adopt each other's children. Lesbian couples were allowed to be registered as the natural, legitimate parents of a child that one of them had born. There were also challenges to the constitutionality of the Marriage Act, which did not then allow for same-sex unions to be recognised as marriages. By late 2005, the Constitutional

Court ruled that the Marriage Act was unconstitutional and gave parliament one year in which to remedy the matter.

However, being 'out of the closet' also meant that LGBTI individuals were also more openly targeted for hate, harassment, victimisation and violence – even as these new laws were passed supposedly protecting their rights.

Although this chapter focuses on violence against black lesbians, it is important to note that the growth in hate crimes was experienced by all members of the LGBTI community, with transgender individuals experiencing even higher levels of violence, as a group, than lesbians or gay men.[3]

This is a good place to discuss why this chapter is about 'black lesbians' and not just lesbians, and also what the concept of 'black lesbians' represents as a group, even though it is quite obviously made up of individual black women who are by no means homogenous because of their sexual preference.

Confronted with the same issue, Mkhize et al., in their book *The Country We Want to Live In: Hate crimes and homophobia in the lives of black lesbian South Africans* (HSRC Press, 2010), go into the topic in quite some detail, and include what I think is an extremely important rationale. The authors write that, while they knew there were risks to 'singling out a particular group of people as targets of gender-based violence', black lesbians were 'doubly vulnerable'. This was because, firstly, although all women in South Africa were vulnerable (to violence), there was a correlation between increased poverty and increased vulnerability and, in South Africa, being black meant that there was a greater association with being poor or having less access to resources:

> [. . .] rape and sexual assault are most frequent where environmental infrastructures (such as secure streets, adequate electricity, strong policing services and safe housing) are inadequate or lacking, and this automatically places poor black women at the forefront of the danger of sexual attack. Black

lesbian women, especially those living in poor neighbourhoods, are as vulnerable to sexual assault, interpellation into gang warfare as rape victims, sexual harassment, childhood sexual abuse, and witchcraft accusations as the heterosexual women living around them. (Mkhize, et al., 2010)

Not only did black women live in environments in which other black women were vulnerable to attack, they also lived in places where cultures were often deeply homophobic, and in which sexual violence had become a 'popular weapon'.

In the 1980s, the rape crisis that emerged in the previous decade continued, and had taken on chilling new aspects, including gang rapes that became known as 'jackrolling'.[4]

Jackrolling initially involved the careful selection and abduction of a victim, usually a woman who (her attackers believed) presented herself as if she was 'better than them' and 'out of reach'. In Steve Mokwena's 1991 paper on jackrolling, he quoted a subject as saying: 'These women think they are better than anyone else, they look down on us, they prefer men who have money and drive in nice cars. When these women get jackrolled it's okay, she likes big men so let them give it to her.'[5]

There were terrifying echoes of these sentiments in the growing number of stories that began to emerge during the 1990s of black lesbian women being targeted, being beaten and raped by men, supposedly as a means of 'teaching them how to be proper women'. This gradually became referred to as 'curative' or 'corrective' rape[6], and involved three distinct aspects: one was punishment of the woman, for her choice of sexual identity and her lifestyle; a second was the humiliation of the victim – as with jackrolling, this was often achieved through gang rapes; the third was the repulsive misnomer of 'transforming' lesbians into heterosexual women through violent penetration.

Even as newspapers carried the occasional story about black

lesbians' struggles for acceptance individually or within their communities (in the context of the changing legislative landscape), almost every single one of these women's accounts also included incidents of violence, most frequently rape. Sometimes these women were even raped with the knowledge of their family members, who either actively encouraged the assault in the hope of ridding the young woman of her homosexuality, or tacitly accepted such attacks as what should happen to 'girls like that'.

Surveys from the time also indicated that fewer than half of such assaults were ever reported to the police, and that nearly three-quarters of gay men and women did not believe the police would take their complaints seriously (a sentiment which, anecdotally, seems to have been backed up by the horrific experiences of those who did go and report their rapes).

It was in this context that, in 2002, photographer and activist Zanele Muholi and poet and activist Donna Smith, both of the Forum for the Empowerment of Women, established a campaign called 'The Rose Has Thorns', which researched and provided legal and other support for black lesbian women who had been raped and assaulted, and began to push for the recognition of these acts of violence (against lesbians) as hate crimes (something that has still not been achieved in South Africa).

While covering the rapes and assaults of black lesbians, newspapers chose simultaneously to give prominent platforms to voices that declared homosexuality as undesirable and 'un-African'. In a letter published by *The Star* in November 2004, Bishop Moagi Khunou (who, according to his current LinkedIn profile, is also a former attorney and a magistrate) wrote that, in his view, it was 'better for a virgin to suffer rape rather than for one to engage in homosexuality'.[7]

The use of rape in the 1990s as an almost socially accepted means of punishment, particularly of black women, needs to take at least one other factor into account and that is the impact of HIV and AIDS in South Africa.

When the first documented case of AIDS was reported in South Africa back in 1982, the patient was described as a homosexual man who had contracted the disease while in California (the human immunodeficiency virus – HIV – which caused AIDS would only be discovered the following year). At that time, like in the United States and other Western countries, AIDS in South Africa was considered primarily a disease that was spread among homosexual men, haemophiliacs and recipients of blood transfusions. The first HIV-related deaths were recorded in South Africa three years later, in 1985. At that time, HIV prevalence in the heterosexual population was relatively low. By the early 1990s, however, this had begun to change, and researchers noted that HIV prevalence in the heterosexual population (which was measured by testing women attending public antenatal clinics) was beginning to double year on year. It should be noted the HIV epidemic that affected heterosexuals was due to a different subtype of HIV (sub-type C) than that which had previously been found among gay men (sub-type B)[8], and was not caused by HIV crossing over from one group to the other. Researchers modelled the spread of HIV among heterosexual populations and showed that sub-type C[9] had been distributed along migrant labour and transport routes in sub-Saharan Africa.

At this stage, HIV and AIDS were still largely considered either a 'gay' problem, or a 'black' problem, neither of which had overly concerned the apartheid government. Although researchers were warning anyone who would listen about what the potential epidemic might mean, as South Africa approached and was delivered into its fraught new democracy, HIV and AIDS took a back seat to liberation.

By the mid-1990s HIV infections were growing at an exponential rate. Between 1993 and 1999, HIV prevalence increased by over 400 per cent, making South Africa the country with the fastest-growing epidemic in the world.

Just as the number of new infections peaked and life expectancy rates plummeted, notorious AIDS-denialist Thabo Mbeki was elected president, and he appointed Manto Tshabalala-Msimang as his Health minister. Their combined programme of public HIV-AIDS denialism, while actively blocking the roll-out of new, lifesaving antiretroviral medications in favour of recommendations of beetroot, African potato, garlic, olive oil and the scam medicine Virodene, meant that, under Mbeki and Tshabalala-Msimang, an HIV infection was a death sentence.

Because of this, and because of the state's deliberate misinformation programmes, the disease remained deeply stigmatised even as infections soared – the secrecy and stigmatisation contributing to new infections. There was widespread confusion, frustration and fear, and this was coupled with rising anger.

In 1998 an HIV activist and educator named Gugu Dlamini was stoned and beaten to death near KwaMashu in KwaZulu-Natal after publicly revealing her HIV positive status. Seven years later, in December 2005, another AIDS activist, Lorna Mlosana, a volunteer with the Treatment Action Campaign, was gang-raped in a bathroom in Khayelitsha. When her five rapists discovered she was HIV-positive, they beat her to death.

Women were punished not only for *being* HIV-positive, they were also punished by being potentially infected with HIV by their rapists. Among the news reports of black lesbians being targeted and gang-raped because of their sexual preferences were also stories of the same women who had found out they were infected with HIV, or who had died of AIDS-related complications a few years after being raped.

In the mid-2000s, these faultlines coalesced in the media.

In February 2006 an openly lesbian soccer player named Zoliswa Nkonyana, who was just nineteen years old, had been at a shebeen in Khayelitsha with another lesbian friend of hers when a group of straight girls had taunted them for being tomboys. Zoliswa apparently replied, 'We are not tomboys, we are lesbians. We are just doing our thing so leave us alone.'[10]

One of the (straight) women went and summoned a group of men, who pursued Zoliswa and her friend across a field, eventually catching up with Zoliswa (the friend managed to get away) before pelting her with bricks and beating her with a golf club until she died. It would take nearly six years and some 60 court appearances before four of the nine men eventually charged with her killing would be found guilty.

This was the first prominent example of a black lesbian who was killed for being 'out' – almost certainly there were other murders, but until 2006, the same year gay marriage was legalised in South Africa, there was nothing in the press about such killings. The media's response to Zoliswa's case also quickly indicated why this might have been the case.

When the *Sunday Times* covered the murder a few days later, the newspaper ran the story together with a photograph of several other lesbian women in Khayelitsha who had been friends or acquaintances of Zoliswa's. As a result of the prominent news coverage, these women, too, were targeted, and there were subsequent reports that at least one of them had been raped. At least one of Zoliswa's friends – a lesbian identified as 'T', who attended court protests at the pre-trial hearings – was stabbed by two men in Nyanga in retaliation for giving testimony.

A similar situation occurred in 2007, after television programme Carte Blanche ran an insert on lesbian rapes and murders, in which a number of other black women were identified as lesbians in the footage, which meant several of the women featured said they were unable to return home after the show was aired as they feared for their safety.

This may have been one of the factors which had inhibited, or which continued to inhibit, reporting of hate crimes and violence against lesbians – because of the very real fear that identifying the victim in one crime would implicate other women, and that this might make them targets in turn.

The state of the nation was also particularly precarious when it came to the issue of women and rape.

The year before, then former Deputy President Jacob Zuma had been accused of raping a 31-year-old family friend identified at the time only as 'Khwezi'.

The court case against Zuma started in March 2006 and was widely attended by large crowds of his supporters – mostly women – who would do things like parade photographs of the victim before burning them, or who would publicly call Zuma's accuser *nondindwa*, or bitch.

During the proceedings it also emerged that Khwezi was HIV-positive, and that Zuma had not used any protection during the act, testifying that he had 'taken a shower' afterwards to minimise the chances of him getting infected. The politician denied the allegations of rape and claimed that the act had been consensual. He was eventually found not guilty.

Khwezi, who was later revealed to be Fezekile Ntsukela Kuzwayo, had to leave South Africa after the trial as she was receiving death threats. She died in exile in 2016.

On paper, the murder of Zoliswa Nkonyana and the rape of Fezekile Ntsukela Kuzwayo had little to do with each other. But, when they are read against the broader narrative of what was happening in South Africa, and what was still to come, it is impossible not to see the links.

When the judgement was announced in May 2006, finding Zuma not guilty of rape, Professor Pumla Dineo Gqola wrote how the case – with its 'ugly and convenient use of culture against African women', where Zuma himself had commented that women 'asked' for sex, and rape, in their dress – had left her 'with a spate of unanswered questions about how to live my life in a democracy that wages an unacknowledged war against those who look like me'.[11]

In her later book *Rape: A South African Nightmare* (2015), Gqola discusses the concept of the 'unrapable' black woman. 'Unrapable' because, in this narrative scheme, black women are considered as 'excessively sexual and impossible to satiate', which then makes them 'legitimate targets of sexual violence'.[12] As Gqola explained at a book launch, this made them 'impossible' to rape just as it was once 'impossible' for a husband to rape his wife, meaning not that the physical act was impossible, but that the act could not be thought of as rape.

Gqola also noted that this violence against women was not just a part of patriarchal culture but, more specifically, it was *heteropatriarchal* culture – where the only 'approved' form of femininity was one where women were cis-gendered heterosexual subjects, had relationships with heterosexual men, and aspired to 'reproductive marriage'.[13] In an earlier paper, Gqola commented that, even under the powerful Constitution of the new South Africa, women's empowerment, 'only really applies to women while they are in the official "public space": in the workplace. A completely different set of rules . . . continues to govern the "private" world of the home, and other spaces in between: public transport, the streets, clubs, restaurants, shebeens, etc.'[14]

From 2006 onward, a pattern began to emerge in media coverage of the rape and murders of black lesbian women, the stories bearing uncanny resemblances to each other even when they were a decade apart.

Almost certainly, these cases that were reported in the news did not represent the extent of such killings in real life. But, as above, there were a number of very real deterrents to reporting these types of crimes (the risk of others becoming targets, the poor treatment of lesbian complainants by the police). Plus, this type of aggravated homicide – the rape and killing of lesbians – was not (and is still not) recognised as a specific category of crime, apart from that of general rape and homicide, so there is no separate police data.

Which means all we have to go on really are these stories, and information collected by various LGBTI organisations around the country (which is usually the basis for any media reporting – journalists are typically alerted to a murder by a local or regional rights group).

Below is a list of some of the incidents that have been reported in the press after 2006, where black lesbians were murdered allegedly because of their sexual orientation. You don't have to read the entire list, and to be honest it's quite hard going, even in summary. But we should all know that this is going on, that this has been going on for some time, and that this shows no signs of stopping. Unless we participate in stopping it.

2007

In April, 16-year-old lesbian **Madoe Mafubedu** was raped and stabbed to death in Soweto. [*There is very limited information about this case, and there are no reports that anyone was arrested for this murder.*]

In June, **Simangele Nhlapho**, a member of an HIV support group co-ordinated by the Positive Women's Network (an HIV/AIDS community programme) was raped and murdered. Her two-year-old child was also murdered during the attack, and it was reported that both of the infant's legs had been broken during the beating. (It is not clear from news reports that Simangele was a lesbian, but her death was very obviously linked with her work in HIV, which had links to lesbian victims the following month.) [*There are no news reports indicating that anyone was arrested for these murders.*]

On 7 July, 34-year-old **Sizakele Sigasa**, a lesbian and gay rights activist and an outreach co-ordinator at the Positive Women's Network, was raped, tortured and murdered together with her friend, 23-year-old **Salome Masooa**. The women's bodies were found lying next to each other just a few metres from the car they had been travelling in. Sizakele had three bullet wounds in her head and three near her collarbone. Salome had a single gunshot wound to the head. Their killers had used Sizakele's underwear and her shoelaces to tie her hands and her ankles. [*Four suspects were originally arrested for these murders but there was no evidence connecting them to the crimes and they were let* free. As of 2017, nobody has been convicted for either of these murders.]

On 22 July, the naked body of 23-year-old lesbian **'Sdo' Thokozani Qwab**e was found in a field near a community hall in Ezakheni, Ladysmith. She had been raped and possibly stoned to death. Two men were arrested and charged with her killing but were acquitted.

2008

On the night of 27 April – Freedom Day – 31-year-old former Banyana Banyana national soccer player, soccer coach and lesbian activist **Eudy Simelane** was attacked by a group of men after leaving a local pub in KwaThema. She was robbed, gang-raped and stabbed 25 times before being left naked to die in a ditch. Five men were arrested in connection with her murder, but only two were convicted. Themba Mvubu received a life sentence plus 35 years and Thato Mphithi was sentenced to 32 years imprisonment.

A month later, on 26 May, 25-year-old lesbian **Khanyiswa (Lhoyie) Hani** was found murdered in New Brighton, Port Elizabeth. She had been stabbed, her throat had been cut, and her teeth knocked out. [*No suspects were arrested.*]

On 20 June, 21-year-old lesbian **Sibongile Mphelo** was raped and murdered, her body discovered in a patch of open veld in Strand in Cape Town. Sibongile had been mutilated during the attack. Her vagina and part of her calf had been cut off. Condoms were discovered next to her body. [*No suspects have ever been arrested.*]

2009

On 19 June, 37-year-old soccer player **Girlie 'S'Gelane' Nkosi** was stabbed in a nightclub in KwaThema (Girlie had played with the late Eudy Simelane in one of the local clubs). She died of her injuries a few days later. Girlie, who had been attacked a number of times before her death, was an outspoken gay and lesbian rights activist, and had been a part of the 070707 Campaign (named after the date of the murders of Sizakele Sigasa and Salome Masooa). [*Girlie's killers were never found.*]

*

In August 2009, Arts and Culture Minister Lulu Xingwana walked out of an exhibition of work by Zanele Muholi which featured black lesbian couples. Xingwana reportedly described Muholi's photographs as 'immoral, offensive and going against nation-building'.

2010

In September 2010, 21-year-old lesbian **Nontsikelelo Tyatyeka** went missing from her home in Nyanga. A year later her body was discovered in a wheelie-bin outside the house of her neighbour, Vuyisile Madikane. The neighbour was subsequently charged with her murder.

In November 2010, another 21-year-old, newspaper seller **Ncumisa Mzamelo** was murdered and her body left in a disused toilet in Bhambayi, KwaZulu-Natal. Ncumiza had been set alight and the body was so badly burned it had to be identified through dental records.

2011

On 28 March, the body of 20-year-old lesbian **Nokuthula Radebe** was found in an abandoned building in Thokoza. Her pants had been pulled down and her face covered with a plastic bag. She had been strangled with her shoelaces.

A few weeks later, on 24 April, the body of 24-year-old mother of two, **Noxolo Nogwaza**, was found in a stream in KwaThema. Noxolo was an activist and a member of the Ekurhuleni Pride Organising Committee. Human Rights Watch reported that the woman's face had been disfigured by stoning, and she had been stabbed multiple times with broken glass. Used condoms were found on and near her body.

Two days after she went missing, on 4 May, the body of 23-year-old **Nqobile Khumalo** was discovered in a shallow grave in Kwa-Mashu. The following year, a man was sentenced to 15 years in prison for her rape and murder. Some news reports mentioned that the killer was a former boyfriend of Nqobile's, who murdered her for having a relationship with a woman.

2012

On 23 June, a gunman wearing a balaclava burst into a home in Mau Mau, Nyanga, Cape Town, and shot 21-year-old lesbian **Phumeza Nkolonzi** three times in front of her mother and her niece. [*No suspect has ever been arrested for her murder.*]

On 30 June, 28-year-old school clerk **Sanna Supa** was shot three times while opening the gate to her driveway at her house in Braamfischerville, Soweto. [*No arrests have been made for her killing.*]

The same day, 30 June, the body of 29-year-old **Hendrietta (Andritha) Thapelo Morifi** was discovered on the bed of her home in Polo Park, Mokopane. Andritha's throat had been slit from ear to ear, and she had been stabbed with a braai fork. Blood-soaked underwear was also found at the scene and it was believed Andritha had been raped. Andritha, who was openly lesbian, was survived by her two-year-old daughter, who was with a relative at the time of the attack. Two men were arrested but were later released, reportedly due to a lack of evidence.

In August, 25-year-old lesbian **Mandisa Mbambo** was raped, beaten and stabbed at her home in Inanda, KwazZulu-Natal. Four men were arrested for the crime, but there is no information in the press as to whether any of the suspects were convicted.

On 23 September, the body of lesbian **Desiree Ntombana Mafu** (also **Ntombana Desire 'Deezay' Mafu**) was discovered in the Roodepoort Cemetery near Dobsonville, Soweto.

On 9 November, 19-year-old **Sihle Sikoji** was stabbed in the chest with a spear by five male gang members in Samora Machel, Nyanga, in Cape Town. Sikoji was a member of Luleki Sizwe, an organisation that supported lesbian, bisexual and transgender women. [*No arrests have been made in connection with her murder.*]

2013

On 21 April, the body of 36-year-old lesbian **Patricia Mashigo** was discovered in Daveyton. She appeared to have been beaten with a brick or stoned to death. Patricia was a saleswoman, and mother of two children. [*No arrests were ever made for her killing.*]

On 30 June, the body of 26-year-old lesbian **Duduzile Zozo** was discovered just ten metres from her home in Thokoza. A toilet brush had been violently shoved into her vagina, and it was reported that she had died as a result of the organ damage this had caused. One of Duduzile's neighbours, Lekgoa Motleleng, was later convicted of her murder and sentenced to 30 years in prison.

2014

In August, 24-year-old lesbian **Disebo Gift Makau**, a college student, was found dead in Tshing location in Ventersdorp. She had been raped and strangled with wire and a shoelace, and a hosepipe had been forced into her mouth. Gift's childhood friend Stoffel Botlhokwane was found guilty of her rape and murder and was sentenced to two life sentences, plus an additional 15 years for theft.

2015

On 16 December, the body of 21-year-old **Pascalina Motshidisi Melamu** was discovered in an open field in Evaton. Her eyes, breasts and vagina had been cut out and her body set alight. Four suspects were arrested, but there are no further news reports indicating if they were charged.

2016

On 19 March, the night of her 19th birthday, student **Lucia Naido** was stabbed to death a few metres from her home in Katlehong. Her mother heard her daughter's screams and ran out to help her, but Lucia died on the way to hospital. [*No arrests have been reported.*]

In May, 47-year-old police clerk **Nosisa Sonjani** was found murdered at her home on the SAPS Faure base in Kleinvlei. She had been stabbed, and strangled with the electric cord from a toaster. Nosisa's employee, Lwando Dubha, was later arrested, after fleeing to the Eastern Cape. Dubha was found guilty and sentenced to 30 years for murder and 15 years for robbery.

In December, 22-year-old lesbian and LGBT activist **Noluvo Swelindavo** was abducted from her home in Driftsands, Khayelitsha, by a group of men. Her body was found the next day near the N2 highway, with a gunshot wound. Noluvo's girlfriend, who had hidden in a gap between the bed and the wall when the attack happened, was able to identify one of the assailants as a neighbour, Sigcine Mdani, who had previously attacked Noluvo because of her sexual orientation. Mdani was later found guilty of abduction and murder and sentenced to 18 years in prison.

2017

On 4 April, a badly burned body was discovered in the township of Maokeng near Kroonstad. A month later, DNA tests confirmed that the victim was 28-year-old **Nonki Smous**, a welder who had lived openly as a lesbian for many years. [*Three men who were arrested in connection with the murder and robbery were subsequently released.*]

In May, 27-year-old **Lerato 'Tambai' Moloi** was raped and murdered in Naledi, Soweto. Her half-naked body was found in an open space by community members who were cutting grass near the railway line. Lerato had been stabbed, and there were rocks near her head. Photographs of Lerato's corpse were widely shared on social media. The following year, Petroos Tsotang Mokhgethi, Lerato's friend and 'drinking buddy', was convicted of her rape and murder. He received two life sentences, one for each charge.

In December, lesbian couple **Joey van Niekerk** and **Anisha van Niekerk*** were tortured, gang raped and murdered. It later emerged that the murders were allegedly part of a plot by a tenant who wanted to take over the couple's land where they lived in Mooinooi. The man believed to be the mastermind behind the plot, Koos Strydom, committed suicide while the case against him was under way.

* *Joey and Anisha were both white women, but they have been included on this list because they were specifically targeted and tortured on the basis of their sexuality, and the fact that they were a married female couple rather than a heterosexual couple.*

2018

On New Year's Day, 23-year-old **Noxolo Xakeka** was harassed, assaulted and then stabbed three times because of her sexual orientation. She died in hospital later that day, leaving behind a six-year-old child. Her killer pleaded guilty and was sentenced to eight years in prison.

Transgender victims

In addition to the lesbians who were murdered, above, each year there are also a number of hate killings of transgender women, including gay men who occasionally dressed as or presented as women. (*The many victims listed below each identified differently; I have tried to refer to them according to their chosen gender and identity, based on available press reports. It is, of course, not possible to ask them how they wish to be identified.*) As with lesbian killings, it is almost certain that these deaths, too, are under-reported in the media, although this may change as transgender individuals become more visible – although even that, of course, sadly remains a risky act in itself.

2008

In June 2008, 25-year-old **Daisy Dube** was shot and killed in Yeoville, Johannesburg while out with four friends who identified as drag queens.

2012

In June 2012, Miss Gay Kuruman pageant winner **Thapelo Makutle**, who identified as both gay and transgender, was attacked in his room and his throat was slit. Later news reports indicated that Thapelo's testicles had been cut off and his penis stuffed into his mouth. Although the crime was evidently committed by more than one perpetrator, only one, Sizwe Tajini, was arrested and convicted. He was sentenced to a 14-year prison term.

Also in June 2012, trans woman sex worker **Sasha Lee Gordon** was stabbed in the heart and left to die on a pavement in Wynberg, Cape Town.

In July 2012, 28-year-old transgender woman **Vuyisa 'Norizana' Dayisi** was murdered in her home in Duncan Village. She had suffered a blow to the forehead, and her pants were pulled down to expose her genitals.

2015

In December 2015, 30-year-old trans woman **Phoebe Titus** was murdered by a 15-year-old boy while she was buying ice lollies in her hometown of Wolseley. The attack took place after the teenager had started verbally abusing Phoebe, shouting homophobic and transphobic slurs. After Phoebe responded by gesturing towards the youth with a plastic crate, he took a knife and stabbed her in the neck. [*The perpetrator was arrested but was later released on bail.*]

2018

In January 2018, 24-year-old **Kagiso Ishmael Maema** was murdered in Seraleng, Rustenburg. Her half-naked body was found next to a stream, and it was suspected she had been strangled and had wounds that may have been caused by an axe.

In February 2018, the body of 30-year-old hairdresser **'Rose' Papi Mogoera Elias Malebatso** was discovered in Welkom. Rose was allegedly murdered when the man she was having a drink with discovered that she was a transgender woman.

In September 2018, 31-year-old **Motlhatlhedi 'Gustav' Modise** was stabbed to death in Ventersdorp; her handbag and wallet and other belongings were left lying next to her body.

9. 'We all know who are the witches here': Witch killings

In January 1986 a school student named Solomon Maditsi – who had been partly crippled from an earlier bout of polio[1] – was shot and killed while taking part in a protest against a local chief in the village of Strydkraal in the heart of what was then the 'homeland' of Lebowa. Solomon came from the neighbouring twin villages of Apel-GaNkoane [Ga-Nkoana] which today fall within Limpopo province.

Solomon's killing – it is unclear whether the bullet that killed him came from the police or one of Chief Masha's men – became the first of what would later become known as the Sekhukhune youth revolt, directed against elderly people in general and the area's chiefs in particular, who were seen as 'puppets of the [apartheid] regime'[2]. It also provoked one of the worst mass witch killings in the country's history.

Solomon's funeral was held in early February 1986 and attracted a large group of mourners, including many young activists from other surrounding villages. After the funeral one of these activists was struck by lightning, which was generally considered to be a sign of witchcraft.[3] Some of the funeral attendees recalled an old woman complaining that the youth were behaving disrespectfully. On this basis a mass meeting was called at which the old woman was identified. She admitted to having expressed a complaint, but she denied having called for the lightning.

The activists motivated to burn the woman immediately. Parents and older political leaders at the meeting called for a little more circumspection, and a delegation was sent off to consult with the local ngaka (a Bapedi traditional healer and diviner, similar to an nyanga), which was the proper approach for dealing with suspected witches. At this consultation, the delegation were given a mixture to drink and experienced visions showing them who was in fact guilty of practising witchcraft. Another envoy was then sent off to consult with a second ngaka in KwaNdebele but, before the envoy returned, three of the people who had been identified in the initial visions were burned to death. A few weeks later, after another lightning strike and another consultation with the first ngaka, two more women were executed for witchcraft.[4]

In the second week of April 1986 a group of youth in Apel-GaNkoane decided to dispense with the formalities of consulting the ngaka and obtaining the chief's approval, and went on a witch-hunt of their own. They began by rounding up villagers at their homes. Historian Ineke van Kessel reported that the 'evidence' included possessing herbs, or that monkeys had been spotted in their gardens – monkeys and other animals were considered to be witches' familiars. Several of the victims were indeed dingaka (but not witches). Some of them were in their eighties, and half-blind.

The youth, chanting and carrying tyres[5], marched each of their victims up the koppie before placing petrol-filled tyres over them and burning them alive. Pillars of black smoke rose off the koppie, marking where the victims lay. On the first night, 21 people were killed. At dawn the next morning the massacre resumed. By the end of two days it was reported that 32 people had been necklaced[6], most of them elderly, two-thirds of them women.

Over a hundred people were subsequently charged with the murders. All of the accused were under the age of 30, and all but one of the accused were male.

A series of trials followed, with mixed results. Because of the large size of the group, many plea bargains were negotiated. Some older perpetrators were found guilty, and some were acquitted. Those who were under eighteen were let off with a few cuts from a sjambok.[7] Those who pleaded belief in witchcraft as a mitigating factor were given lesser sentences than those who claimed not to believe in witches.

There was not, in fact, a long-standing tradition of burning witches in the Northern Transvaal – historically, witches in the area were hanged, stoned or impaled; and usually in smaller numbers, perhaps only two or three witches every rainy season (also when lightning usually strikes). But, from the early 1980s, there had been an increase in these numbers, and an increase in burnings in the broader Northern Transvaal region, even though the Witchcraft Suppression Act of 1957 made it an offence both to practise witchcraft or to accuse another person of being 'a wizard'.

In January 1984 there had been three incidents in which four adults – Maria Kekane, Joshua Morwamotse, Piet Moekwa and Anna Tlanene – had been burned at the stake in the villages of Khureng and Bolahlakgomo, after lightning struck the villages. That same month in Bushbuckridge a man, Abu Malumane, was stabbed and burned and a woman, Sarah Kgoedi, was thrown into a blazing hut after they were accused of sending lightning that had killed two children. In Zebediela in February 1984, an alleged 'witchdoctor', Lester Malanze, and two women, Tshaisa Makhopa and Magrieta Tsela, were placed on a truck in the middle of the veld where old tyres and other materials had been set alight and were burned to death.[8] In March 1984, 45-year-old Mary Modikwe, her husband Bethuel and her brother-in-law Lehong were put into three cars, doused in petrol and set alight at Skilpadfontein, near Bela Bela (Warmbaths). They were accused of causing lightning that had struck a high school pupil.

The act of burning suspected witches was not just symbolic punishment. Burning was said to be a way in which the person's soul was destroyed, severing the spirit's connection to its ancestors.[9] Fire was also a way of effectively destroying the suspected witch's magic items, medicines, and even their familiars – hence the common practice of burning the huts and homes of suspected witches.

Burning witches had become so common during this time that researcher Joanna Ball, in a report for the Centre for the Study of Violence and Reconciliation, suggested that the earliest necklacings (putting a petrol-soaked tyre over a victim, like a 'necklace', and setting them alight) may have been of suspected witches, and not political killings. The first widely reported politically motivated necklacings, of Langa councillor Tamsanqa Kinikini and Maki Skosana in Duduza (both accused of being informers), took place in March and July of 1985, respectively. Lester Malanze, Tshaisa Makhopa and Magrieta Tsela had reportedly had a large tractor tyre placed over them in February 1984. What Ball suggested was that this rural practice had spread to urban areas and townships rather than the other way around. By the time of the Apel-GaNkoane massacre, it was both.

In the townships, necklacing was a way of condemning and punishing traitors and collaborators.[10] Ineke van Kessel explained that, for the youth of Sekhukhuneland, this included many dingaka:

> Previously, the comrades had turned to the dingaka for help when the youth were involved in battling the police and the army. They had demanded a medicine that would turn bullets into water or, alternatively, into bees. When the dingaka proved unable or unwilling to provide this service, the comrades retorted that since the dingaka were able to make lightning and to kill people, it was evident that they did possess supernatural powers. It was now established that they used these powers not to support the freedom struggle but to inflict evil. Therefore, these dingaka were judged guilty of witchcraft. (Van Kessel, 2010)

By bypassing the 'accepted' procedure for smelling out witches – which required consultation with and identification by an ngaka (who could only be consulted by adults), followed by authorisation from the chief – Van Kessel also noted that the Apel-GaNkoane witch killings were a way for the youth to reject the established authorities and elders, and show that they no longer required their legitimisation.

Isak Niehaus wrote about similar youth-led witch-hunts and killings that took place in Bushbuckridge that same year. He explains how the local Youth Organisation, launched in 1986, had attracted a large male following, calling themselves the Comrades. The Comrades boycotted school, asking for free books and an end to corporal punishment. They encouraged boycotts of white-owned supermarkets, and asked villagers not to pay taxes and levies to the local tribal authorities within the Bantustan. And, Niehaus writes, as part of their commitment to eradicating 'evil' from their communities, they began to ask adult men to name the witches they knew.

The Comrades formed their own disciplinary squads, and between April and May 1986 they burned at least 150 homes in the area, killing as many as 36 people accused of 'witchcraft'.[11]

Niehaus also points out that, between 1985 and 1995, judges appeared to be very lenient with those who were accused of witch killings. Only around half of those ever accused were prosecuted, and many of the sentences given were exceedingly light – if they cited their belief as an extenuating factor. In one case at the Venda Supreme Court, a [white] judge considered sentencing four men to death for pleading guilty to a murder, but then reduced the sentence to five years imprisonment because of their claim they thought the deceased person was a witch.[12]

The frenzy around witches evidently suited the apartheid government. In Apel-GaNkoane, the killings gave them the excuse to come in with heavily armed police and army units and arrest at least one high-profile United Democratic Front leader, as well as other political activists who had nothing to do with the killings, at least not directly. Peter Nchabeleng, president of the UDF in the Northern Transvaal, was arrested in Apel on 9 April and died in detention two days later. Peter's son Maurice and another activist, Silas Mabotha, both members of the Sekhukhune Youth Organisation, were arrested together with others accused of the witch-killings. Maurice and Silas were later acquitted but by the time the activists slowly started returning to Apel and GaNkoane, Van Kessel writes that the authority and influence of the youth organisations had collapsed, replaced by the authority of the army – that remained in place – and vigilante groups of adult men.

Newspapers at the time appeared equally happy to report on witches whether they were dead or alive, but devoted an even larger number of column inches to alleged 'muti killings', where humans – particularly children – were supposedly murdered for body parts to be used in dark magical practices. This, too, tied in nicely with the apartheid state's narrative of othering black subjects, while simultaneously titillating and terrorising white South Africans with stories of evil powers – much like it did with the constant fear and threat of encroaching Satanism and the powers of the devil. The Afrikaans-language press in particular took garish enjoyment in regaling readers with stories of 'toordokters' (witchdoctors), and urban legends of white people's body parts being smuggled in loaves of bread. In 1984 *Die Transvaler* claimed that there were an estimated 300 muti murders a year. That same year, Wits anthropologist Dr Anthony van Fossen told the *Sunday Express* that some 75 muti killings annually were committed in Venda alone.

Van Kessel, though, described the witch burnings of the early 1980s as the practice of 'burning social enemies'. The elderly, particularly women, made easy targets in the struggle between generations and ideologies. (I would also suggest that elderly women make easy targets all the time – something that is discussed in the next chapter.) These fractures between individuals and communities were easily exploited by those with other objectives, whether personal or political. Many cases of alleged witchcraft were belatedly ascribed to jealousy between neighbours, between rival dingaka or izangoma, even between family members or families. Isak Niehaus later wrote of witch-hunts as 'multifaceted social dramas' which involved different modes and degrees of participation and had a 'variety of different meanings' for audiences.[13]

As South Africa's political uncertainty persisted, and as political, social and bureaucratic structures paused, then changed (or crumbled) with the approach of democracy, the witch-hunts and witch killings persisted, concentrated in the northern provinces of the country.

As an indicator of how much of a role political and social transition and upheaval played in enabling hate crimes against people – under the guise of alleged witchcraft – in the late 1990s the Northern Province's then MEC for Safety and Security, Seth Nthai, told a conference that between 1990 and 1994 more than 300 people had been killed for witchcraft in the district. Between April 1994 (the date of South Africa's first democratic elections) and April 1995, he added, 228 people were killed for witchcraft *in a single year*.[14] By 1996 this figure dropped to 17 and hovered between the late teens and mid-20s thereafter. But the search for witches was very much still on. In September 1998 *City Press* reported that in the Northern Province 368 people had been 'sniffed out' as witches between January and June. Not all lost their lives, but many lost their homes or were forced to flee. In many instances, individuals, even families accused of witchcraft, would flee to a local police station for safety. During the late 1990s, there were reports of a village in Limpopo that had been set aside as a 'witch sanctuary' and mentioned that it was one of ten such sanctuaries officially recognised by the police (although I could find no record of any others).

In police terms, witches nominally fell under the same general crime category as Satanism. From the mid-1980s, this in itself was considered a big enough problem that the South African police force instituted a dedicated Occult Crimes Unit in 1992, under 'veteran "Satan seeker"' Colonel (later Senior Superintendent) Kobus Jonker. In the January/February 1999 issue of police magazine *Servamus,* an editorial warned its readers that black people in particular were soft targets for Satan, as most of them had grown up with ideas of witchdoctors and witches.[15]

This isn't intended to mock Christianity, but more to highlight the absurd way in which traditional beliefs and practices were understood and categorised by the police force. Given that the Occult Crimes Unit was run by evangelical and born-again Christians singularly obsessed with finding evidence of the Devil in everyday life, it is fair to say that the Unit didn't really have much interest in protecting the lives of people who practised what it probably viewed as something not just transgressive but possibly sinful, and it tended as a rule to want to investigate alleged crimes committed by witches (or Satanists) rather than against them.

The Occult Crimes Unit was supposedly disbanded in 2006, but was quietly reinstated a few years later under what is now known as the Occult and Harmful Religious Practices Unit (it is not clear exactly what is meant by harmful religious practices, but judging from the few media articles about the Unit, this may involve teenagers who wear black clothing and women who have abortions). A South African Police Service press release from late 2018 mentioned the Unit as playing a role in the arrest of five suspects allegedly involved in a ritual killing (aka a 'muti murder'). This is also not to say that ritual killings of humans do not happen in South Africa, just that these are often reported on in hyperbolic and fact-free terms, and tend as a result to be over-reported and to dominate news coverage of traditional healers and practices.

Also, as much as it's easy to poke fun at the flawed agenda of the flagbearers for South Africa's Satanic Panic, the bias and blindspots in the state's official position on witches, whether real or accused, is no laughing matter and continues to be something that daily places the lives of women – particularly elderly women – and men at risk.

The South African Pagan Rights Alliance (which does not represent traditional healers, but is a pagan advocacy and legal rights organisation that has been consistently vocal about drawing attention to ongoing witch-hunts in South Africa) keeps a list on its website of some of the names of the victims of witch-hunts between 2000 and the present. It's a long list, with sometimes ten or more of fatal victims for each year – and which shows that the extent of witch-hunts isn't localised to Limpopo but also takes place in the Eastern Cape, in KwaZulu-Natal, and in the Western Cape. Again, those who are accused of or killed for allegedly practising witchcraft are not always female; but the majority of victims are, and many of them are older than 50 years of age.

This corresponds to research from Dr Yassen Ally[16], who found that both age and gender were a factor in witchcraft accusations – most alleged 'witches' are older women – and that witch-hunts tend to take place in rural communities, particularly poorer communities where there is competition for resources.

Academic and author Silvia Federici has argued that witch-hunts, which are common across Africa (and in Latin America and India, among other places), constitute a secret war on women, and are often used not only to act out violence as an end in and of itself but also as a way of removing 'troublesome' women, or of appropriating valuable assets, including land. In Federici's book *Witches, Witch-Hunting, and Women* (2018) she writes that in Africa in particular 'victims are older women living alone off some piece of land, while the accusers are younger members of their communities, or even of their own families, generally unemployed youth, who see these elderly women as usurping what should belong to them'. She adds that these young attackers may be 'manipulated by other actors who remain in the shadows, including local leaders, who often conspire with business interests'.[17]

In news coverage of witch killings and alleged magic-related violence these factors are typically overlooked, and the murders are reduced to unsophisticated superstition rather than often complex domestic, social, societal and communal underlying issues. Press reports also continue to conflate witch killings with stories of alleged ritual killings, although information suggests that the epidemiology of either are not closely related except through broad systems of belief.

Witch-hunts (which are still often perpetrated by mobs, although there tends now to be a more even distribution of stabbings, beatings, stonings and burnings) have a distinct and separate profile and are not usually incited because of a suspected muti killing but because of things like lightning, or unexplained deaths after accidents or short illnesses (which is particularly common in rural areas where there is limited access to tertiary healthcare).

Alleged muti killings do not appear specifically to target elderly females; if anything the opposite is true. In his research into alleged muti murders, forensic psychologist and former police officer Dr Gérard Labuschagne even noted that the 'elderly are perhaps the only age group who are not targeted in muti murder, presumably because any muti made from an older person would be considered weak and ineffective.'[18]

This means that magic-related killings remain poorly defined, and poorly understood – and, within this, that witchcraft accusations are still being used as a pretext for committing deliberate violence against women, and elderly women in particular.

A note on Satanic panics and 'gangs of black men'

> '27. 4 October 2012 – Mikeila Baillie (25) was murdered in her home in Ruimsig by a gang of 4 black men. Her throat was slit.'
>
> [From a list of 55 white women allegedly murdered by

'unknown Black men', posted on Facebook in February 2013 by Sunette Bridges]

Mikeila Valentine née Baillie was murdered on 4 October 2012. Her killing was one of several violent crimes that had taken place across Johannesburg's West Rand that week. On the Wednesday a Metro Police officer had been killed during an armed robbery at a shopping centre. Three other attacks had taken place between Monday and Wednesday, where victims had been badly injured and hospitalised. Mikeila was stabbed to death in her own home on Thursday morning and discovered in the afternoon. She was found in her own bed, covered in blood. Police urged members of the public to stay calm.

Afrikaans singer and Facebook 'volk' activist Sunette Bridges posted online that Mikeila had been murdered by a 'gang of 4 black men' – this claim appeared on one of Bridges' Facebook pages (she maintained several as she was occasionally blocked for promoting hate speech and racist speech).

Pairs and gangs of black men were a standard cut-and-paste in Bridges' lexicon, as were 'barbare' (barbarians). The language on Bridges' online posts was often reminiscent of apartheid-era newspaper pejorative usage of the word 'Swartes' (blacks) to describe individuals by their colour – for example, in apartheid-era reports it was common to read a farmer had been attacked by 'Swartes', or even one 'Swart' (black), rather than ''n swart man' (a black man) or 'swart arbeiters' (black workers). It's a subtle point to those not used to being on the receiving end of systemic racism and discrimination, but it's the equivalent of saying: 'a man was attacked on his farm by blacks', rather than 'a man was attacked on his farm by a group of black assailants'.

Bridges invoked two or more black men as perpetrators in more than three-quarters of the femicides she wrote about, and 'gangs' of black men specifically in about a third of the cases – even though available police information showed that less than 20 per cent of the incidents she had posted about were believed to involve three or more perpetrators. In fact, in a third of the femicide cases Bridges discussed, the perpetrators were entirely unknown to the police (according to newspaper reports).

Except in the case of Mikeila Valentine, the police did have leads. Within a week of her killing they were investigating the possibility that Mikeila's death was somehow connected to three earlier allegedly Satanic murders: those of Natacha Burger and Joy Boonzaaier, who had been murdered in Boonzaaier's home in Centurion in July; and of pastor Reg Bendixen, who had been murdered in Honeydew in August.

The victims were all connected through a group called Overcomers Through Christ, which supposedly worked helping former Satanists return to Christianity. Mikeila, who had grown up in Heidelberg, had joined the group after leaving the Rhema Church where she had been completing a course at the Bible College. By the time Mikeila left Rhema, she apparently believed it was being controlled by Satanists.

At some point in 2012 there had been a split in Overcomers Through Christ and a splinter group had formed, calling itself Electus Per Deus. Mikeila and her husband Zak Valentine had joined the splinter group. The first point of order for Electus Per Deus was to seek revenge or retribution against the members of Overcomers Through Christ. Natacha Burger was their first victim. They used a friend of hers, Joy Boonzaaier, to write a note asking Natacha to come to her home after work. They then stabbed both women to death. The following month Zak and another member of the group pretended to be police officers and went to Bendixen's home and, after being let in, hacked and stabbed him to death.

Mikeila, though, had decided that she was unhappy with the killings and wanted out of the group, which suddenly made her a liability. Zak and the other group members decided that the best solution was to kill her instead.

On the day of Mikeila's murder Zak went to work so that he would have an alibi. Before he left he put tranquillisers into his wife's coffee, and gave a gate remote and set of keys to fellow Electus Per Deus member Marinda Steyn, who, together with her then 14-year-old daughter Marcel, killed Mikeila by hitting her on the head with a hammer and, when Mikeila woke up and recognised Marinda, stabbing her to death.

The remaining members of Electus Per Deus would kill a total of eleven people between 2012 and 2016 when they were finally arrested, including murdering a homeless man so they could fake Zak Valentine's death in order to claim his life insurance money. In August 2019, Zak Valentine was sentenced to eight life sentences, to be served concurrently, plus an additional 78 years, also to be served concurrently.

Why Mikeila Valentine's death is notable even within this bizarre and terrible spree is that it marked the quite deliberate intersection of a number of tropes that exist within South African homicide myths – first, that she had been murdered by a 'gang' of 'unknown black men'; and, second, that her death was then implied to be due to Satanist or cult activities.

The purpose of both of these spectres, commonly invoked and readily believed in the South African context, is typically the same: to draw attention away from the fact that our biggest threat comes from inside our own homes (by which I mean intimate partners and family members); and deliberately to create and foment fear, often in order to justify and boost support for political ideologies – this was something the apartheid government was particularly good at and even encouraged, and something Sunette Bridges and others in the 'white genocide' brigade proactively employed across social media over the last decade. None of the early news reports (neither in *Beeld* nor the local *Heidelberg/Nigel Heraut* in Mikeila's home town) on Mikeila's death mentioned either the number of suspects or the race of those who had killed Mikeila. This means that Bridges or one of her contributors potentially just made it up.

There are parallels between these devices – which create and allow for only particular pre-approved narratives, and also enable disinformation to be shared more easily – and the way in which society (and the media) covers other crimes and criminals, particularly those we have determined to be 'deviant'.

Professor Brett Bowman describes how paedophiles, for example, embody not only a threat to specific children but also to the 'broader moral fabric that ideally constitutes our South African society'.[19] Within this, he continues, there is a paradox: the threat of the paedophile is both internal and external – often it is a family member, a trusted caregiver. But, at the same time, there is a deliberate objectification, a creation of 'otherness' that allows this contradiction to hold. Bowman describes this as a 'tenuous tightrope' – between otherness and familiarity – and how this, ultimately, allows us the relief of disidentification: the monster is *not* like us.

Although I can't see any evidence that there is a specific connection between alleged Satanism and femicide – compared to witchcraft, where there is an obvious and deliberate agenda against women, even though attacks also include men as victims – the role that 'the Devil' (or 'gangs of black men') play in how we narrate crime to ourselves is important; and it is important that we see these features as narrative devices specifically employed to stop us from easily seeing the truth. Stanley Cohen calls these 'folk devils': the clear villain, on whom all our ills can be blamed. The man who shot Reeva Steenkamp invoked exactly such a figure when he claimed to have been afraid of an imaginary black stranger hiding in his bathroom.

Margie Orford – in what I think is still probably the best and most insightful piece of writing about the entire Steenkamp murder, and which was later appropriated by Jacqueline Rose in a longer article on the 'Bantu in the Bathroom' – wrote how this claim inserted 'a third body into an all too familiar narrative of domestic violence. This imaginary body of the paranoid imaginings of suburban South Africa has lurked like a bogeyman at the periphery of this story for the past year. It is the threatening body, nameless and faceless, of an armed and dangerous black intruder.'[20]

Margie continued, explaining how the 'figure of the threatening black stranger has driven many South Africans into fortress-like housing estates, surrounded by electric fences, armed guards and the relentless surveillance of security cameras'.

At the end, Margie asks whether this fear – the fear of the man who wasn't there – was not in itself a kind of possession.

There is, of course, an inverse of this, which is a paradox created between 'a black man is always a suspect' and the fact that, in a country with a population that is more than 80 per cent black African, the perpetrator is often a black man.

I once presented a paper about ideal victims and 'super predators' at a university symposium, and one of the audience members commented that in their research many black men expressed that they felt like they were being 'painted into a corner' through constant depictions of black men as perpetrators of violence. And, of course, this is true (that black men are depicted as suspects), and on one level it is unfairly so. But, on another level, it is true and it is accurate. Black women are not beaten or killed by invisible entities. They are, by and large, attacked by black men. The problem is that for centuries – certainly for the last four decades – black men have been depersonalised, dehumanised and represented almost continuously as a violent 'collective' rather than as individual perpetrators of violence. This is something we need to be cognisant of, and which needs to change. Particularly if we are to start really confronting intimate partner violence and gender-based violence in black communities.

10. The 'ideal victim': Elderly women and farm murders

In 1986 a Norwegian criminologist and sociologist by the name of Nils Christie presented a concept he described as the 'ideal victim'. This wasn't a person who saw themselves as a victim, nor was it necessarily those who were at the greatest risk of victimisation or who were most often victimised. What Christie was discussing was a 'person or category of individuals who – when hit by crime – most readily is given the complete and legitimate status of being a victim'.[1]

Christie was interested in the 'sociology of the phenomena' of victims and victimisations, and he started his presentation by saying that being a victim was not in itself 'a thing, an objective phenomenon. It will not be the same to all people in situations externally described as being the "same". It has to do with the participants' definition of the situation.'

Victims and victimhood, Christie continued, could be seen or understood at both individual or personal levels (someone seeing themselves as a victim, or even as the opposite – as a champion), or at a systemic social level, that is, who society readily views as a victim. Christie suggested that, in this framework, a 'victim' had the same public status (and a similar type and level of abstraction) as, for example, a 'hero', or a 'traitor'.

To explore this concept, Christie made up a construct of an 'ideal' victim. He suggested a little old lady who, while on her way to assist a sick family member, is accosted and assaulted by a drug user who is unknown to her.

Christie's hypothetical victim involved six requirements: first, the victim should be weak, which typically includes elderly women, pregnant women and young children; second, the victim should be involved in a respectable activity (so, not a sex worker, for example); and, third, at the time of the crime, she should be at or en route to a place that is 'beyond reproach' – she cannot be heading to or from a bar; fourth, the perpetrator must be able physically to dominate the victim and be able to be described in negative terms; fifth, the victim must not know the perpetrator, and there must be no relationship between them; and, finally, the victim should have enough status or influence to assert her 'victim status' without threatening society's vested interests.[2]

These criteria are quite important in terms of understanding how society understands femicide in general. Any deviation from these rules and we slip back into a comfortable mode of victim blaming – where we assign fault to the victim of the crime for not only putting herself in harm's way but actively inviting risk into her life by participating in dangerous behaviours like having a job, wearing clothes, taking public transport, driving her own car, walking in a park, and so on.

Of course, dead women can't really assert much about their own victimhood, and so after a murder it is often the media that does this in the victim's place. This also implies that news media has an interest in assigning and promoting victim status to particular victims (which we can link back to media effects theories like agenda setting[3], which states that there is a strong correlation between the issues that mass media emphasises, and the importance that mass audiences attribute to these issues – the media covers issues it thinks are important; and audiences think that the issues the media covers are the important issues). Through these processes, media stories about crime legitimise certain views and certain victims while marginalising or excluding others. This, in turn, creates consistent and even predictable messages through mass media about who matters most in our society.

If we look at South African media coverage of femicide, very specific profiles and patterns start to emerge around both victims and perpetrators.

Although they are not a simple binary, victim and perpetrator are often defined in relation to each other – and they cannot really exist without each other. In order for a victim to exist, there first has to be a source of harm.[4] This relationship is important, too, in terms of media coverage, and the demographics of the victim and the perpetrator often help to determine the 'newsworthiness' of a crime, and its prominence in the media.[5]

One of the things I had noticed fairly early on in my research, when I was comparing the victims in my media database with crime information from the Medical Research Council's studies on femicide, was that there were noticeable differences in the victims' age profiles. While the median[6] ages of intimate-femicide victims were largely consistent across both sets (between 29 and 30 years of age), the median age of non-intimate femicide victims in news stories (47.5 years old) was substantially older than the median ages of similar victims in the autopsy-based studies (37 years of age in 1999; and 41 years of age in 2009 respectively).

Although one of the earlier studies (Mathews et al., 2004) had indicated that elderly women were at a higher risk for non-intimate femicide, this suggested that older women were possibly overrepresented – in news stories – compared to other age groups. The same issue emerged when I compared my media-based data with the age profiles of femicide victims in the data the South African Police Services had given me for 2012/2013. Here I couldn't check which cases were intimate or non-intimate femicides, because SAPS didn't provide me with that level of information. But it was clear that, in the police data, there was a single age 'bulge' for victims between the ages of 25 and 30 (which is expected because this fits entirely with the data we have on the ages of intimate femicide victims); however, in the victims mentioned in the media, there were two bulges: one at around 25–30 years, and *another*, between 60 and 70 years of age.

Violin graphs showing age distribution and density of femicide victims in the media survey (left) and SAPS data (right)*

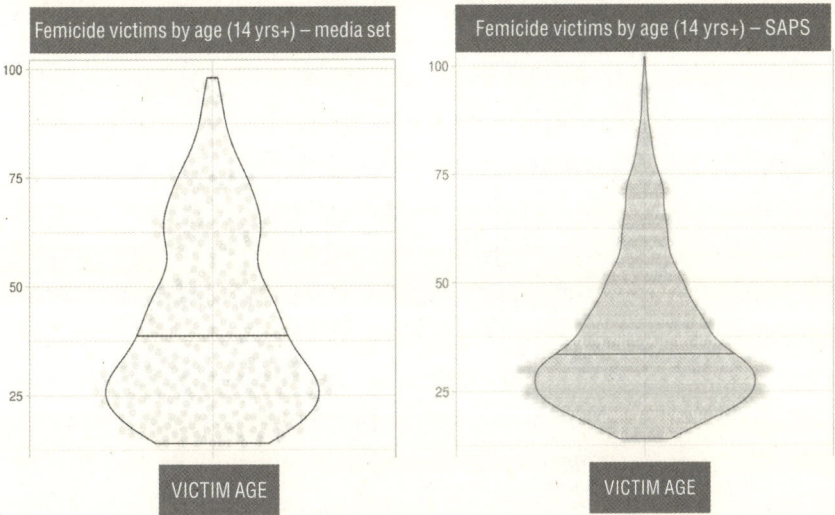

Sources: Own media survey; SAPS female homicide data

* These violin plots give a graphic representation of the distribution of victims (X axis) by age (Y axis) and density (number of dots). [horizontal line = median]

Several international studies[7] had previously claimed that 'older people' were statistically the least likely to be victims of crime[8] but were more likely to *fear* being victims of crime because of their heightened vulnerability (physical infirmity, living alone), and because of the serious consequences of being a victim of crime – the after-effects of physical violence are generally much worse for a 75 year old than for a physically strong 20 year old.

But in South Africa, this was not necessarily the case – or at least, it was not the entire picture. National mortality surveys[9] had found that while South Africa's 'eldercide' rate (eldercide meaning the murder of persons aged 60 years or older) was less than half the murder rate for young and middle-aged adults, it was still more than five times higher than the global average – again, not dissimilar to other types of homicide, for example, our femicide rate is five to six times the world average.

167

A 2019 study published by Dr Lu-Anne Swart, Sizakele Buthelezi and Professor Mohamed Seedat from Unisa's Institute of Social and Health Sciences, looking at eldercides in the Johannesburg region[10], found that the largest number of eldercide victims were black (which is to be expected, because the majority of the population is black) and white – there were actually nearly as many elderly white victims as elderly black victims. This is extremely significant but also needs to be read in the context of several other details, which include the fact that whites make up a larger proportion of Johannesburg's population than they do nationally, and that white murders overall were just five per cent of that of black murders for the same period (so the sample size is relatively small). This also shows why it's important that we discuss the role of race in crime and violence, because more than two-thirds of black homicide victims in Johannesburg (in this study) were between 15 and 34 years of age, while less than a third of white victims were younger adults – in fact, whites older than 60 years of age had a three times higher risk of being murdered than young white adults, while for black victims the reverse was true. Eldercides among whites also involved a significantly higher number of female victims. Which brings us back to our 'ideal' victims.

More than 20 per cent of all victims identified in my media research were women aged 60 years and older. When this was broken down into intimate and non-intimate femicides (the relationship between the victims and perpetrator was not always known, or evident in news stories, and was only available for 293 out of 408 cases), it emerged that nearly *50 per cent* of the non-intimate femicide cases covered by the media were of elderly women. This was significantly higher than figures from the Medical Research Council's first femicide study in 1999, which found that women aged 60 years and older made up eleven per cent or less of non-intimate femicides. This also meant that elderly women made up the single largest clear sub-set of (non-intimate) femicide victims.

Many of these findings made sense, instinctively. Firstly, elderly women are at a much lower risk of intimate-partner murder because more of them are single or widowed in their later years, or (if their male partners are still alive), their partners are less likely to pose a physical threat to them. Secondly, although the annotation of 'ideal victim' was not intended as an empirical construct, older women *are* often targeted because they typically live alone, they are easy to dominate physically and they may have a source of income, such as a pension, or other assets worth robbing. One of the things I noted in articles about several of the elderly victims, particularly older black women in more rural or in lower-income areas, was that many of the stories mentioned small failures, warning signs that had preceded the woman's death: for example, that the victim had previously been targeted for robbery or petty theft, but had either not reported it to or had not been helped by the police. There were also several cases where the killers were out on bail or had prior convictions for violent crime. At least one woman was murdered in an incomplete government housing development, where the local authorities had been warned for months that the construction site was being used by criminals, but had failed to make it safe. These details suggested that as much as political leaders loved to make speeches about 'protecting the elderly', the reality on the ground was that there was little support or protection to be had.

I would also argue that elderly women appear to make ideal *targets*, in much the same way as black elderly women were targeted for violence through witchcraft allegations, because elderly women, in all societies, present a convenient and accessible object against which male rage can easily be expressed.

I can't honestly claim to understand any of the crimes I have studied over the past several years, the random ones, the planned ones, the lines that get crossed from one moment to the next, but the aggressive and deliberately cruel ways in which elderly women are killed – including, frequently, being *raped* before or after her death (more than a quarter of the elderly victims in my study had been raped) – seem so gratuitous that, at some point, I have had to accept it is not an accident but a feature of why men choose to kill such defenceless and vulnerable people. And, also, because there seem to be few consequences for perpetrators.

Indeed, arrests were reported in fewer than half the cases where elderly women had been murdered, and convictions in under a quarter. Where the perpetrator was known, a little over ten per cent of the elderly victims had been killed by immediate family members, with a similar number of women killed by strangers. Only two of the 85 victims were killed by their intimate partners – Hester Salmans, who was beaten and burned by her husband in Sedgefield (he also tried to kill his step-daughter in the incident); and Australian tourist Jette Jacobs, who was killed in Johannesburg by a Nigerian boyfriend she had met online, and who was trying to scam her for money.

Including these two intimate-partner femicides, the 85 elderly victims in my (media-based) group ranged in age from 60 to 98 years old. There were near-equal numbers of reported black and white victims (37 white victims and 36 black victims), along with two coloured victims, two Indian victims, and eight women of undetermined race. But this is not to say that all elderly victims were considered equal by the press. The majority of black victims were reported on in five or fewer articles – fourteen of them warranting just a single mention. Only two white victims received single mentions, and nearly a third received media coverage of fourteen articles or more (an 'article' is not necessarily an entire news story about the victim and often consisted of a single-line mention in a bigger story).

Once I started looking at which elderly victims got the most prominent coverage, another sub-pattern emerged. With the exception of a Delmas day-care owner named Margrietha de Goede, who was murdered together with a baby in her care, of seven elderly female victims that received coverage in 21 or more articles (this is a significant number – the median number of articles for a femicide is three articles per victim), six were farm murders and five of these were incidents in which the women had been killed with their husbands. Taken together, these six farm killings represented more than a third of all media coverage of elderly women overall.

Farm murders

Farm attacks and farm murders occupy a prominent place in the landscape of violence in democratic South Africa. The terms (including, in Afrikaans, 'plaasanval' and 'plaasmoord') are used in the press almost exclusively to refer to attacks or killings of white farmers ('boere') by black perpetrators, and not to rural killings of black or coloured men and women, even if they are smallholders or farm workers.[11]

In the context of media reporting, farmer killings are the *most reported* type of murder in South Africa. Research by minority white-rights organisation AfriForum found that more than 70 per cent of farm murders were reported in the press[12] – compare this to femicide, where less than 20 per cent of the murders ever appeared in the media[13] (this juxtaposition does need to be contextualised – the highest number of reported farm murders in a single year was 153 deaths, recorded in 1997/98 and is estimated at around 62 farm murders for the 2017/2018 year, although these numbers are disputed).

Farm murders are an extremely controversial topic, partly because, for an extended period, SAPS stopped providing official data on farm attacks and farmer killings – which opened the floodgates for false information, speculation and rumours of a government conspiracy against farmers. There is also ongoing debate as to what does and does not qualify as a 'farm attack', who qualifies as a 'farmer', and how many 'farms' (and even what counts as a 'farm'?) should or shouldn't be included in such data. But, related to the above, it is also because the victims of such attacks are often white, (although this should not come as a surprise given that, even as late as 2017, 72 per cent of privately owned agricultural land in South Africa was held by white owners[14]) particularly white and often Afrikaans speaking. As a result, farm attacks have increasingly become framed as race crimes, or 'hate crimes' against whites. On the N1 highway between Mokopane and Polokwane there is a 'witkruismonument' (white cross monument) where thousands of white crosses are planted on a hillside to mark white victims of farm attacks (the woman who maintains the site has declined to plant crosses for black victims of farm attacks).

The farm murder narrative is also a central lobbying issue exploited by Afrikaans minority-rights groups such as AfriForum, and political parties like the Vryheidsfront Plus, plus occasional British and American (and a few South African) D-list celebrities who fly in looking to gain attention and financial remuneration by promoting disproven claims of an alleged 'white genocide' on their social media channels.

I'm not sure if I can claim the distinction of being the *very* first person formally to debunk claims of a white genocide in South Africa. But this (the debunking) is what I did back in July 2013, when I wrote a report for Africa Check looking into a series of false claims about murders of white people that had been broadcast by popular Afrikaans singer Steve Hofmeyr (and which later resulted in Hofmeyr, Sunette Bridges and several others, including the Vyrheidsfront Plus, charging me with hate speech against white men).

One of Hofmeyr's claims was that a white farmer was murdered in South Africa every five days. When I looked at data collected by the Transvaal Agricultural Union, I found that, between 1990 and 2012, they calculated an average of 70 people a year were killed in farm attacks – which works out to one murder every 5.2 days – but (and this is important), nearly fourteen per cent of these victims were black. So Hofmeyr's statement would only have been true if he considered farm attack victims of all races. (He did not, and would not.) This was backed up by separate research from white Afrikaans trade union Solidariteit, which previously found that over 38 per cent of farm attack victims were black or coloured. New research (which I will discuss below) shows this figure is even higher.

I've been accused, repeatedly, of been a farm attack denialist. I will repeat that farm attacks and farm killings in South Africa are a genuine and significant crime, and a security problem that needs urgent intervention and solutions – but that these solutions and interventions need to be based on facts, not prejudice (and that these solutions should include everyone on farms and smallholdings, not only white farmers and their families).

I believe that farm killings should be treated with the same swift condemnation and decisive justice response that all the other murders in this book should command. But that is also the problem, because our police and justice system right now aren't just failing farm attack victims, they're failing pretty much all of us, almost uniformly.

One of the things I hope this book shows, in quite devastating range and detail, is that the idea that there are 'exceptional' killings, is not true. Every year, without fail, there are not just a few, but literally *hundreds* of cases of murder that are shocking in their violence, and in their gratuitousness. To somehow imagine or claim that it is worse for some people but not for others shows the most callous sort of indifference; and this is also why the narrative of farm murders has become such a fraught space, because it persistently attempts to humanise white farmers through dehumanising black victims – by simply ignoring them, by pretending they don't exist, by saying that black victims are not a white problem because violence is just 'their culture', as if 400 years of white colonisation of southern Africa wasn't literally built on murder and violence.

Research from the past two decades has also consistently shown that farm killings are, in the overwhelming majority, criminally motivated and are not hate crimes (like, for example, the killings of black lesbian and transgender women, which *are* hate crimes, even if they are not yet legally recognised as such), nor are they politically motivated[15] – although political, social and economic instability may indeed drive violent crimes including an increase in violence against vulnerable people such as the elderly, as can clearly be seen in the chapter on witch killings. In fact, reviewing data for this book it occurred to me that a large number of farm murders appear to have a great deal in common with other eldercides, which is an aspect that is currently under-explored in research.

The absolutely grim reality is that, in many instances, criminals appear to commit extreme acts of violence against victims simply because they can. Dr Johan Burger, senior researcher in the Crime and Justice Programme at the Institute for Security Studies, explains that, '[u]nlike urban areas, farms and smallholdings are much more isolated and removed from immediate police or other security services, including close neighbours. This relative isolation provides attackers with more time and freedom to commit crimes against their victims, which are often extremely violent, including the gratuitous use of torture.'[16]

Having said that, as with every other chapter in this book, it is quite frankly impossible to 'rationalise' the ways violence is meted out against people. As an example: in January 2013, two elderly couples were murdered within days of each other – 79-year-old Elna[17] van Heerden and her husband Rudolf, who were killed at their home in Belfast, Mpumalanga; and 76-year-old Annetjie[18] van Rooyen and her husband Ernest, who were killed at their farm tuckshop in Parys in the Free State. Both Elna and Rudolf had been beaten, their hands and feet bound, and their bodies jammed into a freezer. Annetjie's body was also found in a freezer, her hands tied with shoelaces and her feet bound with wire. Annetjie and Ernest had been stabbed (his body was left on the tuckshop floor).

During the murder trial it emerged that Annetjie had suffocated to death in the freezer, and the pathologist explained that he had to wait for her body to defrost before he could conduct the autopsy.

It's easy to see how these kinds of murders – just four out of many, from just one year – would provoke outrage, and anger. And rightly so. But when this becomes loaded with emotion and rhetoric, we also sometimes miss the bigger picture. Sometimes, it has even been obscured. I believe this is particularly true with farm attacks, not just because they represent white victims but also because farms and farmers themselves represent something much bigger in the narrative and history of white Afrikaans-speaking South Africans. In Afrikaner history, farmers were quite literally the pioneers who settled the land (and, in another narrative, they were the ones who stole the land) – and not just any land, but, for the boers, God-given land. Land to which the farmers had, and still have, a deep-rooted connection.

Stolen land or not, the connection between person and place is as real for many farming families as it is for families who were forced off the same ground. This is a fraught prospect (emotionally, and also legally), and farm attacks should be seen as an extension of both histories: the heroic creation myth of the Boer states; and the violent theft of water and land from local populations. It's such a formative part of South Africa's colonial history that, in Nigel Worden's book on slavery in Dutch South Africa, he describes how, in the early eighteenth century, colonist farmers 'lived in a constant fear of slave violence' and the threat of attacks by either Khoekhoe or runaway slaves or, worse, both. It was the fear of such attacks that led farmers in the Stellenbosch region to form their own commandos[19] – which would later become quite formal commando systems, performing what was essentially a paramilitary-type neighbourhood watch service for farmlands.

The current white-right narrative likes to position farm killings as something far more recent – either from the mid-1980s, when the ANC leadership in exile broadcast calls for workers to seize back the land; and, more specifically to the early 1990s, after the release of Nelson Mandela and the unbanning of the African National Congress, the South African Communist Party, the Pan Africanist Congress and other liberation organisations. TAUSA's statistics on farm attacks, which it started keeping in the late 2000s during the government moratorium, only date back to 1990 specifically.

These more recent narratives centre around the supposedly self-evident political motives for black violence against white farmers, and the post-1990 version in particular seems to make the point (taken up by Hofmeyr and his friends) that democracy was in itself bad for white people.

Except – even if we overlook accounts from the eighteenth and nineteenth centuries – press records clearly indicate that farm attacks and farmer killings were already a problem by the late 1970s, particularly (according to news reports) in the Northern Transvaal. Which, not coincidentally, was where we were starting to see other flare-ups of violence (see: witch killings), and at a similar period in time. While the violent witch-hunts were linked to political instability and inter-generational confrontations in the Bantustans, the reports on farm murders (by which I mean mostly white farmers) had more in common with the 'white fear' narrative I discussed previously, in my chapters on intimate partner murders. Which is to say, in the late 1970s crimes against white victims, even on farms, were framed within a bigger – and quite deliberately foregrounded – threat of terrorism.

In November and December 1978, there was a spate of stories in the press about farm killings, particularly elderly victims – in November an 80-year-old woman and her 35-year-old daughter were killed at their farm in Beestekraal, the younger woman's battered body found in the chicken run. A few weeks before that, another elderly couple had gone missing from their smallholding in Potgietersrus, a neighbour finding only bloody walls. Another couple was shot dead on their farm in Nylstroom. In a separate killing, a husband and wife and the husband's sister were killed on their farm in the Western Transvaal...[20]

In many stories, it was mentioned or alluded to that several of these attacks were suspected to be linked to terrorists. This was obliquely emphasised by other stories, of killings of white farmers in Namibia by SWAPO 'terrorists', and by the growing number of stories about attacks on white-owned farms and white farmers in Zimbabwe (then Rhodesia) during the latter years of the Bush War. Even when the local police spokesperson would comment that they believed a particular farm attack to be a case of regular armed robbery, the newspapers (and readers' letters) would often imply that there was a more sinister force behind the violence.

This was, of course, complicated by a number of actual politically motivated attacks on farms and farmers – which included the deaths, in 1985, of several labourers and farmers who were killed by landmines which had been planted close to the border with Zimbabwe. The South African government told reporters that three men had been seen planting the mines, and that it was assumed they were operatives from the then banned ANC. In the early 1990s, the armed wing of the Pan African Congress, APLA (the Azanian People's Liberation Army), also embarked on a deliberate campaign against white farmers, designed to 'drive white farmers off the land so that it could be reclaimed by the African people'[21], and engineered to seize weapons from the farmers. In that same year, at a memorial rally for Communist Party leader Chris Hani, who had been assassinated by white supremacists in April 1993, ANC Youth League president Peter Mokaba chanted the phrase, 'Dubula ibhunu' (Shoot the boer).

AfriForum later published data which, they said, showed that Mokaba's incitement had directly contributed to a 135 per cent increase in farm murders in the month immediately after the incident[22] – the increase may indeed have been correct (the sources of the figures are not given in the paper, so it's hard to check), but given that it was also the month after the assassination of one of South Africa's most important black liberation leaders, it might not be entirely fair to assume that it was Mokaba's speech rather than the unstable environment in general that would have contributed to any spike in attacks.

Hani's murder quite literally set South Africa at the brink of a civil war. What AfriForum's report does not mention is that, in the wake of Hani's killing, right-wing Afrikaner organisations like the Afrikaner Weerstandsbeweging (AWB) drove around townships threatening black residents they would suffer the same fate as Hani had. In an extremely volatile time – which saw a two- to four-fold increase in conflict and violence between mid-1993 and the first democratic elections in 1994 – Mokaba's chants were, in all likelihood, only one of many factors that contributed to violent actions. But, and this is a consistent flaw with the arguments and allegations of these right-wing lobby groups, the inability to see black people at all (except as threats) has meant an almost crippling blindspot in their ability to contextualise or analyse farm attacks in any other way except a race-based one.

This isn't just betrayed in racist behaviours and language (and a volk nostalgia for relics like the old South African flag, or a time when 80 per cent of the country had no rights), but it also displays a persistent rejection of other data, which at some point can no longer be seen as ignorance and must perhaps be regarded as malice.

A SAPS docket analysis from 2015/16 showed that 47 per cent of farm murder victims that year were *black*, and 42 per cent were white.[23] To claim farm killings as a whites-only tragedy is bizarre, and quite plainly untrue.

This brings me to another crucial point, which is that we have to be able to say 47 deaths (SAPS's figure for farm killings in 2017/18) is too much; *and* also be able to acknowledge that the killing of 47 people in one year is a tiny drop in the ocean of violence in which all South Africans are swimming. It is not clear how the white right lobby, with its posturing and misspelling of victims' names, the fake postings of bloody images, the courting of right-wing white organisations in America, Europe and Australia, groups and individuals who can't even be bothered to acknowledge one black person's death at Ysterberg, expects empathy from other South Africans, never mind their support.

One of the reasons I believe this has happened – not just because people are inherently bigots, or because politicians and lobbyists have exploited these deaths to make names for themselves and exploited antagonism rather than genuinely sought solutions – is that our newspapers, our news sources, don't really teach us much about each other when it comes to understanding the shared burden of violent crime and death. In the next chapter, I explain what the media gets 'wrong' in its coverage of femicide, which includes quite worrying discrepancies when it comes to the races of murder victims.

News stories, I should add, also don't usually cover the full extent of what a murder means, and what it does to a family (and how could you, with so many murders each day?) – unless it is the man who shot Reeva Steenkamp, in which case we know more about him than we could have ever reasonably desired.

Sometimes I would catch glimpses of lives that unravelled after a death. I would read a case about a mother who was killed at the entrance to her farm, which did make the news. And then, a few years later – maybe even after the trial, where two culprits had been found guilty – I would come across a notice that the same farm was up for auction (I found this because I would Google family members' names, in case they showed me additional news stories related to the crime). And just that simple notice, the sale of the farm, told an entire story in itself. That it was too much, that it had been too much for the family to bear. That they had lost something, someone, who was most important to them, and that they never fully recovered. That they were never able to recover.

Perhaps this is my imagined narrative, from the viewpoint of a mother who wonders how the woman's nine-year-old son – who had just been dropped off at school before his mother was shot – coped. He would be a teenager now. This part usually doesn't make the news.

PART THREE

The media and the message

11. Mega cases, race and rape: What the media gets wrong about femicide

Murders are considered to be among the most newsworthy crimes. But not all murders are equally newsworthy, and some are not even considered newsworthy at all. There are supposed to be certain factors that predict the likelihood of greater news coverage. These include things like rarity – the more uncommon an event, the more likely it is to be reported in the news – and often relate to victim characteristics, like race (white victims tend to get more coverage); gender (female victims are less common and therefore more 'newsworthy' than males); socioeconomic status (middle-class versus low-income victims); the victim's age (we pay more attention to crimes committed against the very old and the very young); and the location of the crime, mostly as a proxy for class, for example, suburban versus inner city (but also, practically, because remote areas may have fewer news outlets or fewer reporters). But these findings are not universal and there are regular exceptions.

A lot of what we 'know' about how newspapers and other professional consumer media (so, not social media, or lobby sites) cover crime comes from studies of media in what we might call Western or First World countries, where white people constitute a majority and brown people form a minority, where violent crime may be increasing but is often still relatively low compared to developing nations, where police and justice institutions are relatively robust and efficient, and where media institutions are relatively prolific and well resourced and, generally, have some protections in terms of things like freedom of speech. Across the Global South these criteria are often reversed: white populations are the minorities; class and status play out along different lines, including tribe and caste, as well as wealth; there may be lower levels of policing, and certainly lower levels of accountability or transparency of policing and justice; media systems are also frequently under-resourced, and often vulnerable to threats from those in power.

Writing and reading violence within the Global South requires an understanding or at least an acknowledgement of these phenomena, and also an inherent recognition that what constitutes the 'Global South' as a collective is, essentially, the persistent effects of colonialism, which have contributed to what Brazilian writer and editor Natália Maria Félix De Souza describes as residual systems of violence.[1] It is not a coincidence that we see commonalities in patterns of murder between India, Brazil, South Africa, Jamaica and Mexico. This might be hard to appreciate for readers who insist that we should already forget the brutality of apartheid, which ended less than 30 years ago, but those of us who study history and society have little challenge in demonstrating the direct links between slavery, forced removals, indigenous genocides and other features of colonial capitalism, even from four centuries ago, and showing how they have directly influenced the geographies of violence that exist today.

The Global South can generally be understood to include Central and South America and the Caribbean, Africa and Central and South Asia, including India. It is not specifically a *territorial* concept, however; rather it is a political and historical one, which emerged from a 'shared experience of subjugation under contemporary global capitalism'.[2]

Scholarship from the Global South specifically challenges and critiques the dominant focus on material, ideas and histories that emerged from Europe, Britain and North America, and can be seen as part of broader post-colonial and decolonisation movements – that, in my view in any rate, don't outright reject 'Northern sociologies of knowledge'[3] but acknowledge that these were both prejudiced and flawed because they specifically excluded scholars and scholarship that was not traditionally white and male. Scholarship from the Global South also locates research and knowledge *within* these regions, rather than simply locating these regions within ethnographic studies.

In this context in particular, South Africa represents an important location for the research of violence. This is partly because of the country's extremely high rate of inter-personal violence – we may as well be experts at the things we have in abundance: minerals, fossils and violence – but also because of several other significant features. South Africa has a mid-size population (approaching 59 million people in 2019), which is highly urbanised (more than 63 per cent by 2016), but which still has a substantial rural portion.[4] In addition, South Africa has a well-established body of academic and epidemiological work on violence, particularly focused on violence under apartheid, violence during the transition from apartheid to democracy, and violence in the post-apartheid state. The scope and depth of this research provides a strong foundation for understanding violence as a phenomenon rooted in *both* the present and the past.

South Africa also boasts a mature, diverse and relatively free press[5], located within a relatively democratic society which has a strong Constitution and both freedom and protection of information laws. Or at least it does now. Our news archives, though, are important evidence of a very different time and have unwittingly (and occasionally probably intentionally) preserved the flaws and failings and hypocrisy of apartheid South Africa with quite incredible detail. When we study how our news outlets have chosen to cover crime in general and femicide in particular over the last four decades, we often gain insights into the world outside of the page – for example, that South Africa in the late 1970s was not only obsessed with the threat of terrorism, but that it was also gripped by fears surrounding the potential collapse of the nuclear family as the country's new 'no fault' divorce laws went into effect (in 1979).

Stories that are published by news outlets don't manifest by magic, fully formed and untouched. Even by the time a piece of information arrives at a news desk, or a journalist or editor pitches an idea in a diary meeting, the 'news' has already been filtered, shaped and modified by hundreds of interactive processes, including societal and personal biases, and a host of political, legal and even practical issues. Journalists and editors are shaped by the societies in which they live, and they internalise many of those societal values while simultaneously reflecting and shaping them in their professional endeavours. News platforms also reflect and shape particular social values and encourage those values within their editorial content – for example, some newspapers consider themselves to be more 'family oriented', while others might not. Researchers Michele Lloyd and Shula Ramon describe a prescribed 'allegiance to a newspaper's ideological worldview'.[6]

News stories, then, emerge from and within media ecosystems which are simple and complex in different parts. The systems include roles like journalists, photographers, news editors, production editors, managing editors, copy- and sub-editors, retouchers, designers and publishers, who, variously, work with a variety of stakeholders, including readers, media owners, advertisers, press ombudsmen and media councils, even the state. There are deadlines, printers, distribution agencies and resellers, circulation boards and bureaus, regulatory bodies and statutory codes. Each of these parts, processes or systems can impact on a story just as much as the ability of a single reporter to 'sniff out' a good headline. Also (in spite of what TV series and movies insist), reporters don't usually make decisions as to what gets onto the page – that's typically the function of various editors. Similarly (also in spite of what television may have taught you), for non-political crimes there is typically very little involvement from publishers. In this context, the 'newsroom' should be seen as a gestalt system – it is much more than merely the sum of its parts.

And its relationship with the society in which it is situated is dynamic and reciprocal. News shapes the public agenda. Public interest influences the news. These dynamics can be as wide and long as ocean currents, and a successful news platform or publication has to be able to gauge all of them at a glance.

Today the trend is to measure audience engagement through page impressions, clicks, and so on. In the past – not that we were ever oblivious to circulation – we used to have to rely on our gut instincts (in journalistic biology, directly related to having a nose for a good story) to suss out what might capture the audience's attention. This 'gut' was usually developed through years spent in an actual newsroom, passed on osmotically by cranky, chain-smoking news and sub-editors.

When I interviewed a news editor who used to run South Africa's largest news wire agency, he described how, in November 2010, they got a tip-off about a couple who appeared to have been kidnapped in Gugulethu, and that one of the couple was missing and presumed dead. On the surface, he said, it was a routine crime story, mundane even in South African terms. But, tucked away in the tip-off was the information that the couple were British citizens, which immediately moved the case up from everyday to the story of the day. The missing woman, who was later found dead from a single gunshot wound, was Swedish citizen Anni Hindocha. Her new husband, Brit Shrien Dewani, initially claimed that it was a botched hijacking gone wrong. But soon he was accused of hiring a crew of local South Africans, including his taxi driver, to kill his wife and make it look like a crime (not entirely unheard of – it was literally the playbook for how Omar Sabadia had killed his wife Zahida).

The murder of Anni Hindocha in 2010 turned into one of the biggest news stories of the year – between 2010 and 2011 there were more than *five hundred* newspaper stories about her killing and the subsequent attempts to extradite her widower Shrien (who had returned to the UK) to stand trial in South Africa.

When Dewani was eventually tried in 2014, he was found not guilty and the killers – who had attempted to mitigate their own punishments by 'turning state's witness' and testifying against Dewani – were found to have lied. The high-profile court case once again dominated local news, generating hundreds of stories, receiving exponentially more coverage than almost every single other femicide case that year.

Cases like the killing of Anni Hindocha are what are referred to as 'mega cases'[7], murders that receive the most prominent coverage and eventually come to represent what we consider to be general 'knowledge' about homicide – by which I mean, almost everything we think we 'know' about murder, police and the criminal justice system typically comes from these mega cases rather than personal knowledge or experience or a wide reading of cases.

The best example of a mega case is undoubtedly the fatal shooting of model Reeva Steenkamp by her celebrity sportsman boyfriend, on Valentine's Day 2013. I had never met Reeva, but had interviewed her killer a few years before, for a story in the *Sunday Times*. I still clearly remember receiving a phone call from a colleague of mine, about what was initially described as some sort of mistaken identity type shooting (the first version I got was that Reeva had been shot and killed trying to break into her boyfriend's home to surprise him for Valentine's Day).

Reeva's murder was mentioned in over 1 800 press clippings on the Sabinet service alone – that was without including online news services which, based on my research, would easily have doubled that figure – and that's only using South African news sites. These figures suggest that the murder of Reeva Steenkamp received more coverage in the press than every single other femicide that was committed that same year. *Combined.* As best as I can tell, it is the most-covered (non-political) killing in the country's history.

At the time, I found the media's coverage of the case quite grotesque and self-serving (not unlike the ANC Women's League in some respects) – as long as the stories continued to drive sales, the media was quite prepared to meet the demand. On some days, there would be four to six different stories about Reeva or her killer in the same newspaper.

Some of my colleagues who were reporting on the case and subsequent trial would tell me that the coverage was important because it boosted coverage and awareness of femicide overall. I know they meant well and possibly believed this sentiment to be true. But I have no evidence that this was the case. If anything, my data shows that while mega cases may provide an extremely localised short-term boost in femicide coverage (in the first weeks following Reeva's killing, slightly more femicides were reported in the press than usual), this is followed by a slump in other coverage as media space and resources – and public attention – is consumed and exhausted by the main case (the month after Reeva's death had the lowest number of femicides reported in the press that year).

Not only do mega cases drown out news of other murders (and other court cases for older murders), these effects can persist for years. Every court case, anniversary or parole application will tend to generate significant coverage again. In some instances, one mega case can actually influence or even create another – across oceans. For example, South African news coverage of the gang rape and brutal murder of Delhi student Jyoti Singh in India in December 2012 was *directly* linked to local press interest in the rape and murder of Bredasdorp teenager Anene Booysen in South Africa in February 2013, and without which Anene's death would almost certainly have gone unremarked or only mentioned in passing. The subsequent murder of Reeva Steenkamp, a week later, again boosted coverage of the Bredasdorp killing, as media scrambled to prove they didn't *only* cover successful and attractive white victims. Anene's death eventually also became the second-most reported femicide in the 2012/2013 year, after Reeva's death.

But those events had little impact on the coverage of two other horrific gang rape-homicides, of Thandiswa Qubuda and Thandeka Madonsela, that took place within weeks of Anene's death.

It would be easy to blame the paucity of coverage on reporters or editors. But this is simplistic, and perhaps naive. I remember, during a session at the chaotic Summit on Gender-Based Violence that was held in late 2018, one of the attendees tearfully insisted that the media *had* to cover all stories of gender-based violence. To which I responded: with what resources?

Nearly 3 000 women are murdered in South Africa each year. That's an average of eight femicides every single day. Can you imagine trying to report not only on the eight new female murders that day, while also reporting on the investigations, arrests, court cases and all the other narratives of every other murder that preceded them? You wouldn't just need an entire newspaper, you'd need a phone book every few hours (if anyone remembers what phone books are), manned by an actual army of journalists. And that's *just* for femicides. The reality is that most newsrooms no longer even have dedicated crime or justice reporters, never mind separate police and courtroom reporters. There is also fierce competition for space on the page – even with online platforms, prime property is at a premium. Professional news platforms and publications are usually commercial ventures, which means they need to be profitable or at least sustainable. And that means telling stories that your readers believe are important or interesting, sometimes at the expense of other stories that are perhaps just as important or worthwhile but which, for various reasons, don't appeal to your readers. Activists sometimes like to pretend as if this is not the case, in the same way some people pretend carob tastes just the same as chocolate. But it's not only media who are mercurial and base and driven by trashy celebrity news and tabloid gossip. Audiences are too. It's why we raise voices and arms in protest against the killings of Karabo Mokoena and Uyinene Mrwetyana, and don't know even the name of the unemployed woman who lived in a shack and got drunk with her husband on Friday night and then they argued, and he didn't realise he had beaten her to death until he tried to wake her up the next morning.

Like it or not, we are equally fickle and frequently hypocritical when it comes to which victims matter *to us*, which bodies count. And we show this year after year, by deciding that some cases matter more than others. Which is not to say that these mega cases don't matter – of course they do. The killings of Valencia Farmer, Eudy Simelane, Anni Hindocha, Anene Booysen, Reeva Steenkamp, Jayde Panayiotou, Susan Rohde, Marthella and Christel Steenkamp, Teresa van Breda, Karabo Mokoena, Uyinene Mrwetyana, Zolile Khumalo, Franziska Blöchliger ... these are, individually, stories of great pain and horror, and which devastated families and communities. But they are also not representative (at all) of the reality of femicide in South Africa; nor do they represent the challenges and limitations of the current police and justice systems. Uyinene's killer, for example, was arrested, tried and sentenced within three months of her murder. More typically, cases can take months or even years to get to court – and that is if the perpetrators are ever arrested. Coverage of mega cases makes the average South African intimately familiar with concepts like 'dolus eventualis' but leave us poorly informed about the comparatively banal or mundane aspects of everyday femicide, including any real understanding of who is at risk.

One of the most interesting and perhaps problematic examples of how this plays out can be seen not through mega cases, but by analysing how South African media covers femicide stories by race.

Let's start by discussing at how overall media coverage of femicide breaks down by race.

This requires a slightly expanded discussion on race in the context of news reporting and murder. The attribution, identification and experience of race in South Africa is still strongly aligned with apartheid-era categorisations and has specific meanings and connotations that are not necessarily common with other regions.

Statistics South Africa includes five categories under race in its Census: black African, White, Indian or Asian, Coloured and Other, but these are not explained (in the Census or other statistical documents) and are self-described by Census participants rather than enumerators.[8]

In the broader South African context 'black' or 'African' usually means black African, and may include some mixed-race individuals; 'white' typically means Caucasian; 'Indian' refers to South Africans of Indian origin; similarly, 'Chinese' (both 'Indian' and 'Chinese' may be used to refer to recent, that is, first-generation immigrants who were born in those countries, or equally to individuals whose families have lived in South Africa for multiple generations); 'Coloured' refers to 'a phenotypically diverse group of people descended largely from Cape slaves, the indigenous Khoisan population and other people of African and Asian descent'[9], often described as being of mixed-race origin but associated with specific communities and histories rather than being a catch-all for mixed-race individuals. Unlike the use of the term in North America, 'Coloured' in the South African context is not the same as 'black', although coloured individuals may choose to identify as black.

Gender and race also influence risk profiles for violence, which is why it is important to make these factors explicit in research about violence. The Medical Research Council notes that while the 'concept of "population group" or "race" and its constituents, i.e. "Asian", "Black", "Coloured" and "White" are social constructs and are not meant to signify any inherent genetic or biological differences between these groups', they are 'used as demographic markers where such profiling allows for identifying vulnerable populations in order to plan and implement effective prevention and intervention programmes.'[10]

Within this exceedingly complex context, which cannot adequately be covered in this book, the notion of race is important and relevant to understanding societal data including crime, but it is contested and unfixed. Which means that attributing or inferring race to victims of crime, particularly to deceased individuals, is a challenging proposition – even at a medical level.

In South Africa the official cause-of-death certification (form DHA-1663) is supposed to be filled out by the 'medical practitioner/ professional nurse/forensic pathologist'[11] who determined the cause of death, and includes a section where the practitioner is asked to '[s]elect the race group' that they consider the decedent to belong to. The Medical Research Council's femicide studies and other similar mortality studies in South Africa use racial categorisations derived from either police and/or post-mortem reports, but even these can include a sometimes large proportion of uncertainty. In the 1999 femicide study, for example, 15.6 per cent of non-intimate victims' race was categorised as unknown.

These ambiguities obviously make it challenging to infer racial identification from news reports, as this information is not generally explicit. It is nonetheless important to include data on race in order to examine the potential role played by the race of both the victim and the perpetrator in media coverage of violence against women.

In my media research, information about victims' race was determined where possible using a combination of provided information that could be used to positively include or negatively exclude a victim or perpetrator from a race category. This included photographs of the victim or the victim's family, using the victim's surname (for example, 'Singh' is likely to be Indian, while 'Dlamini' is likely to be black), or using her location – for example, an elderly victim living in a rural village in the Eastern Cape is more likely to be black. However, these approaches do include an unknown degree of uncertainty and recorder bias. Where information included in news reports was insufficient to include or exclude a victim or perpetrator from specific race groups, their race was recorded as unknown.

In the total sample included in my initial femicide study, if we look at the 408 victims, 57% of the women were black, 18% white, 5% were coloured, 3% Indian, and in 18% of cases the race of the victim could not be determined from the information supplied in the news reports. What appears to be a possible over-reporting of the proportion of white victims is partly explained by the fact that most newspapers are situated in urban areas, which have higher proportions of white residents – whites make up less than 9% of South Africans overall but in Gauteng they might make up as much as 16% of the population. The under-reporting of black and coloured victims would probably be offset to some extent by the 'missing' race information in the unallocated 18% of cases noted.

When we look at the *number* of stories per victim, by race, though, a completely different profile emerges – and one which shows that, although white victims only make up 18% of the total number of victims, their deaths dominate news coverage by the sheer volume of stories. More than 56% of news stories about femicide were of white victims, while news stories of black and coloured victims only made up 26% and 15% of news coverage respectively.

My database of media coverage also allowed me to identify which titles or platforms had the highest number of unique stories about femicide, and exactly which stories they had covered. When I started separating out cases and coverage by title, another picture emerged.

Out of nearly 200 media titles included in my survey, I found that just 24 titles published 50 or more unique femicide stories (about victims who were killed in 2012/2013). And that, together, these top 24 titles represented more than three-quarters of all news media coverage of femicide in South Africa. I also found that the coverage within these titles was typically dominated by prominent coverage of a small number of high-profile femicides, rather than lots of coverage of multiple femicide events. The types of stories that each newspaper chose to focus on also tell quite a story about the newspapers themselves (for this section I excluded coverage of Reeva Steenkamp because the massive number of stories would have skewed the sample).

Nearly half of femicide stories in *Volksblad* (Afrikaans medium, distributed predominantly in the Free State and Northern Cape) were about the Steenkamp family murders in Griekwastad, while close to 60 per cent of femicide coverage in the *Cape Times* (English medium, Western Cape and Eastern Cape) was about the murder of Anene Booysen. By contrast, *Volksblad* only covered Anene Booysen's death in eight news reports, and *The Star* (English medium, primarily distributed in Johannesburg) covered the Griekwastad killings in just 14 out of 192 femicide stories. This reveals quite stark differences in the perceived 'newsworthiness' of these stories and shows that editorial selection differs significantly between newspapers – and even depending on language and location. *Beeld* (Afrikaans medium, distributed in Gauteng, Limpopo, North West and Mpumalanga) featured similar coverage for the Steenkamp family and Anene Booysen murders but did not cover the Cape Town-region murders of teenager Charmaine Mare or clown and stilt-walker Rosemary Theron[12]. None of the top-reporting titles gave prominent coverage (I defined this as ten articles or more in one publication) to all four of the top-reported femicide incidents for that year (Steenkamp family, Booysen, Mare, and Theron).

Another significant finding was how the coverage broke down by race when I took language into account. Here again, a distinct profile emerged: in the English-language newspapers, the majority of female homicide victims reported on were black (this was true even for the English-medium *Cape Argus*, where the majority of the city's population is coloured). However, in the Afrikaans-language newspapers, the majority of victims covered were white:

in *Beeld*, 62% of victims were white; in *Volksblad*, the proportion was 53%; and in *Die Burger* (Afrikaans medium, Western and Eastern Cape), it was 48% (whites were the largest single group but not a majority). Every single femicide victim covered by weekly Afrikaans national newspaper *Rapport* was white, with the lone exception of Anene Booysen. As an observation, if one's sole source of news was the Afrikaans-language media, the narratives of an alleged 'white genocide' or of a particular and deliberate epidemic of 'violence against whites' becomes perhaps a little more understandable.

More than any other approach, this provided perhaps the strongest indicator of how the problem position of femicide is specifically, and often narrowly, presented to South African readers by the different media they consume.

What should also be noted here is that none of the journalists or newspaper editors I spoke to specifically set out to present a skewed picture of murder, particularly by race. If anything, they were increasingly conscious of the need to be more representative. But here again is where a number of practical considerations often come into play – factors not often taken into account by newsroom studies which focus on philosophical attributes rather than pragmatic ones.

Editors don't typically exclude femicide stories because the victim is black, or poor. They exclude them, rather, because their network of informants (in the case of *Volksblad*, for example) are predominantly white and probably unaware of murders outside of their own immediate community. Or because they only have one reporter available to go to court, and so they choose to go to the closer and more accessible magistrate's court, which will also allow the journalist to file his or her stories on time – rather than a smaller court that is farther away, which might involve additional travel costs, or might mean a reporter is not able easily to make deadlines. There is also the gruesome reality of news coverage in a high crime country: as much as audiences 'demand' we cover more femicide, we don't actually want to read about more murders. It's depressing. If the newspaper in question has already covered three or four gruesome murders that week, a fourth or fifth or sixth one might make audiences disinclined to keep reading. And readers aren't the only ones to experience crime fatigue. Reporters, too, may eventually become overwhelmed by the unrelenting violence they are exposed to every day. Even studying this violence from a relative distance, it doesn't leave you. For court and crime reporters, those who sit through court testimonies, who hear pathologists and police describe bodies and crime scenes, this can be unbearable. Reporters have nightmares. One reporter, who is now an editor, recalled covering one case where a three-year-old girl had been raped to death. The perpetrator had penetrated the victim so deeply that her kidneys had ruptured, and the child's body had gone into hypovolemic shock, which had killed her.

So, it is easy to criticise what newspapers get wrong – easy to criticise the police, too, who see even more, and even worse than we do. But we also need to appreciate that, while we can and should (must) acknowledge our shortcomings and even failings when it comes to press coverage, we also realise that this same coverage takes place within a difficult, sometimes almost impossible situation. As with many other discussions, it requires a greater degree of empathy, even while we work to improve the status quo.

12. Fuck the hashtag

In November 2018, the South African government hosted a National Summit against Gender-based Violence and Femicide, which was held at a sprawling and maze-like conference centre near Pretoria. The summit was attended by President Cyril Ramaphosa, a gesture to the protesters who had participated in the #TotalShutdown march to the Union Buildings a few months earlier, which had precipitated the summit, and where crowds of red-and-black-clad women and gender non-conforming people had waited until late in the evening for the president to arrive and receive their list of demands.

I had been asked to help moderate a breakaway session on gender-based violence and media but, at the last minute, this role was taken over by someone from GCIS (the Government Communication and Information System department) together with a representative from the #TotalShutdown movement. The media session took place shortly after the large opening session, where President Ramaphosa had been in attendance and where silent protesters had held up bloody underwear and a survivor had stripped naked to show the president the scars on her body following a brutal attack. Women were crying, sobbing, shouting. Emotions were extremely high.

The media group was a total mess. Within minutes of starting, any resemblance to the original agenda was abandoned as more survivors – obviously those who had not been picked to go on stage in the previous session – felt the need to stand up and give their testimonies, even though they had no relation to the session that was supposed to be taking place. People wanted a space to be heard, and they wanted the opportunity to speak their pain in public. I understand this was necessary for many women, individually and collectively, but it also meant that any proposed discussion around the role of media was quickly drowned out by anger and memory.

For me, personally, it was overwhelming. I was deep in my own research, spending my days and nights reading and re-reading information about hundreds of femicides. It was physically and emotionally traumatic to be ambushed, without my consent, by a succession of women demanding that I hear about how they had been violated and brutalised and harmed. I am a survivor of sexual abuse myself (it was a long time ago and thankfully long healed, but it will always be a part of my reality), and I also experienced the testimonies as a form of non-consensual violence against me. It was extremely triggering, on many different levels. I had stepped out of the earlier opening session, not prepared to engage with the intensity of the emotional spectacle.

I walked out of the media session less than an hour after it started. I realised my presence was not only pointless (nobody was interested in talking about the media from a pragmatic point of view), but also that staying would continue to expose me to the constant assault of other women's pain. (I can't emphasise enough how important it is that women are able to opt *out* of this as well as opt in.) I left the summit feeling angry – angry that I had been exposed to repeated emotional violence; and angry that what I had naively believed was going to be a genuine opportunity to discuss best practices (not just in media, but other sectors) had been completely hijacked by rhetoric and emotion.

I know that there are many people – those who have been working for far longer in the gender activism space – who have worked exceptionally hard to redeem some value from this and other similar gender events, and that there are many dedicated, experienced and competent people who have worked and who continue to work towards an agenda that will not only be adopted by government but which will actually one day translate into or at least support practical and pragmatic initiatives that might improve the situation. But what I saw, on that day, was millions of rands being spent on people venting emotion instead. And the government, in turn, being able say: yes, we did it, we listened to you the way you asked us to. We have ticked the box you asked us to tick. But, of course, it also meant they weren't really required to do anything about it beyond provide a platform for the spectacle.

I remain circumspect about the value of the #TotalShutdown, or any other hashtag, except in that it gives people the public opportunity to participate in mass emotion, anger and the unrealised promise of catharsis.

More than this, I saw first-hand not just at the 2018 summit but many times since, how the group mentality of these procésses can actually undermine (or just drown out) the smaller, or the longer-term, less vitriolic responses to our country's violence crisis. The Gender Summit gave a platform to many new voices, but it also prioritised those voices that were the loudest – not necessarily those voices that were the most relevant. Many long-established NGOs and other organisations were excluded, or relatively sidelined on the day, in favour of those who were behind the #TotalShutdown movement. Maybe this is necessary – maybe we need more new voices. But, at the time, it smacked of petty politics rather than any real desire to find solutions.

I was in India the following year when the body of missing university student Uyinene Mrwetyana was found in Cape Town, after she had been raped and murdered by Post Office employee Luyanda Botha.

There were more protests then and more hashtags, and once again I had scores of journalists and editors contacting me for comment: can we interview you, can you write us a thought-piece on femicide, and so on. I said no to all of them because first of all I was in another time zone and I was swamped with other work. But I also knew that what I wanted to say was not what people wanted to hear. At least, not that week. That week, and in the weeks that followed, people wanted to wear black and express outrage, and ask #AmINext. And, again, I understand this was valuable and even necessary. But it did nothing to change the bigger picture. In fact, from my perspective it showed a remarkable ability to ignore the bigger picture.

More than two years before Uyinene's death, during the outcry that accompanied the murder of Karabo Mokoena in Johannesburg, I gave an interview to an online news site, explaining that what many women perceived as a spike in gender-based violence was really just a spike in media coverage. Women were (and are) being murdered all the time. Every day. Eight times a day. Nearly three thousand women a year. But we protest about one, because she (whoever she is, depending on the year) made us realise how close the violence really was. And then we allow ourselves to forget again.

When we make cardboard placards and banners, and dress in black and stand outside parliament or the stock exchange, we seem to express brief solidarity in fear, and ambiguity when it comes to asking for solutions. This vagueness is a real weakness and it needs to be addressed.

I looked back at the 'demands' that were issued in 2018 by the #TotalShutdown movement – which included things like the 'development of a National Action Plan on gender-based violence whose terms of reference will be determined by [a] review process' and the 'establishment of accountability and oversight mechanisms to ensure that an adopted National Action Plan is implemented' and 'provision of prevention services and information on GBVAW [gender-based violence/violence against women] with a view to raising awareness on the different forms of GB-VAW, preventing violence and changing attitudes'.

The phrasing of these sentences is so abstract that they are rendered almost meaningless. As supposed 'actions' they fare poorly, particularly in a highly bureaucratic government environment where even a review process can take years to constitute, never mind complete. I understand there is an argument here that, leveraged correctly, protests might increase political will to drive actual progress; but if we don't ask for meaningful and specific results, we should not be surprised when we get what we ask for.

The #TotalShutdown also included demands like the '[r]ecognition that intersecting forms of oppression heightens women's vulnerability to GBVAW and that these factors are taken into account during the investigation, prosecution and sentencing'. What is the appropriate response to this? If the state says – as Ramaphosa essentially did – that he sees and acknowledges the women, the victims in front of him; if the government says: 'Yes, we recognise there are intersecting forms of oppression,' is that sufficient? Does the demand compel the state to actually *do* anything about this, or just 'recognise' the problem? It's like the old joke, with the dying woman lying on the ground, and she says to a passer-by, 'Please, call me an ambulance.' And the passer-by says, 'You're an ambulance.'

The vagaries of these demands also obscured the fact that, buried within the righteous and the ambiguous, were some real and sensible and important requests, like for places of safety and care for survivors of gender-based violence, for shelters and for interim housing, for Legal Aid assistance, and for the proper application and implementation of existing laws and prescribed sentencing for perpetrators of gender-based violence.

But even those were problematic at times. For example, there was a request for the publication of 'a monthly list of police stations and police officers who have been reported to the Independent Police Investigative Directorate for failing to provide services to survivors of GBVAW'. It sounds good and important on paper but fails to take into account the current mandates of either the South African Police Service or IPID. For example, SAPS is compelled to provide certain assistance to victims of abuse under Section 18(4) of the Domestic Violence Act, but this Act does not encompass broader 'gender-based violence' (which is not actually mentioned or defined in the Independent Police Investigative Directorate Act of 2011). How would the IPID comply with this demand, when no formal broad or inclusive crime category (gender-based/violence against women) exists?

Also, having previously submitted requests for data to SAPS and given that we are currently only able get basic public information about crime on an *annual* basis, an expectation of publicly available (and presumably, given the serious nature of the allegations, one would hope audited or at least checked) monthly IPID updates on charges against individual police officers at individual stations seems quite frankly unrealistic (and, even if it was possible, probably would not be the highest priority in terms of the kinds of monthly crime data that might be useful).

This is becoming a consistent feature of the hashtag brigade: that even when 'practical' requests are made, they are often knee-jerk responses cast in anger, tailor-made for Tweeting and immediate relief of emotional pain, rather than actions that might achieve positive systemic change. More than that, I believe that many of these requests are potentially dangerous – barely disguised calls for the right to perform mob justice under the label of 'monitoring'.

It is understandable why so many people express a desire to bypass the criminal justice system. People have no faith in the system, because they can see where it is not working. But most of us don't see the parts where it *is* effective and necessary (the foundations, clearly spelled out in our Constitution, for example), which contain myriad countless tiny checks and balances, put in place by thoughtful jurists, specifically to provide a counterweight to our biases and to crowds' bloodthirsty desires for 'citizen' justice.

Since the murder of Uyinene Mrwetyana in 2019[1], I have seen repeated calls, including an online petition, asking for the National Register for Sex Offenders to be made public (the Register is currently available only to certain employers, such as schools, creches and hospitals, to check whether a potential employee is fit to work with children or people with mental disabilities). I find this ironic, and also problematic. Ironic because it inherently says: 'We don't trust the system to look after us', but then also asks the very same system to provide the data on who is supposedly 'safe', and who is not.

First, it must be noted that the Register only contains information on individuals who have been convicted of sexual offences against minors and people with mental disabilities. It is not a comprehensive registry of all people convicted of sexual offences (i.e. against adults); and it is *not* a register of people who have been accused of or even charged with sexual offences, because even though we all think we are better and smarter than everyone else, we are not, in fact, a replacement for a court of law. I think that, at the heart of the petitions, this is what people really want to get at – the shared whisper-gossip of accusation, a new version of a makgotla. And the consequences of this can be fatal. The Institute for Security Studies has reported that at least two people *a day* die in South Africa as a result of vigilante or group attacks[2].

Second, even if it *was* a record of all convicted sexual offenders, this would only represent a minute proportion of actual sexual offences in South Africa. Research has consistently indicated that the majority of sexual offences that are committed go unreported. And, of those that are reported, only a very small proportion end in convictions. A Medical Research Council study of rape cases reported in 2012[3] found that just under nine per cent of cases were finalised (that is, the trial was completed) with a verdict of guilty of a sexual offence. Let's also keep in mind that, if you are caught and charged with a sexual offence, notwithstanding the frequent ineptitude and apathy of the system, if you are wealthy (and, often, white), you have a better chance of navigating the system in your favour, as opposed to an accused who cannot afford bail or his own choice of legal representation. So, an offenders' registry, which only represents a fraction of actual offenders, is always more likely to represent poor, brown and black men, than wealthier and white men. Or, in other words, just because a man is not listed on the registry, doesn't mean he's not a threat.

Also, the entire point of *correctional services* is that, once a prisoner is convicted and has served time, we assume that there is the potential for correction and rehabilitation. Not 'damnation in eternity' (we seem to want to not only be judge and jury, but also gods). Making a sexual offenders' registry completely open and searchable to the public would, in effect, confer a life sentence on all convicted offenders – and, contrary to popular social media sentiment, prisoners and ex-convicts *do* have rights.

More than this, a publicly searchable registry wouldn't just expose the offender to further punishment, it would expose their families[4] ('Did you know Joan's dad was a rapist?') and, potentially, their victims ('Hey, Joan, I saw your dad was convicted of sexual offences against a minor. Did he molest you?').

Multiple studies on sex offender registries have also shown that registries and notification protocols (in districts where convicted sex offenders are required to notify law enforcement, or the public, about their status) don't reduce recidivism (re-offending), tend to create community panic and incite vigilante attacks against the offenders, and, in some studies, may actually reduce convictions for sexual offences as individuals plead guilty to lesser non-sexual (and therefore non-notifiable) offences.

Which is partly the point of my criticisms (which I am sure will not be well met in many quarters) – that the very nature of hashtags, of emotionally loaded mass protests around gender-based violence, of calls for citizen justice, ultimately undermines the possibility of appropriate interventions in favour of meaningless but popular rhetoric.

And that is a pity because there *are* a number of specific actions that would have an immediate and longer-term meaningful impact in reducing violence against women. But these rarely make it onto the placards at protests (admittedly they may be harder to fit on an A3 cardboard sign, but if we are not asking for specific remedies, then we will never make the kind of progress we need).

One important 'small' action would be to install street lighting in poorly lit areas in informal settlements and townships. The Khayelitsha Commission of Inquiry found that inadequate and ineffective lighting contributed to crime, while also making policing of crime more challenging. In response, a Khayelitsha lighting master plan was developed, with an estimated cost of R12.93 million. The plan, which was supposed to be rolled out in 2019/2020, has had less than half this amount allocated to it by the City of Cape Town – and the funds have been allocated for *all* lighting upgrades across 'Area East', which stretches from Mitchells Plain to Gordon's Bay.

Instead of constantly upbraiding SAPS, we should also keep calling for training and support that would allow police officers to properly investigate violence against women, including femicide. South Africa's police services are facing a number of urgent challenges, including a demoralised workforce following years of poor senior management, and a rising wave of violent crime that shows no signs of stalling. Within this, though, a patriarchal culture or at least tolerance of violence, in particular domestic or intimate partner violence, still permeates across SAPS ranks. This is evident both in the high number of police officers involved in intimate partner violence, including fatal incidents, and in the way in which police treat complaints of partner violence from citizens. Members of the police services need to be trained not only to provide better support to victims of domestic and gender-based violence, but also to investigate cases of such violence with greater integrity. Of course, this same point has been made and repeated for many years now and has yielded little real systemic change. At the Commission for Gender Equality's

Public Investigative Hearings held in December 2019, it was evident that SAPS had little data on its own officers, and it emerged that only four per cent of SAPS members were going through the required training about how to deal with domestic violence and gender-based violence. As a related concern, SAPS needs to improve its investigation into all forms of domestic violence and violence against women, particularly femicide (which may also require SAPS to re-think its own currently limited definition of the term). This would require additional resourcing, not only training of SAPS members but, for example, provision of rape kits and related support from forensic services, and so on.

What we also need is to put tighter controls in place for gun owners who are accused or convicted of domestic violence or gender-based violence. Pro-gun rhetoric has been a part of South Africa's mythos since at least the 1970s, but the current narrative has also expanded to included nonsense justifications and even statistics borrowed from the United States in particular. There is no data that indicates private gun ownership has any positive effect on reducing crime overall, or violent crime in particular. In addition, there is significant evidence that increased private gun ownership in South Africa increases gun homicides (including femicides), and also suicide. Previous studies have conclusively shown that tighter restrictions regarding gun ownership, including the compulsory renewal of gun licences, can decrease gun deaths.

As part of the above, we also need to take guns away from abusive cops and security officials. Gun control mechanisms need to account for the fact that nearly five per cent of South Africa's entire population is employed either in the security industry or the police force, and that there are proportionally exceptionally high rates of fatal intimate partner violence related to these professions. Domestic violence complaints against current and even former members of the police services in particular need to treated much more seriously; and male police officers who are accused of violence against a partner should not be allowed to continue working with their service weapons without further evaluation.

Media plays an important role in how we understand the 'problem' of violence against women, and also what we believe might be solutions. Because of this, media reporting on gender-based violence and femicide should be held to higher standards of accuracy and accountability, including protecting the dignity of victims of gender-based violence.

South African media would do better to give up on the folly of 'Sixteen Days' and rather focus its resources on developing better practical and ethical standards for the reporting of violence against women, including femicide. My study of media coverage of femicide in South Africa indicates that there are major discrepancies between news coverage of femicide and actual femicides, and that this coverage perpetuates incorrect stereotypes around who is at risk and who is a perpetrator of violence. Media also needs to put more effort into getting its data and numbers right. Publishing false or inflated information about violence against women or femicide does *not* help to raise the profile of the problem; it just introduces or entrenches mythology around violence, which influences what people believe are potential solutions to decrease violence.

While we are working on all of these, we also need interim measures. The state needs to provide suitable funding and support for shelters and care centres for victims of gender-based violence. Shelters are not a solution to ending gender-based violence. But, as the Commission for Gender Equality explains, they provide a means 'for survivors to escape the cycle of abuse and avoid further harm'. This means that shelters can save lives, while we work out how to fix the underlying problems. Understanding, undoing and repairing the fractures in our violent society is the work of generations, not just a single electoral term. While this work continues, it is essential that shelters are properly funded, are adequately resourced, are properly managed and monitored so that women are able to access them when they need them and so that shelters do not, in turn, become places of abuse. Shelters need to be more inclusive, able to accommodate women with infants and babies, and also to provide safety and shelter to members of the LGBTQI communities and any non-conforming individuals who need assistance. The South African government also needs to take steps to legalise sex work. Sex work is work, and its continued stigmatisation continues to place sex workers at risk of violence.

Fuck the patriarchy

Then there is the 'big' question: how do we change men's attitudes towards women? How do we defeat misogyny, how do we fight the patriarchy? (None of which, I might add, can be achieved without also fighting racism and other bigotry.) This is a question that researchers around the world are trying to confront. Some studies have suggested that teaching girls about self-defence and teaching boys about respecting women's bodily autonomy can, together, reduce gender-based violence. But there is nothing empirical. There is no behavioural vaccination that will suddenly fix thousands of years of abusive and controlling male behaviour towards women. Our laws may have made progress over the last 40 years, but our societies have not. Nowhere is this more clear to me than when I read news reports from, say, 1978, explaining why men feel entitled to shoot and kill their wives: because they feel undermined, because they feel like they are losing their position of authority in our society, because they are struggling to get or keep a job and it is hard not to be the 'provider', because women are taking men's jobs, because women's independence threatens their status quo. How many generations do we have to endure men feeling pathologically threatened by the mere fact of women's personhood?

This also presents a supplementary challenge, which is how to talk to men about the violence they commit. And I'm not just talking about men who kill women. I'm talking about the everyday violence men commit against women. Which doesn't just mean men who hit women, or who control women's behaviour, or who cat-call or leer at a woman because they can, or who call women bitches online because they didn't respond (or didn't respond the way the man wanted them to). I also mean every man who has seen that kind of behaviour, and who has said or done nothing against it. (Which is pretty much all men.)

More than once I have been told that saying things like 'all men are trash' is counter-productive, because it alienates men instead of trying to get them to be our allies.

Even without having spent the better part of a decade researching violence against women, I am honestly so tired of being told I should be *nicer* to men about this. The implication that I should smile more and wear a flattering but modest dress when I talk about how not just one man but a group of men participated in raping and murdering a woman, and how these men (more than one man!) inserted broken bottles into a woman's vagina and inserted an avocado pip into her rectum.[5] Or how a male police officer – who tried to kill his girlfriend, also a police officer, by shooting her four times – forbade his partner from washing herself or even changing her clothes before he got home, because he believed such actions were used to hide her supposed infidelity. I should also be 'nice' about husbands who allege their wife hanged herself with hairdryer cord in her bathroom. And, and, and.

I don't know how to explain these things nicely. I don't know, really, why men think such a thing is possible, never mind that they are also entitled to having this violence sanitised and made palatable for them because they did not, personally, rape and beat a woman to death. Because I don't have that luxury. We (women, and LGBTQI people) all walk around wondering if we are next, but the perpetrators of these acts are, like so many newspapers suggest, invisible. 'Woman shot in home' and so on. Nobody is doing the shooting or the stabbing or the strangling. No man. Certainly not all men.

This is the real challenge of allyship. I know (or see) men who claim to support women's rights, who speak out against individual violence against individual women, even societal violence against women, but who stop short at ever taking responsibility for their own accountability. 'Other men did this, but not me,' they say, never once pausing to ask themselves, exactly what were they doing while these other men were doing that.

The answer is: if (as a man) you are not actively fighting against violence against women, if you are not only taking full responsibility for your own behaviour (no cat-calling, no groping, no leering, no trying to have drunk sex with your female friend who has said no five times but is now just tired), if you are not calling out every male you see behaving that way towards a woman, if you are not stepping up with your male body and voice when you see a woman being abused in a public space, if you are not stepping up when you see a woman being abused in a domestic space... if you are not doing all of these things, then what you are is the lookout. You are the lookout at the door, making a safe space for the man inside the room who is doing all of those violent things.

Women are not just dying in South Africa. Men are killing them. We need our male allies to stop being the lookouts for patriarchy.

Acknowledgements

Much of this book is based on research conducted for my doctoral thesis on media coverage of femicide. I would like to take the opportunity to once again thank my supervisors, Professors Shireen Hassim and Scott Hazelhurst, who played a much more important role in getting me through my PhD than perhaps either of them realise (and who also made the experience brilliant for me). Prof. Hassim also raised funds and made the decision to award me a scholarship under the Mellon Foundation Governing Intimacies programme, which allowed me to focus on my PhD research full-time.

There are also many other researchers whose work has been absolutely critical to my own understanding of violence, of murder, of femicide, who have been working with this kind of material for far longer, and who are still studying violence so that we can one day make this country a safer place. I would like to acknowledge each of these people – some I have only read (and cited, extensively), some I have developed correspondence relationships with, some have become mentors and colleagues. I have such abundant respect and gratitude for their excellent and important work, and, where this applies, for their input, support and guidance. To Lisa Vetten, Brett Bowman, Naeemah Abrahams, Richard Matzopoulos, Lizette Lancaster, Gareth Newham, Chandre Gould, Rachel Jewkes, Shanaaz Mathews, Lorna Martin and Garth Stevens – thank you.

Also to the Wits Institute for Social and Economic Research (WiSER) and Professor Srila Roy, who took over the Governing Intimacies programme, and gave me an incredibly rich context within which to work: a supportive space that was full of ideas and shared learning, and where I was able to connect with other academics from the Global South. There is a lot of (sometimes deliberate) misrepresentation of what it means to decolonise academic thought and praxis. For me, a large part of that is starting to shift the conversation, and the notion of what is knowledge, away from the North or the West, whatever you like to call it, and allow countries like India and South Africa (and Brazil, Mexico, Argentina) to not just contribute to but actually lead the conversation on violence against women.

Finally, thank you to Na'eemah Masoet at Kwela, for wanting to publish this book in the first place, and for giving me the freedom to try and explain femicide in such unflinching terms.

NECHAMA BRODIE is a multi-media journalist, author and academic based in Johannesburg, South Africa. In a career spanning nearly 25 years she has worked as a feature writer, editor and publisher of women's magazines, a radio talk show host, a TV writer and director, and has written for leading newspapers, including the *Mail & Guardian*, *Sunday Times*, *City Press*, the UK *Guardian* and the Indian *Hindustan Times*. Between 2013 and 2018 Nechama worked with independent fact-checking organisation Africa Check, launching and heading up the group's training and research division TRI Facts. She has trained researchers, journalists and students in South Africa, Nigeria, Kenya and Zimbabwe, and collaborated with fact-checking organisation Chequeado in Argentina, developing and teaching fact-checking, verification and reporting methods. Nechama is an occasional lecturer at the University of the Witwatersrand's school of journalism where she recently completed a PhD looking at South African media coverage of femicide.

Nechama is the author of seven books, including two novels. She has twice been long-listed for the *Sunday Times* Alan Paton Award for non-fiction, and once for the *Sunday Times* Barry Ronge Award for fiction. Her first novel, *Knucklebone*, was shortlisted for a Nommo Award for African speculative fiction.

Notes

2. Everywoman's femicide

1. 2000 Data from Statistics South Africa, 2004. 'Mid-year population estimates, South Africa: 2004'.
2. United States Overseas Security Advisory Council (OSAC) report: https://www.osac.gov/Country/Jamaica/Content/Detail/Report/1d98b2df-fd4b-485f-aa62-15f4aed245ef.
3. Statistical Institute of Jamaica data for 2018, from: https://statinja.gov.jm/Demo_SocialStats/Newpopulation.aspx.
4. Statistics South Africa Mid-Year Population Estimate: 2018. 'https://www.statssa.gov.za/publications/P0302/P03022018.pdf'.
5. Africa Check https://africacheck.org/factsheets/factsheet-south-africas-crime-statistics-for-2018-19/.
6. UNODC, Global Study on Homicide 2018 (Vienna, 2018). Downloaded from https://www.unodc.org/documents/data-and-analysis/GSH2018/GSH18_Gender-related_killing_of_women_and_girls.pdf.
7. There are also 'lawful' killings, which may include self-defence, or certain killings during a time of war and so on.
8. Canadian Femicide Observatory for Justice and Accountability.
9. Vetten, L. 1995. 'Intimate Femicide'. *Agenda* 11(27): 78–80.
10. Russell, D.E.H. 2011. '"Femicide" – The Power of a Name'. http://www.dianarussell.com/femicide_the_power_of_a_name.html
11. Seedat, M. 1999. 'The Construction of Violence in South African Newspapers: Implications for Prevention'. *Peace and Conflict: Journal of Peace Psychology* 5(2): 117–35.
12. The definitions here are taken from the United Nations' Vienna Declaration on Femicide signed in 2012, and the Latin American Model Protocol from 2014.
13. Honour killings are murders of women by a close male relative, or several male relatives, for allegedly committing an act which caused shame or brought dishonour to the family. These kinds of killings are more common in India and Pakistan, and in communities of Indian and Pakistani descent. Dowry killings are more common in India, and occur when a woman is killed by her husband or in-laws for failing to meet their dowry (bride price) demands.
14. Abrahams, N., Mathews, S., Jewkes, R., Martin, L.J., and Lombard, C. 2012. 'Every Eight Hours: Intimate Femicide in South Africa 10 Years Later! South African Medical Research Council Research Brief, August 2012'. http://www.mrc.ac.za/sites/default/files/attachments/2016-06-27/everyeighthours.pdf

15   Dworkin, A. 1997. *Life and Death*. New York: The Free Press.
16   Statistics South Africa. 2018. 'Report 03-40-05: Crime against Women in South Africa'. Downloaded from http://www.statssa.gov.za/publications/Report-03-40- 05/Report-03-40-05June2018.pdf
17   Personal correspondence with the South African Police Service.
18   A third femicide study is under way and is expected to be published in 2021.
19   Mathews (2005) explains that 'the age category 14 years and older was used as the study aimed to determine the incidence of intimate partner homicide, as very little dating or few sexually intimate relationships occur before the age of 14'. In: Mathews, S. 2005. 'Intimate Femicide-suicide in South Africa: The Epidemiology of Male Suicide Following the Killing of an Intimate Partner'. Masters thesis, University of Cape Town, Department of Public Health.
20   Abrahams, N., Mathews, S., Martin, L.J, Lombard, C., Jewkes, R. 2013. 'Intimate Partner Femicide in South Africa in 1999 and 2009'. *PLOS Medicine*, April 2013. https://doi.org/10.1371/journal.pmed.1001412.

3. Urban legends
1   Makou, G. 'Statistic that a child goes missing every 5 hours in SA incorrect'. *Africa Check*. 12 October 2016. Viewed at https://africacheck.org/reports/statistic-child-goes-missing-every-5-hours-sa-incorrect/.
2   SAPS Common-Law Offences Definitions: https://www.saps.gov.za/faqdetail.php?fid=9.
3   Silverman, C. 2012. 'Visualized: Incorrect information travels farther, faster on Twitter than corrections'. Poynter Institute. 7 March 2012. Viewed at: https://www.poynter.org/reporting-editing/2012/visualized-incorrect-information-travels-farther-faster-on-twitter-than-corrections/.
4   With some notable exceptions, of course.
5   I don't want to get side-tracked into a longer discussion here about algorithms and text-based searches of news archives. There are, of course, studies that use computer programmes to scan tens of thousands of articles for word matches or word frequencies, but these emphasise breadth (which may not be accurate and may not be relevant) over depth. This is to say, they may tell us one thing, but they also only tell us that one thing. Searching for the number of appearances of the word 'femicide' might show its popularity or use over time, but it doesn't tell us how the word was used – whether it referred to policy, to actual cases, and so on.
6   Halliday, S. 2001. 'Death and miasma in Victorian London: an obstinate belief'. *British Medical Journal*, 323(7327): 1469–1471. doi: 10.1136/bmj.323.7327.1469.
7   I later expanded this to 456 femicides, when I conducted a comparative survey using a different media clippings/archive service, LexisNexis, which helped me to find an additional 48 deaths I had not previously included.
8   Sabinet, personal communication.
9   Sabinet, personal communication.

PART 1: INTIMATE FEMICIDE
4. 'A love story gone wrong': Finding the words

1. Hadley Kavin may also have intended to kill himself but obviously did not succeed.
2. 'Could your spouse turn into a killer?' *Sunday Express*, 12 October 1980.
3. Between 1987 and 1989 Steyn heard 87 capital cases in the Transvaal Provincial Division, of which 33 were 'competent' death penalty cases, meaning the accused were convicted of a crime for which the death penalty could be imposed. Steyn handed down a death sentence in ten (30 per cent) of these, placing him among the top 'scoring' death sentence judges in the Transvaal, based on how frequently he handed down the death sentence. (Angus, L. and Grant, E. 1991. 'Sentencing in Capital Cases in the Transvaal Provincial Division and Witwatersrand Local Division: 1987–1989'. *South African Journal on Human Rights*. Vol. 7, 1991 – Issue 1).
4. As an interesting side note, because Kavin was not found guilty of murdering his wife, he remained eligible to inherit her portion of their joint estate, thereby setting a new precedent in South African inheritance law. See Gafin v Kavin 1980 (3) SA 1104 (W).
5. Similarly, in the United States the use of the term 'domestic violence' to mean violence within the family home only came into common use as late at the 1990s.
6. The apartheid government regularly imposed 'banning orders' on people it viewed as a threat to state security, including communists, anti-apartheid activists, trade unionists, and so on. Banning orders meant the banned person could not leave his or her home and could not be seen with more than one person at a time. It was also illegal to quote or publish a banned person. Between 1950 and 1990 more than 2 000 people were banned. For more information visit South African History Online at sahistory.org.za.
7. Which, at that time, was still illegally administered by South Africa despite United Nations resolutions aimed at securing Namibia's independence.
8. For an introduction to SWAPO, Namibia's independence, and the Angolan civil war, go to South African History online at www.sahistory.org.za.
9. The men, named as P.G. Faught, P.A. Liebenberg, I.G. Bernardo, and B.L. van Zyl, were sentenced to two years military detention.
10. *The Citizen* had been launched the year before, in 1976, and consistently took a pro-National Party line. It was later revealed that the newspaper had been secretly funded by the apartheid government's Department of Information.
11. Blake, L. 'Women must be able to use gun'. *The Citizen*, 18 August 1977.
12. 'Are we gun crazy?' *The Citizen*, 9 February 1978.
13. 'Are we gun crazy?' *The Citizen*, 9 February 1978.
14. 'Could your spouse turn into a killer?' *Sunday Express*, 12 October 1980.
15. 'Could your spouse turn into a killer?' *Sunday Express*, 12 October 1980.
16. 'Battered wives ...' *Pretoria News*, 24 April 1978.
17. Mike Cohen. 'Tragedy Haunts Families'. *The Star*, 27 August 1983.
18. 'A grim year of crime and death'. *The Star*, 21 December 1977.

19 'Family abuse due to stress, say experts'. *Evening Post*, 6 December 1982.
20 '249 Murdered in Pretoria'. *The Citizen*, 29 December 1984.
21 Cohen, S. 2002. *Folk Devils and Moral Panics: The Creation of the Mods and Rockers*. London: Routledge.
22 'Blacks plan crackdown on crime and rape'. *Weekend Post*, 21 January 1978.
23 At the time, the law only recognised 'rape' as being the forced penetration of the vagina by a penis. Other acts of penetration, including vaginal penetration by an object other than a penis or penetration of the mouth or anus were regarded as 'indecent assault'. This was amended in 2003 to include all types of forced or non-consensual penetration, and coerced penetration. Common law also did not recognise rape within marriage.
24 'SA Crime Highest in World Claim Officials'. *The Daily News*, 27 March 1979.
25 'Blacks plan crackdown on crime and rape'. *Weekend Post*, 21 January 1978.
26 Kingdom Lolwane and Mzikayise Edom. 'Gunmen slay five'. *Post*, 19 August 1980.
27 Butchart et al. 1991. 'Epidemiology of non-fatal injuries due to external causes in Johannesburg-Soweto'. *South African Medical Journal*. Vol. 79, 20 April 1991. And: Butchart, A. and Brown, D. S.O. 1991. 'Non-Fatal Injuries Due to Interpersonal Violence in Johannesburg – Soweto: Incidence, Determinants and Consequences'. *Forensic Science International*, 52 (1991): 35–51.
28 For inter-personal injuries.
29 Seedat, M. 1999. 'The Construction of Violence in South African Newspapers: Implications for Prevention'. *Peace and Conflict: Journal of Peace Psychology*, 5(2), 117–135.
30 Butchart, A. and Brown, D.S.O. 1991. 'Non-Fatal Injuries Due to Interpersonal Violence in Johannesburg – Soweto: Incidence, Determinants and Consequences'. *Forensic Science International*, 52 (1991), 35–51.
31 Jackie Cock, quoted by Pat Schwartz and Marilyn Elliot in: 'Rights or a rape – a new look at a law'. *Rand Daily Mail*, 19 June 1979.
32 Kaganas, F. 1986. 'Rape in Marriage: Developments in South African Law'. *The International and Comparative Law Quarterly*, Vol. 35, No. 2 (April 1986), 456–61.
33 Walker coined the phrase 'battered woman syndrome' to describe the psychological effects and behaviours of women living in abusive relationships.
34 'Battered wives . . .' *Pretoria News*, 24 April 1978.
35 Wanda Edkins. 1979. 'Battered wives – the widespread problem society chooses to ignore'. *Daily Post*, 10 July 1979.
36 Early histories of Rape Crisis also showed that the model initially adopted by the organisation's founders did not really attempt to be more understanding or inclusive of black women, but assumed a suburban whiteness or middle classness as the default mode. See SA History Online's archive on the History of the Rape Crisis Trust at: https://www.sahistory.org.za/article/history-rape-crisis-trust-cape-town.
37 Vogelman, L. & Eagle, G. 1991. 'Overcoming Endemic Violence Against Women'. *Social Justice*, Vol. 18, Nos 1–2.

38 In the early 1980s, the then minister of Law and Order Louis le Grange even deliberately withheld crime statistics for the Cape Peninsula, most likely because the area was already showing signs of incredibly high crime rates, including murder – a situation which persists to this day.
39 Segal, L. 1991. 'The Human Face of Violence: Hostel dwellers speak'. *The Journal of Southern African Studies*, Vol. 18, No. 1, March. Viewed at: https://www.csvr.org.za/publications/1794--the-human-face-of-violence-hostel-dwellers-speak.
40 The first State of Emergency was declared in July 1985, initially only for parts of the Eastern Cape and the PWV (Pretoria-Witwatersrand-Vereeniging) districts, but later extended to include the Western Cape and other districts. After briefly lifting the emergency in early 1986, in June of that year a State of Emergency was implemented nationwide, and largely held until 1990.
41 Ertürk, Y. and Purkayastha, B. 2012. 'Linking Research, Policy and Action: A Look at the Work of the Special Rapporteur on Violence Against Women'. *Current Sociology* 60(2): 142–60, https://doi.org/10.1177/0011392111429216.
42 UN Department of Public Information, 2000.
43 Marika Sboros. 'Women wake up an ignorant world'. *The Star*, 12 May 1995.
44 'More haste less speed? The South African Domestic Violence Act'. *Gender Links*. n.d. Downloaded from https://genderlinks.org.za/wp-content/uploads/imported/articles/attachments/13451_more_haste_less_speed.pdf.
45 Vetten, L. 1995. 'Intimate Femicide'. *Agenda*, 11(27): 78–80.
46 Vetten, L. 1996. '"Man Shoots Wife": Intimate Femicide in Gauteng, South Africa.' *Crime and Conflict* 6 (Winter): 1–6. From: https://www.csvr.org.za/index.php/publications/1627-man-shoots-wifeq-intimate-femicidein-gauteng-south-africa.html.
47 Parliamentary Monitoring Group presentation, 2003.
48 Schönteich, M. & Louw, A. 1999. 'Crime Trends in South Africa 1985–1998'. Paper commissioned by the Centre for the Study of Violence and Reconciliation as part of a review of the National Crime Prevention Strategy carried out for the Department of Safety and Security, June. Viewed at: https://www.csvr.org.za/publications/1518-crime-trends-in-south-africa-1985–1998.
49 Hamber, B. and Lewis, S. 1997. 'An Overview of the Consequences of Violence and Trauma in South Africa'. Research report written for the Centre for the Study of Violence and Reconciliation. https://www.csvr.org.za/publications/1778-an-overview-of-the-consequences-of-violence-and-trauma-in-south-africa.
50 Seedat, M. 1999. 'The Construction of Violence in South African Newspapers: Implications for Prevention'. *Peace and Conflict: Journal of Peace Psychology*, 5(2): 117–35.
51 'Powa seeks to give abused women solace'. *City Press*, 28 April 1996.
52 Amma Ogan. 'A woman dies while an overburdened system struggles to get to grips with domestic violence'. *Sunday Independent*, 6 December 1995.
53 Samuel Sithole was later sentenced to eleven years imprisonment.
54 Estelle Ellis. 'Third time unlucky for wife killer Di Blasi'. *Cape Argus*, 14 June 2002.

55 S v Di Blasi (429/94) [1995] ZASCA 111; online.
56 A question: why does a woman marry a man who has already killed one of his wives?
57 Waheeda Amien and Mohamed Paleker. 'Women and the Law'. *South African Human Rights Yearbook*, Vol. 8, Issue 1, January 1997, p.321–391.
58 'The year of living salaciously'. *Mail & Guardian*, 23 December 1997.
59 Mathews, S., Abrahams, N., Martin, L.J., Vetten, L., Van der Merwe, L., and Jewkes, R. 2004. '"Every Six Hours a Woman is Killed by her Intimate Partner": A National Study of Female Homicide in South Africa'. South African Medical Research Council Policy Brief No.5, June 2004.
60 Abrahams, N., Martin, L., Jewkes, R. Mathews, S., Vetten, L., and Lombard, C. 2008. 'The Epidemiology and the Pathology of Suspected Rape Homicide in South Africa'. *Forensic Science International*, 178(2–3): 132–8. Mathews et al., 2004.
61 Abrahams, N., Martin, L.J., Mathews, S., Vetten, L., and Lombard, C. 2009. 'Mortality of Women from Intimate Partner Violence in South Africa: A National Epidemiological Study'. *Violence and Victims*, 24(4): 546–56.
62 Abrahams et al., 2009.
63 Matthews et al., 2004.
64 UN High Commissioner for Human Rights. 2014. 'Latin American Model Protocol for the Investigation of Gender-related Killings of Women (Femicide/Feminicide)'. Downloaded from: http://lac.unwomen.org/en/digiteca/publicaciones/2014/10/modelo-de-protocolo.
65 Mathews et al., 2004.
66 Zelda Venter. 'Man sorry he killed cheating wife'. *Pretoria News*, 12 February 2004.
67 Ilse de Lange. '"Pain" of a man who shot cheating wife'. *The Citizen*, 13 February 2004.
68 Zelda Venter. 'Wife killer "not a dangerous man"'. *Pretoria News*, 11 February 2004.
69 Finkelstein, J.J. 1968/69. 'The Laws of Ur-Nammu'. *Journal of Cuneiform Studies*, 22(3/4): 66–82.
70 Carnelley, M. 2013. 'Laws on Adultery: Comparing the Historical Development of South African Common-law Principles with those in English Law'. *Fundamina*, 19(2): 185–211.
71 Centre of Islamic and Middle Eastern Law, n.d.
72 Luopajärvi, K. 2003. 'State Responses to Honour Killings'. Abo Akademie. From: https://www.abo.fi/wp-content/uploads/2018/03/2003-Luopajarvi-Honourkillings.pdf.
73 Barret Broussard, D. 2012. 'Principles for Passion Killing: An Evolutionary Solution to Manslaughter Mitigation'. *Emory Law Journal*, 62(1).
74 https://www.bbc.com/news/world-us-canada-45225183.
75 Janey Starling. 2018. 'Dignity for dead women'. Level Up. Downloaded from https://static1.squarespace.com/static/5741ba638a65e2e0809f8d25/t/5be2a3f3562fa70e48500b21/1541579769061/web-report.pdf.

5. 'Two die in tragedy': Femicide-suicide and family killings

1. Mathews, S. 2005. 'Intimate Femicide-suicide in South Africa: The Epidemiology of Male Suicide Following the Killing of an Intimate Partner'. Masters thesis, University of Cape Town, Department of Public Health.; Mathews, S. Abrahams N., Jewkes R., Martin L.J., Lombard C., Vetten L. 2008 'Intimate femicide-suicide in South Africa: a cross-sectional study'. Bulletin of the World Health Organisation. Jul;86(7):552-58.
2. Sussman, P. & Kotze, C. 2013. 'Psychiatric features in perpetrators of homicide-unsuccessful-suicide at Weskoppies Hospital in a 5-year period'. *South African Journal of Psychology*, 19 (1), 15–18. DOI: 10.7196/SAJP.384.
3. Jason Bantjes and Ashraf Kagee. 2013. 'Epidemiology of suicide in South Africa: Setting an agenda for future research'. *South African Journal of Psychology* 43 (2) 238–251. DOI: 10.1177/0081246313482627.
4. Flisher, A.J. et al. 2004. 'Suicide trends in South Africa, 1968–90'. *Scandinavian Journal of Public Health* 2004; 32: 411–418.
5. Sussman, P. & Kotze, C. 2013. 'Psychiatric features in perpetrators of homicide-unsuccessful-suicide at Weskoppies Hospital in a 5-year period'. *South African Journal of Psychology*, 19 (1),15–18. DOI: 10.7196/SAJP.384.
6. There are, of course, also cases where the maternal perpetrator was suffering from mental ill health, including, prominently, post-partum depression. See Townsend, K.L. 2003. 'A pilot investigation into the phenomenon of murder-suicide in Durban, KwaZulu-Natal'. Master's thesis. University of KwaZulu-Natal.
7. From a suicide note written by a father, before shooting his wife and two children with an R1 rifle in Sasolburg in May 1978. (Translated from Afrikaans by the author). In: Metelerkamp, P. 'Wat laat ouers hul kinders vermoor?' *Huisgenoot*, 14 December 1978.
8. If you take an average for femicide figures between 2016 and 2018, and assume that 57 per cent of these deaths are intimate partner killings – using South African Medical Research Council proportions from the 2009 femicide study – 20 per cent of this = 317.
9. Wilkinson, K. '#5facts: The sad extent of suicide in South Africa'. *Africa Check*, 16 October 2017. From: https://africacheck.org/reports/5facts-sad-extent-suicide-south-africa/.
10. The 2012 Burden of Disease study is the last reliable national data of this nature.
11. Breckenridge, K. 2005a. 'Towards the Theory of the Biometric State'. Last retrieved February 2019 from: http://www.kznhass-history.net/seminars/breckenridge/2005. And Breckenridge, K. 2005b. 'The Biometric State: The Promise and Peril of Digital Government in the New South Africa'. *Journal of Southern African Studies*, 31 (2): 267–82.
    Breckenridge, K. 2014. *Biometric State: The Global Politics of Identification and Surveillance in South Africa, 1850 to the Present*. Cambridge: Cambridge University Press.
12. Breckenridge, K. 2005b.
13. Dorrington, R., Bradshaw, D., and Wegner, T. 1999. 'Estimates of the Level and Shape of Mortality Rates in South Africa Around 1985 and 1990 Derived

by Applying Indirect Demographic Techniques to Reported Deaths'. Medical Research Council: http://www.mrc.ac.za/sites/default/files/files/2017-05-26/1999report.pdf.

14   Flisher, A.J. et al. 2004.
15   Bloomberg, S. 1972. 'The Present State of Suicide Prevention – an African Survey'. *International Journal of Social Psychiatry*. https://doi.org/10.1177/002076407201800204.
16   The Sabinet database only starts from late 1977, so it's impossible to know to what extent the term 'gesinsmoord' pre-dates this period in popular usage.
17   'Gesinsmoorde – niemand kan verwyt'. *Oggendblad*, 25 May 1978.
18   Metelerkamp, P. 'Wat laat ouers hul kinders vermoor?' *Huisgenoot*, 14 December 1978.
19   'Ouers het in 20 jaar 70 kinders vermoor. *Hoofstad*, 27 November 1978.
20   Hamber, B. and Lewis, S. 1997. 'An Overview of the Consequences of Violence and Trauma in South Africa'. Research report written for the Centre for the Study of Violence and Reconciliation. From: https://www.csvr.org.za/publications/1778-an-overview-of-the-consequences-of-violenceand-trauma-in-south-africa.
21   Falkof, N. 2013 'A "Bloody Epidemic": Whiteness and Family Murder in Late Apartheid South Africa', *Safundi*, 14:3, 307–325, DOI: 10.1080/17533171.2013.812866. See also Falkof, N. 2018. *The End of Whiteness: Satanism and Family Murder in Late Apartheid South Africa* (Jacana).
22   Pieterse, P. 'Gesinsmoorde: is dit aansteeklik?' *Huisgenoot*, 26 February 1980.
23   Pauw, J. 1988. 'Gesinsmoord: hoe lyk die man wat so iets beplan?' *Huisgenoot*, 23 June 1988.
24   'South Africans first in race to grave'. *Cape Herald*, 25 November 1978.
25   O'Hara, G. 1980. 'Why do some parents kill their children?' *Rand Daily Mail*, 30 October 1980.
26   'Blacks reject report's high suicide rate findings'. *The Daily News*, 17 October 1978.
27   Themba Molefe. 'Spate of suicides as stress takes its toll on policeman'. *Sowetan*. 15 October 1986.
28   Tyler, H. 'South Africa's black police: focus of black civilian hostility. Called on to enforce the law, they encounter threats, violence, in a job where opportunity seemed to beckon'. *Christian Science Monitor*, 9 April 1985.
29   Robinson, K. 'Horror of family murders'. *Independent on Saturday*, 10 July 1999.
30   Nix, J. 1998. 'To Protect and Abuse: An Exploratory Study Discussing Intimate Partners of Police as Victims of Domestic Abuse'. Paper presented at the Centre for the Study of Violence and Reconciliation, Seminar No. 4, 4 June. From: https://www.csvr.org.za/publications/1461-to-protect-and-abuse-an-exploratory-study-discussing-intimate-partners-of-police-as-victims-of-domestic-abuse.
31   Independent Complaints Directorate. 2009. *Femicide: A Case Study on Members of the South African Police Service*. Pretoria: Independent Complaints Directorate.

32 Newham, G., Masuku, T. and Dlamini, J. 2006. *Diversity and Transformation in the South African Police Service. A Study of Police Perspectives on Race, Gender and the Community in the Johannesburg Policing Area*. Centre for the Study of Violence and Reconciliation.
33 Simpson, G., Mokwena, S. & Segal, L. 1992. 'Political Violence: 1990'. In Robertson, M. & Rycroft, A. (eds.), *Human Rights and Labour Law Yearbook 1991*, Vol. 2, Cape Town: Oxford University Press. Viewed at: https://www.csvr.org.za/publications/1800-political-violence-1990.
34 Jena, S., Mountany, L., and Muller, A. 2009. 'A Demographic Study of Homicide-suicide in the Pretoria Region over a 5-year Period'. *Journal of Forensic Legal Medicine* 16(5), 261–5, DOI:10.1016/j.jflm.2008.12.009.
35 Englebrecht, C. et al. 2017. 'Suicide in Pretoria: A retrospective review, 2007 – 2010'. *South African Medical Journal*, Vol. 107 No. 8, Cape Town, August 2017. http://dx.doi.org/10.7196/samj.2017.v107i8.12034.
36 Naidoo, SS. and Schlebusch, L. 2014. 'Sociodemographic characteristics of persons committing suicide in Durban, South Africa: 2006–2007'. *African Journal of Primary Health Care & Family Medicine*. (Online) Vol. 6 No. 1, Cape Town, January 2014. Read on Scielo.org at: http://www.scielo.org.za/scielo.php?script=sci_arttext&pid=S2071-29362014000100006.

6. 'Man Shoots Woman': Firearms and femicide in South Africa

1 Abrahams, N., Jewkes, R., and Mathews, S. 2010. 'Guns and Gender-Based Violence in South Africa'. *South African Medical Journal*, 100(9): 586–8.
2 Meek, S. 2002. 'Getting A Grip On Guns: Rolling out the Firearms Control Act'. *South African Crime Quarterly* 1, https://doi.org/10.17159/2413-3108/2002/v0i1a1087.
3 This is important because critics of the Act have suggested that, as firearm deaths did not begin to decline in 2000, the decline in gun murders should not be attributed to the Act. However, as multiple researchers have made clear, the terms of the Act only began to be rolled out several years after its passing. And indeed, from 2003/4 onward we see a marked decline in firearm deaths.
4 Matzopoulos, R., Thompson, M., and Myers, J.E. 2014. 'Firearm and Non-firearm Homicide in 5 South African Cities: A Retrospective Population-Based Study'. *American Journal of Public Health*, 104(3): 455–60. DOI:10.2105/AJPH.2013.310650. Quote used with permission from the American Journal of Public Health.
5 Matzopoulos, R. et al. 2018. 'A retrospective time trend study of firearm and non-firearm homicide in Cape Town from 1994 to 2013'. *South African Medical Journal*. Vo. 108, No. 3.
6 Matzopoulos et al., 2014.
7 Matzopoulos et al., 2014.
8 In one of the amateur 'critiques' of Matzopoulos's research, some people have pointed out that this figure must be false because the FCA was only implemented from 2004. But when you take into consideration that up to or even more than 50 per cent of all homicides were caused by gunshot – not to

mention the thousands of suicides annually – the figure of 4 500 lives saved could quite easily represent a period of little more than a year.
9   Statistics South Africa. 2013. 'Statistical release P0302: Mid-year Population Estimates'. From: https://www.statssa.gov.za/publications/P0302/P03022013.pdf.
10 Matzopoulos, R., Groenewald, P., Abrahams, N., and Bradshaw, D. 2016. 'Where Have All the Gun Deaths Gone?'. *South African Medical Journal* 106(6): 589–91. See also Matzopoulos et al., 2018.
11 Matzopoulos et al., 2016: 591.
12 Caryn Dolley. 'Ex-cop in guns-to-gangs case should be charged with murder – lawyer'. *News24*, 8 June 2018. Viewed at https://www.news24.com/SouthAfrica/News/ex-cop-in-guns-to-gangs-case-should-be-charged-with-murder-lawyer-20180608.
13 Burger, 2018b; Cross, 2003; Hennop, 2000; McKenzie, 1999. Cited by Claire Taylor in 'Gun control and violence: South Africa's story'. Gun Free South Africa, 2019.
14 Captain A.L.S. Hudson. 1980. 'Infantry Weapons in SA, 1652–1881'. *Scientia Militaria*, South African Journal of Military Studies, Vol. 10, No. 2, 1980. http://scientiamilitaria.journals.ac.za.
15 Bopape, L.S. 2008. 'The Impact of the Firearm Control Act 60/2000 in Restricting Gun Ownership for At Risk Individuals in the Pretoria North Firearm Registration Centre Policing Area'. M.Tech thesis. University of South Africa. Viewed at: http://uir.unisa.ac.za/bitstream/handle/10500/792/dissertation.pdf.txt.
16 Keegan, M. 2005. 'The Proliferation of Firearms in South Africa, 1994–2004'. Gun Free South Africa.
17 Keegan, M. 2005.

PART TWO: NON-INTIMATE FEMICIDE
7. 'A fate worse than death': Rape and homicide
1   The trip and workshop were part of the Mellon Foundation-funded Governing Intimacies programme, which had also given me a scholarship for my PhD.
2   This research will be published as part of a forthcoming book with Wits University Press.
3   Wilkinson, K. 2014. 'Why it's wrong to call South Africa – or any country – the world's "rape capital"'. *Africa Check*. 28 January 2014. https://africacheck.org/reports/why-it-is-wrong-to-call-s-africa-or-any-country-the-rape-capital-of-the-world/.
4   Mason, P. and Monckton-Smith, J. 2008. 'Conflation, Collocation and Confusion: British Press Coverage of the Sexual Murder of Women'. *Journalism* 9(6): 691–710, DOI:10.1177/1464884908096241.
5   Mason, P. and Monckton-Smith, J. 2008.
6   Molefe, I.J. 2016. 'Violence against Women. Epidemiology and Pathology of Femicides and Suspected Sexual Homicides in Cape Town: A 10-year Follow-up Study'. MMed thesis in Forensic Pathology, University of Cape Town.

7   This is consistent with the introduction of the Criminal Law Sexual Offences Amendment Act No. 32 of 2007, which, among other things, expanded the definition of rape to include any act of sexual penetration without consent (Centre for Applied Legal Studies, 2008).
8   Abrahams, N., Martin, L., Jewkes, R. Mathews, S., Vetten, L., and Lombard, C. 2008. 'The Epidemiology and the Pathology of Suspected Rape Homicide in South Africa'. *Forensic Science International*, 178(2–3): 132–8.
9   Abrahams et al., 2008.
10 Abrahams, N., Mathews, S., Martin, L.J, Lombard, C., Jewkes, R. 2013. 'Intimate Partner Femicide in South Africa in 1999 and 2009'. *PLOS Medicine*, April 2013. https://doi.org/10.1371/journal.pmed.1001412.; Abrahams et al., 2017.
11 Abrahams, N., Mathews, S., Lombard, C., Martin, L.J., Jewkes, R. 2017. 'Sexual homicides in South Africa: A national cross-sectional epidemiological study of adult women and children'. *PLoS One*. 2017; 12(10): e0186432.
12 Dale Hes. 'Courts have no mercy on sex offenders'. *Vuk'uzenzele*, 2nd edition, November 2018.
13 Jordaan, L. 'The principle of fair labelling and the definition of the crime of murder'. *Journal of South African Law/Tydskrif vir die Suid-Afrikaanse Reg*, Vol. 2017, No. 3, August 2017, 569–84.
14 After a four-year moratorium, which started in 1990.
15 Machisa, et al. 2017. 'Rape Justice in South Africa: A Retrospective Study of the Investigation, Prosecution and Adjudication of Reported Rape Cases From 2012'. Pretoria, South Africa. Gender and Health Research Unit, South African Medical Research Council.
16 The Andhra Pradesh Disha Bill 2019 (Andhra Pradesh Criminal Law Amendment Act 2019).
17 Tshabalala v S; Ntuli v S (CCT323/18;CCT69/19) [2019] ZACC 48 (11 December 2019). http://www.saflii.org/za/cases/ZACC/2019/48.html#_ftn15.
18 Tshabalala v S; Ntuli v S (CCT323/18;CCT69/19) [2019] ZACC 48 (11 December 2019). http://www.saflii.org/za/cases/ZACC/2019/48.html#_ftn15.
19 Moffett, H. 2006. '"These Women, They Force Us to Rape Them": Rape as Narrative of Social Control in Post-Apartheid South Africa'. *Journal of Southern African Studies*, 32(1): 129–44.

8. 'We only write about them when they are dead': Hate killings of black lesbians in South Africa

1   During apartheid, that is, pre-1994, while people of all races, of course, could read the commercially published newspapers, there were very clear splits between market segments, and only a handful of newspapers (like the *Post*, *Express*, and later *The Sowetan* and *City Press* and *Daily Sun*) served a predominantly black readership.
2   Deon Delport. 'It's not so gay being locked in the closet'. *The Sunday Star*, 28 April 1985. Male homosexuality, of course, generally had an even worse rap than female homosexuality, and was blamed for everything from turning men

into potential enemy agents, and even used to ban things as ordinary as primary school poetry books.

3   Mkhize, N., Bennett, J., Reddy, V., and Moletsane, R. *The Country We Want to Live In: Hate crimes and homophobia in the lives of black lesbian South Africans*. HSRC Press. 2010.

4   Vogelman, L. & Lewis, S. 1993. Gang Rape and the Culture of Violence in South Africa. https://www.csvr.org.za/publications/1631-gang-rape-and-the-culture-of-violence-in-south-africa

5   Mokwena, S. 1991. In Vogelman, L. & Lewis, S. 1993.

6   These terms are contentious, because, of course, they are violent and absurd. But I use them because, firstly, they are more commonly understood and, second, they bluntly depict the violence and intent of the perpetrators.

7   Moagi Khunou. 'Rape better than same-sex intercourse'. *The Star*, 10 November 2004.

8   Karim, Q.A. and Karim, S.S.A. 2002. 'The evolving HIV epidemic in South Africa'. *International Journal of Epidemiology*, Vol. 31, Issue 1, February 2002: 37–40, https://doi.org/10.1093/ije/31.1.37

9   There are also a large number of sub-types of sub-type C.

10 Bienne Huisman. 'Teen beaten to death for being a lesbian'. *Sunday Times*, 19 February 2006.

11 Gqola, P.D. 'Bleeding on the streets of South Africa'. *Mail & Guardian*, 18 May 2006.

12 Nicholson, T.J. 2016. 'A Call to Action'. *Psychology in Society*, 52: 121–24, http://dx.doi.org/10.17159/2309-8708/2016/n52a15.

13 Gqola, P.D. 2016. 'A Peculiar Place for a Feminist? The New South African Woman, True Love Magazine and Lebo(gang) Mashile'. *Safundi*, 17(2): 119–36, DOI:10.1080/17533171.2016.1178470.

14 Gqola, P.D. 2007. 'How the "Cult of Femininity" and Violent Masculinities Support Endemic Gender-based Violence in Contemporary South Africa'. *African Identities*, 5(1): 111–24, DOI:10.1080/14725840701253894.

9. 'We all know who are the witches here': Witch killings

1   From testimony given by Solomon's mother, Christina Maditsi, to the TRC, 17 July 1996. Viewed at http://www.justice.gov.za/trc/hrvtrans/pieters/maditsi.htm.

2   Oomen, B. 2004. 'Vigilantism or alternative citizenship? The rise of Mapogo a Mathamaga'. *African Studies*, 63:2, 153–171, DOI: 10.1080/00020180412331318751.

3   The account of Maditsi's funeral and the events that followed are based on information drawn from Ineke van Kessel's book, *Beyond Our Wildest Dreams*, from Peter Delius's text 'Witches and Missionaries in Nineteenth Century Transvaal', and from various news reports published at the time of the witch-hunt. Ineke van Kessel. 2010. *Beyond Our Wildest Dreams: The United Democratic Front and the Transformation of South Africa*. University Press of Virginia; and Delius, P. 1996. 'Witches and Missionaries in Nineteenth Century Transvaal'. *Journal of Southern African Studies*. Vol. 27, 2001 – Issue 3

4   Ineke van Kessel. 2010.

5   Capel, D. 'Night of the Necklace'. *Saturday Star*, 20 April 1986.

6. Abel Mabelane. 'Relatives say aged women necklaced'. *The Star*, 16 April 1986.
7. Ineke van Kessel, 2010.
8. Dianna Games. 'Three "witches" burnt to death'. *Rand Daily Mail*, 21 February 1984.
9. Minnar et al., 1992. Cited in Ball, J. 1994. 'The Ritual of the Necklace'. Research report written for the CSVR. Viewed at https://www.csvr.org.za/publications/latest-publications/1632-the-ritual-of-the-necklace.
10. Although Joanna Ball points out that it was not *only* used in political killings, but in fact more widely used against people who had committed social misconduct or criminal conduct, including rapists, murderers, other ethnic groups and anyone who could be categories as what Van Kessel described as a 'social enemy'.
11. Niehaus, I. 2012. 'Witchcraft and the South African Bantustans: Evidence from Bushbuckridge'. *South African Historical Journal*, Vol. 64, No. 1, March 2012, 41 http://dx.doi.org/10.1080/02582473.2012.640829.
12. Isak Niehaus, 2012.
13. Niehaus, I. 1988 'The ANC's Dilemma: The Symbolic Politics of Three Witch-Hunts in the South African Lowveld, 1990–1995'. *African Studies Review*, Vol. 41, No. 3, December 1998: 93–118.
14. 'SA witch-burning "new phenomenon"'. *The Citizen*, 8 September 1998.
15. Fourie, M. 'Slaves of Fear'. *Servamus*. January/February 1999.
16. Ally, Y. 2009. 'Witch Hunts in Modern South Africa: An Under-Represented Facet of Gender-Based Violence'. Medical Research Council. Cited in South African Pagan Rights Alliance report 'Witch-hunts in South Africa Advocacy against human rights abuses committed as a result of accusations of witchcraft and violent witch-hunts. (2014)'. Viewed at http://www.whrin.org/wp-content/uploads/2014/06/SAPRA-Advocacy-against-witch-hunts-2014.pdf.
17. Federici, S. 2018. *Witches, Witch-Hunting, and Women*. PM Press.
18. Labuschagne, G. 2004. 'Features and investigative implications of muti murder in South Africa'. *Journal of Investigative Psychology and Offender Profiling* 1(3): 191–206, June 2004.
19. Bowman, B. 2005. 'Children, Pathology and Politics: Genealogical Perspectives on the Construction of the Paedophile in South Africa'. PhD thesis, University of the Witwatersrand.
20. Margie Orford. 2014. 'Oscar Pistorius trial: the imaginary black stranger at heart of the defence'. *The Guardian*, 4 March 2014.

10. The 'ideal victim': Elderly women and farm murders

1. Christie, N. 1986. 'The Ideal Victim'. In E.A. Fattah (ed.), *From Crime Policy to Victim Policy*. London: Palgrave Macmillan.
2. Lindgren, M. and Nikolić-Ristanović, V. 2011. *Crime Victims: International and Serbian Perspective*. Organization for Security and Cooperation in Europe, Mission to Serbia, Law Enforcement Department. Van Wijk, Joris. 2013. 'Who Is the 'Little Old Lady' of International Crimes? Nils Christie's Concept of the Ideal Victim Reinterpreted'. *International Review of Victimology*, 19(2): 159–79.

3   McCombs and Shaw (in Scheufele, D. and Tewksbury, D. 2007. 'Framing, Agenda Setting, and Priming: The Evolution of Three Media Effects Models'. *Journal of Communication*, 57(1): 9–20.).
4   Holstein and Miller. 1990, cited in Jankowitz, Sarah. 2017. 'Intergroup Struggles over Victimhood in Violent Conflict: The Victim–Perpetrator Paradigm'. *International Review of Victimology*, 24(3): 259–71.
5   Taylor, R. 2009. 'Slain and Slandered: A Content Analysis of the Portrayal of Femicide in Crime News'. *Homicide Studies*, 13(1): 21–49.
6   Median is a way of calculating the mid-point in a set, rather than just using an average, which can be misleading. For example, if you had a dataset that included five different salaries, four individuals receiving R5 000 a month and one individual earning R100 000 per month, the 'average' salary would be R24 000, but it's not a fair representation because it is skewed by one exceptional entry. The median number here would be R5 000. For demographic data, using the median is often more useful than calculating an average.
7   e.g. Clarke, R., Ekblom, P., Hough, M., and Mayhew, P. 1985. 'Elderly Victims of Crime and Exposure to Risk'. *The Howard Journal of Crime and Justice*, 24(1): 1–8.; Pain, R.H. 1995. 'Elderly Women and Fear of Violent Crime: The Least Likely Victims? A Reconsideration of the Extent and Nature of Risk'. *British Journal of Criminology*, 35(4): 584–98.; Powell, J., Wahidin, A., and Zinn, J. 2007. 'Understanding Risk and Old Age in Western Society'. *International Journal of Sociology and Social Policy*, 27(1/2): 65–76, https://doi.org/10.1108/01443330710722760.
8   'Older person' is often poorly defined and may refer, variously, to people older than 60 or people older than 65 years of age.
9   Matzopoulos R., Prinsloo M., Pillay-Van Wyk V., et al. 'Injury-related mortality in South Africa: A retrospective descriptive study of post-mortem investigations'. Bulletin of the World Health Organisation 2015; 93(5), 303–13. https://doi.org/10.2471/BLT.14.1457714. World Health Organization. Global Status Report on Violence Prevention 2014. Geneva: WHO, 2014.
10 Swart, L., Buthelezi, S. and Seedat, M. 2019. 'The incidence and characteristics of homicides in elderly compared with non-elderly age groups in Johannesburg, South Africa'. *South African Medical Journal*, June 2019, Vol. 109, No. 6.
11 Research into farm attacks may include workers and smallholders, but when a headline speaks of a 'farm murder' it almost always implies the murder of a white farmer by a black perpetrator or perpetrators.
12 Ironically, when AfriForum published their findings, they mentioned this finding as if it was a poor reflection of the extent to which media covered attacks against farmers (that is, 'only' 70.9 per cent of murders were covered).
13 There is no data on what proportion of homicides are covered in the press.
14 Department of Rural Development and Land Reform Land Audit (2017) cited in Pretorius, L. and Makou, G. 2019. 'Frequently asked questions about land ownership and demand in South Africa'. *Africa Check*. 26 April 2019. https://africacheck.org/factsheets/frequently-asked-questions-about-land-ownership-and-demand-in-south-africa/.

15 There are, of course, exceptions to this, such as the farm attacks carried out in the early 1990s by members of APLA (the Azanian People's Liberation Army), the Pan African Congress's military wing.
16 Burger, J. 2018. ISS Policy Brief. 'Violent crime on farms and smallholdings in South Africa'. Downloaded from https://issafrica.org/research/policy-brief/violent-crime-on-farms-and-smallholdings-in-south-africa.
17 Also spelled Elma in press reports.
18 Also spelled Annatjie in press reports.
19 Worden, N. 1985. *Slavery in Dutch South Africa*. Cambridge University Press.
20 Greeff, C. '1978 – The year of the killer'. *The Star*.
21 Truth and Reconciliation Commission testimony cited by Tshepo Lephakga (2018) in 'APLA and the Amnesty Committee of the TRC? An ethical analysis of the Amnesty Committee of the Truth and Reconciliation Commission of South Africa'. *Studia Hist. Ecc.* Vol. 44, No. 1, http://dx.doi.org/10.25159/2412-4265/2379.
22 Roets, E. 2017. 'Kill the Farmer: A Brief Study on the Impact of Politics and Hate Speech on the Safety of South African Farmers'. AfriForum. Viewed at https://www.afriforum.co.za/wp-content/uploads/2019/08/Kill-the-farmer.pdf.
23 Willemien Brümmer. 2019. 'Plaasaanvalle: Hoekom swyg ons oor swart lyding?'. *Netwerk24*, 13 August 2019. https://www.netwerk24.com/Stemme/Aktueel/plaasaanvalle-hoekom-swyg-ons-oor-swart-lyding-20190812.

PART THREE: THE MEDIA AND THE MESSAGE
11. Mega cases, race and rape: What the media gets wrong about femicide

1 De Souza, N.M.F. 2019. Introduction: Gender in the Global South: Power Hierarchies, Violence and Resistance in the Postcolony. *Contexto Internacional*, 41(1), 9-14. https://dx.doi.org/10.1590/s0102-8529.2019410100001.
2 Mahler, A.G. 2017. 'Global South.' *Oxford Bibliographies in Literary and Critical Theory*, ed. Eugene O'Brien. Last viewed August 2019 at: https://www.oxfordbibliographies.com/view/document/obo-9780190221911/obo-9780190221911-0055.xml.
3 Connell, R., Collyer, F., Maia, J. and Morrell, R. 2017. 'Toward a global sociology of knowledge: Post-colonial realities and intellectual practices'. *International Sociology*. Vol. 32(1) 21– 37. DOI: 10.1177/0268580916676913.
4 Statistics South Africa, 2013; Parliamentary Monitoring Group, 2016.
5 Reporters Without Borders, 2019 World Press Freedom Index.
6 Lloyd, M. and Ramon, S. 2017. 'Smoke and Mirrors: U.K. Newspaper Representations of Intimate Partner Domestic Violence.' *Violence Against Women*, 23(1): 114–39.
7 Soothill, K., Peelo, M., Pearson, J. and Francis, B. 2004. 'The Reporting Trajectories of Top Homicide Cases in the Media: A Case Study of the Times'. *Howard Journal of Criminal Justice* 43(1): 1–14.
8 Section A, P-05; Statistics South Africa Census 2011, Questionnaire A.
9 Adhikari, M. 2006. 'Hope, Fear, Shame, Frustration: Continuity and Change in

the Expression of Coloured Identity in White Supremacist South Africa, 1910-1994'. *Journal of Southern African Studies.* Vol. 32, No. 3. DOI: 10.1080/03057070600829542.
10 A. van Niekerk, S. Suffla, and M. Seedat (eds), *Crime, Violence and Injury Prevention in South Africa*: 296 *Data into Action*. Cape Town: Medical Research Council-University of South Africa Crime, Violence and Injury Lead Programme.
11 Statistics South Africa, 2012.
12 Teenager Charmaine Mare was murdered and dismembered by the boyfriend of her friend's mother. Rosemary Theron was murdered by her daughter, Phoenix Racing Cloud, and her daughter's boyfriend, Kyle Maspero. Both victims were white women. Their murders received coverage of over 100 news stories.

12. Fuck the hashtag

1 Uyinene's killer had previously been convicted for armed robbery, and had also been charged with rape but the case had been withdrawn, according to the National Prosecuting Authority.
2 Lancaster, L. 2019. 'Is mob violence out of control in South Africa?'. https://issafrica.org/iss-today/is-mob-violence-out-of-control-in-south-africa.
3 'Rape Justice In South Africa: A Retrospective Study Of The Investigation, Prosecution And Adjudication Of Reported Rape Cases From 2012'. South African Medical Research Council, 2017. http://www.mrc.ac.za/sites/default/files/files/2017-10-30/RAPSSAreport.pdf.
4 This is something that is well documented, and a very real concern – see for example Levenson and Tewksbury, 2009. 'Collateral Damage: Family Members of Registered Sex Offenders'. *American Journal of Criminal Justice* 34(1), 54–68.
5 A case recorded by Dr Lorna Martin, reported by Charlene Smith in 'SA rape gets more violent'. *Mail & Guardian*, 11 June 1999.

Index

abductions 25-31
Abrahams, Naeemah 106-107, 123
activists 57-60, 190, 198-206
adultery 79-80
Africa Check 25-26, 27, 33-34, 88, 118, 172
African National Congress (ANC) 114, 176, 177
AfriForum 171, 172, 177-178
Afrikaans-language media 34, 154, 195-196
Afrikaans-speaking white South Africans 34, 86, 94-95, 99, 172-173, 175, 178
Afrikaner Weerstandsbeweging (AWB) 84, 178
age 22, 66, 157-158, 166-170, 183 *see also* elderly women
agenda setting 165
AIDS *see* HIV and AIDS
Ally, Yassen 157
amnesia *see* memory lapses
ANC *see* African National Congress
apartheid
    arms industry 113-114
    crime statistics 11
    domestic terrorism 48-50
    family killings 47-52, 94-95
    immorality laws 131
    impact of 184-185
    media coverage under 31, 59-62, 159, 161
    population registers 89
    race 192
    rape 52-59, 125
    suicides 95-96
    witch killings 153-154
Apel-GaNkoane massacre 149-154
APLA *see* Azanian People's Liberation Army

Arms and Ammunition Act (1969) 108, 113
arms industry 113-114
arrests 33, 170, 191
autopsies 120-121
AWB *see* Afrikaner Weerstandsbeweging
Azanian People's Liberation Army (APLA) 177

Baillie, Mikeila 158-161
Ball, Joanna 152
Bantustans *see* homelands
'battered women', use of term 57-60, 62
BBC 81
Beeld 195-196
Beeton, Brenda 78-79
Beeton, William 78-79, 81
Bellingan, Janine 71-72
Bellingan, Michael 71-72
Bendixen, Reg 160
biases 31-32, 34-35, 129-130
Births and Deaths Registration Act (1992) 89-90
black people
    'black-on-black' violence 61, 96
    definitions 192
    elderly women 168-170
    family killings 99-101
    farm murders 171-174, 178
    firearms 113
    'gangs of black men' 158-163
    inequality 75
    intimate femicide 77
    media coverage 51-56, 59-61, 65-66
    policemen 96, 98-99, 100
    statistics on 88-89
    suicide 88-89, 95-96, 99-101
    use of term 'blacks' 159
    see also hate killings of black lesbians

blame 50-52, 78-82, 91, 165
Bloomberg, Sam 49-50, 91-92, 93, 95
Boonzaaier, Joy 160
Booysen, Anene 117-119, 189-190, 191, 195-196
Botha, David 84
Botha, Luyanda 200
Botlhokwane, Stoffel 144
Bowman, Brett 162
break ins 5-9
Breckenridge, Keith 89
Bridges, Sunette 159-160, 161, 172
Burger, Die 196
Burger, Johan 174
Burger, Natacha 160
burnings 149-155

Cape Argus 195
Cape Times 195
capital punishment 125-127
Carte Blanche (TV programme) 137
cause-of-death certification 193
celebrities 172
Centre for the Study of Violence and Reconciliation 59, 61, 66-69, 73, 99, 152
Chaba, Henry 96
chalk signals 35-36
Charlewood, Carole 58
children 18, 25-31, 92-93
'Chinese', use of term 192
cholera 35
Christie, Nils 164
Citizen, The 49-50, 51, 61, 65-66, 78
City Press 155
Cohen, Stanley 52-53, 162
'collective' violence 55, 59-60, 96, 163
colonialism 112-113, 173, 175, 184
colour-coded rubbish 35-36
coloured people 38, 77, 100, 170, 173, 192
commercial media, definition of 41-43
Commission for Gender Equality 206-207, 208
common purpose doctrine 127-128
communal, black violence as 55, 59-60, 96, 163
Comrades (youth organisation) 153
Conroy, Bea 50
Constitution of South Africa 64, 131-132, 139

convictions 18, 33, 77, 123-127, 170, 204-205
'corrective' rape 21, 133-134
Country We Want to Live In, The 132
crime fatigue 197
'crime of passion' 80
criminal justice system 22, 33, 173, 191, 203
Criminal Law (Sexual Offences and Related Matters) Amendment Act 124
Criminal Law Amendment Act (India) 125
Criminal Procedure Act 65, 131
'culpable homicide', definition of 16
'culture of violence' 93-94
Cunliffe-Jones, Peter 35
'curative' rape *see* 'corrective' rape

Daily News 54, 57
data collection methods 37-43
Dayisi, Vuyisa 'Norizana' 147
death penalty 125-127
definitions 15-24
De Goede, Margrietha 170
De Kock, Eugene 114
'Delhi gang rape' 119 *see also* Singh, Jyoti
demographic data 90
De Souza, Natália Maria Félix 184
Dewani, Anni 187-188
Dewani, Shrien 187-188
Di Blasi, Guiseppe 70-71
dingaka 149-150, 152-153
Dlamini, Gugu 136
dockets, missing 75
domestic violence 48-49, 58, 64, 207-208 *see also* femicide-suicide and family killings
Domestic Violence Act (1998) 67-68, 74, 202-203
dowry killings 17, 20-21
Dube, Daisy 147
Dubha, Lwando 145
Durban 100
Dworkin, Andrea 19, 80

École Polytechnique massacre 19
elderly women
    eldercides 167-170

farm murders 171-180
'ideal victims' 164-165, 168-170
media coverage 37-38, 165-171, 179-180
statistics 166-170
see also witch killings
Electus Per Deus 160-161
English-language media 195
erasure, as form of violence 17
'estranged', use of term 97

Facebook 159
Falkof, Nicky 94
false information see misinformation
family killings see femicide-suicide and family killings
family members, as perpetrators 122, 161-163, 170
farm murders 171-180
Federici, Silvia 157-158
'female homicides', definition of 17, 22
female perpetrators 73, 86
'female total homicide' 14-15
femicide, definition of 15-24
femicide rate 1, 14
femicide-suicide and family killings
    under apartheid 47-52, 94-95
    Bronkhorstspruit family killing 84-85
    definitions 85-86, 95
    legislation 89-90
    media coverage 83-84, 90-96, 101
    motives 86-87
    by policemen 96-99
    statistics 85-86, 88-90, 95-96, 99-101
    types of 86-88
feminist organisations 57-60
firearms
    femicide-suicides and 49-50, 85, 101
    gun lobbies 103-104, 106, 110, 112
    history of 112-114
    illegal 111-112, 114
    intimate femicide and 103
    legislation 107-112, 207-208
    licenced 103, 104-107, 112, 114
    media coverage 102-103
    ownership of 103-107, 207-208
    service weapons 98, 208
Firearms Control Act (2000) 108-112
#FixedIt campaign 81

'folk devils' 162
Forum for the Empowerment of Women 134

'gangs of black men' 158-163
Gauteng 13, 38
gender-based homicide, definition of 23
Gender Links 67-68
Gigaba, Malusi 26
Gilmore, Jane 81
'Girls on Fire' campaign 103-104
global phenomenon, femicide as 76-77
Global South 33, 183-185
Gobbi, Francesca 70-71
Gordon, Sasha Lee 147
Government of National Unity 69
Gqola, Pumla Dineo 128, 138-139
Griekwastad killings see Steenkamp family murders in Griekwastad
Group Area laws 58-59
Gun Free South Africa 112
Gun Owners of South Africa 103-104, 112
guns see firearms

Hamber, Brett 68
Hamilton, Susan 70
Hani, Chris, murder of 177-178
Hani, Khanyiswa (Lhoyie) 141
hashtags 200-201, 205-206
hate killings of black lesbians
    black women 132-133
    'corrective' rape 21, 133-134
    HIV and AIDS 134-138
    'jackrolling' 133-134
    'Khwezi' 138
    legislation 131-132
    media coverage 129-131, 134, 136-137, 139-148
    transgender victims 132, 146-148
    'unrapable' black woman concept 138-139
hate speech against white men, allegations of 33-34, 172
Hindocha, Anni 187-188, 191
HIV and AIDS 90, 134-138
Hlomza, N 98
Hofmeyr, Steve 172-173, 176
homelands 11, 69, 89, 113

homicide, definition of 15-16
homicide-suicide *see* femicide-suicide and family killings
'honour killings' 17, 21, 80
Huisgenoot 92-93, 94
Human Rights Watch 142-143
Human Sciences Research Council 54
Hyderabad killing 126

'ideal victims' 164-165, 168-170
illegal firearms 111-112, 114
Independent Police Investigative Directorate (IPID) 98, 202-203
India 20-21, 117-118, 125-126
Indian South Africans 77, 100, 170, 192
inequality 62, 75, 126-127
infidelity 79-80
informal settlements *see* townships
Institute for Security Studies 174, 204
International Tribunal on Crimes Against Women 16, 58
intimate femicide, definition of 23
'invisible perpetrators' 81
IPID *see* Independent Police Investigative Directorate

Jabela, Constance 55
'jackrolling' 133-134
Jacobs, Jette 170
Jamaica 12
Johannesburg 168
Joint Monitoring Committee on the Improvement of the Quality of Life and Status of Women 68
Jojo, Buhle 97
Jonker, Kobus 156
Jooste, Stephanus 60
Jordaan, Louise 124
judges 47, 70-71, 153
'Justice for Women' campaign 66-67, 73
justice system *see* criminal justice system

Kavin, Denise 47-48, 50, 70
Kavin, Hadley 47-48, 50
Kekane, Maria 151
Kgoedi, Sarah 151
Khayelitsha 206
Khumalo, Nqobile 143

Khunou, Bishop Moagi 134
'Khwezi' 138
kidnappings 25-31
Kinikini, Tamsanqa 152
Kriel, Gabriel Ernst 60
Kriel, Magdalena Julia 60
Kuzwayo, Fezekile Ntsukela ('Khwezi') 138

Labuschagne, Gérard 158
land 175
Latin America 15, 76-77
legislation 15-16, 57, 61-62, 64-65, 79-80, 107-112, 125-128, 131-132
Le Grange, Louis 90
Lépine, Marc 18-19
lesbians, black *see* hate killings of black lesbians
Level Up 81-82
Lewis, Sharon 68
LexisNexis 38, 43
LGBTQI communities 131-132, 139, 209
see also hate killings of black lesbians
licenced firearms 103, 104-107, 112, 114
Life and Death 80
lighting *see* street lighting
lightning 149-150, 151, 152, 158
litter, colour-coded 35-36
Lloyd, Michele 186
lookouts 127-128, 211
'Lover's Lane' killer 54

Mabotha, Silas 154
Mabuza, Julia 55
Madikane, Vuyisile 142
Maditsi, Solomon 149-151
Madonsela, Thandeka 119, 190
Maduna, Elizabeth 96
Maema, Kagiso Ishmael 147-148
Mafu, Desiree Ntombana (Ntombana Desire 'Deezay') 143
Mafubedu, Madoe 140
Mahlangu, Joseph 54
Mail & Guardian 74
Maintenance Act (1998) 67
Makau, Disebo Gift 144
makgotlas *see* neighbourhood makgotlas
Makhopa, Tshaisa 151, 152

Makutle, Thapelo 147
Malanze, Lester 151, 152
male
  behaviour towards women 209-211
  homicides 1-2, 16-17, 60
  suicides 85-86
Malebatso, 'Rose' Papi Mogoera Elias 148
Malumane, Abu 151
Marais, Eugene 84-85
Marais, Tania 84-85
Mare, Charmaine 195
marital rape 56-57, 64
Marriage Act 131-132
Martin, Lorna 121
Marx, Lida 49
masculinity 52
Mashigo, Patricia 144
Masia, Nonhlanhla Martha 105
Mason, Paul 119-120
Masooa, Salome 140-141, 142
Mathews, Shanaaz 85-86
Matzopoulos, Richard 108-109, 111
Mbambo, Mandisa 143
Mbeki, Thabo 136
Mdani, Sigcine 145
media coverage
  Afrikaans-language media 34, 154, 195-196
  under apartheid 31, 59-62, 159, 161, 185
  audiences 37, 187, 190-191, 197
  biases 31-34, 208
  black people 51-56, 59-61, 65-66
  crime fatigue 197
  elderly women 37-38, 165-171, 179-180
  English-language media 195
  factors that influence 183-187
  'femicide', use of 64, 70
  femicide-suicide and family killings 47-52, 83-84, 90-96, 101
  firearms 102-103
  guidelines 81-82, 208
  hate killings of black lesbians 129-131, 134, 136-137, 139-148
  'mega cases' 188-191
  rape 52-55, 118-120
  research on 2, 24, 37-38, 179-180, 193-196
  resources, lack of 190, 196

urban legends 25-31
white people 37-38, 194
witch killings 154, 158
'mega cases' 188-191
Melamu, Pascalina Motshidisi 144
memory lapses 79, 81
Metelerkamp, Petrovna 92-93
misinformation 3, 28-31, 34-36, 158-163, 171-174
misogyny 16, 18-19, 76, 101, 209
missing children *see* abductions
Missing Children South Africa 25
missing dockets 75
Mkhize, N 132-133
Mlosana, Lorna 136
Mngadi, Doreen 97
Modikwe, Bethuel 151
Modikwe, Lehong 151
Modikwe, Mary 151
Modise, Motlhatlhedi 'Gustav' 148
'mods and rockers' 52-53
Moeketsi, Shirley 55
Moekwa, Piet 151
Moffett, Helen 128
Mofokeng, Betty 122
Mofokeng, Morena Petrus 122
Mokaba, Peter 177-178
Mokhgethi, Petroos Tsotang 146
Mokoena, Karabo 190, 191, 201
Mokwena, Steve 133
Moloi, Lerato 'Tambai' 145-146
Monckton-Smith, Jane 119-120
'moral panic' 52-54
moratorium on crime statistics 90
Morifi, Hendrietta (Andritha) Thapelo 143
mortality rates 89-90
Morwamotse, Joshua 151
Mothobi, SP 96
motive 18-19, 21, 123
Motleleng, Lekgoa 144
Mphelo, Sibongile 141
Mphithi, Thato 141
Mrwetyana, Uyinene 190, 191, 200-201, 203
Muholi, Zanele 134, 142
murder, definition of 15-16
murder rate 1, 11-13
'muti killings' 154, 156-158

Mvubu, Themba 141
Mzamelo, Ncumisa 142

Naido, Lucia 145
names of victims, in media 83
National Injury Mortality Surveillance System (NIMSS) 23-24, 90, 109-110
National Summit against Gender-based Violence and Femicide 190, 198-200
Nchabeleng, Maurice 154
Nchabeleng, Peter 154
necklacings 150-152
neighbourhood makgotlas 53-54
'newsworthiness' 166, 183, 195
ngakas 149-150, 152-153
NGOs see non-governmental organisations
Nhlapho, Simangele 140
Niehaus, Isak 153, 155
NIMSS see National Injury Mortality Surveillance System
Nix, Jennifer 97-98
Nkolonzi, Phumeza 143
Nkonyana, Zoliswa 136-138
Nkosi, Girlie 'S'Gelane' 141-142
Nogwaza, Noxolo 142-143
non-governmental organisations (NGOs) 27, 59, 200
non-intimate femicide, definition of 23
'not all men' 128, 210-211
Nthai, Seth 155
Ntuli, Annanius 127-128
Nxumalo, Mbali 105
Occult and Harmful Religious Practices Unit 156-157
Ogan, Amma 69-70
online archives 40
Orford, Margie 162-163
'othering' 36, 130, 154, 162
Overcomers Through Christ 160-161
Oxley, Paul and Lynette 112

PAC see Pan Africanist Congress
paedophiles 162
Pan Africanist Congress (PAC) 59, 176, 177
Pappas, Lorraine 51
Pappas, Peter 51
patriarchy 17, 94, 139, 209-211

Pauw, Jacques 94-95
People Opposing Women Abuse (POWA) 58-59, 63-64, 69
percentages 13-14
perpetrators
   female 73, 86
   'invisible' 81
   media coverage 32-33, 165-167
   sympathy with 75, 78-82
   unidentified 18, 123
Pieterse, Petra 94
police
   under apartheid 53-54, 59-61, 96
   challenges of 18, 76, 191, 202-203
   elderly women 166-167, 169
   farm murders 171, 173, 178
   femicide-suicides by policemen 66, 73-74, 96-99, 100, 206-208
   firearms and 98, 105, 108, 111-112, 207-208
   hate killings of black lesbians 134, 139
   rape 126
   Satanism 156-157, 159-160
   service weapons 98, 208
   statistics by 10-11, 20, 21-22, 87, 95
   sympathy with perpetrator 75
   training for 76-77, 206-207
   urban legends 28
   witch killings 155-157
political violence 56, 59-62, 69, 113-114, 152, 154-155, 174, 176-178
Population Registration Act 89
post-traumatic stress 9
poverty 132-133, 157-158, 183
POWA see People Opposing Women Abuse
power 52, 127-128
pregnant women 122, 165
prejudice 129-130
Pretoria News 50, 57, 78
Pretorius, Braam 78-79
Prevention of Family Violence Act (1993) 64-65
private security companies 36
protection orders 68, 73-74
protests 198-206

Qubuda, Thandiswa 119, 190
Qwabe, 'Sdo' Thokozani 141

237

race 59, 77, 90-92, 99-101, 183, 191-196
'race crimes' 172
racism 34, 61, 209
Radebe, Nokuthula 142
Ramaphosa, Cyril 198, 202
Ramon, Shula 186
Ramontoedi, Sandy 73-74
Ramontoedi, Yvonne 73-74
Rand Daily Mail 55, 96
rape
    under apartheid 52-55
    convictions 123-127
    'corrective' 21, 133-134
    definitions 120-121
    elderly women 169-170
    'jackrolling' 133-134
    legislation 65, 125-128
    marital 56-57, 64
    media coverage 52-55, 118-120
    murder and 119-121
    murders of Jyoti Singh and Anene Booysen 117-119
    poverty 132-133
    statistics 118, 121-123
    strangulation 122-123
    'township rape crisis' 52-55
    'unrapable' black woman concept 138-139
Rape: A South African Nightmare 128, 138-139
Rape Crisis 58-59
'rape-homicide', use of term 120
Rapport 196
Recognition of Customary Marriages Act (1998) 67
right-wing organisations and individuals 3, 11-12, 34, 84, 175-176, 178-179
risk profiles 22, 34, 161-163, 191-192
ritual killings *see* 'muti killings'
Rose, Jacqueline 162-163
'Rose Has Thorns' campaign 134
Russell, Diana 16-17, 20-21

Sabadia, Omar 72-73, 187
Sabadia, Zahida 72-73, 187
Sabinet SA Media news clippings service 38-41, 43, 188
Salmans, Hester 170
same-sex marriages 131-132

SAPS *see* police
Satanism 154, 156-163
school boycotts of 1976 53-54
Schwarz, Dave 74
Schwarz, Sonia 74
Sekhukhune youth revolt 149-154
sentences 33, 124-127
Serfontein, Jan 51
Serfontein, Lorraine 51
Servamus 156
service weapons 98, 208
sex offenders registry 126, 203-205
sexual assault 52-55, 121, 132-133 *see also* rape
sex work 18, 209
shelters 58, 208-209
Sigasa, Sizakele 140-141, 142
Sikoji, Sihle 144
Silverman, Craig 31
Simelane, Eudy 19, 141, 191
Simpson, Graeme 68
Singh, Jyoti 117-119, 125, 189
Sithole, Sam 70
Skosana, Maki 152
Small Arms Survey 76
Smit, Robert 48
Smith, Donna 134
Smous, Nonki 145
Smuts, Adriaan 84
Snopes.com 28, 29
Snow, John 35
'social enemies' 154-155
social media 11-14, 28-31, 42-43, 103-105, 159, 161, 172
societal values 31-32, 129-130, 186
sodomy 131
Solidariteit 173
solutions 35, 201-209
Sonjani, Nosisa 145
South Africa, research on 107, 185-186
South African Journal of Military Studies 112-113
South African Law Commission 77
South African Medical Journal 111
South African Medical Research Council 22-24, 33-34, 55-56, 74-77, 85-86, 88, 90, 101, 110, 121-122, 192-193, 204
South African Pagan Rights Alliance 157

South African Police Service *see* police
Sowetan, The 65-66, 96
Soweto 53-55
Spectrum (TV show) 58
Star, The 51, 64, 65-66, 94, 134, 195
States of Emergency 61
statistics 10-14, 61, 90
Statistics South Africa 19-20, 90, 110-111, 192
Steenkamp, Reeva 119, 162-163, 179, 188-189, 191, 195
Steenkamp family murders in Griekwastad 191, 195
stereotypes 34-35, 53, 61, 129-130, 208
Steyn, Irving 47
Steyn, Marinda 161
Steyn, Tessa 105
storytelling 36-37
strangulation 122-123
street lighting 206
Strydom, Koos 146
suicide 20, 49-50, 86, 88-97, 107, 207 *see also* femicide-suicide and family killings
Sunday Express 50, 154
Sunday Times 137
Supa, Sanna 143
suspected rape homicide, definition of 23
Suzman, Helen 58
'Swartes', use of term 159
Swelindavo, Noluvo 145
Syria 76

'T' 137
Tajini, Sizwe 147
TAUSA *see* Transvaal Agricultural Union of South Africa
Tembisa criminal gang 127-128
terrorism 48-50, 176-178
Theron, Rosemary 195
Titus, Phoebe 147
Tlanene, Anna 151
#TotalShutdown movement 198-203
townships 32, 51-55, 206
transgender victims 132, 146-148
Transvaal Agricultural Union of South Africa (TAUSA) 172, 176
Transvaler, Die 154

travel industry 25-26
TRC *see* Truth and Reconciliation Commission
Trump, Donald 106
Truth and Reconciliation Commission (TRC) 72, 84-85
Tsela, Magrieta 151, 152
Tshabalala, Jabulane 127-128
Tshabalala-Msimang, Manto 136
Tshwete, Steve 90
Twitter 28-31
Tyatyeka, Nontsikelelo 142

United Nations (UN) 58, 62-64
United Nations Office on Drugs and Crime (UNODC) 1, 15
United States 106
University of South Africa 55-56
UNODC *see* United Nations Office on Drugs and Crime
'unrapable' black woman concept 138-139
urban areas 95-96, 194
urban legends 3, 28-31, 34-36, 158-163, 171-174

Vaderland, Die 94
Valentine, Mikeila (née Baillie) 158-161
Valentine, Zak 160-161
Van Fossen, Anthony 154
Van Heerden, Elna 174
Van Heerden, Rudolf 174
Van Kessel, Ineke 150, 152-153, 154
Van Niekerk, Anisha 146
Van Niekerk, Joey 146
Van Rooyen, Annetjie 174-175
Van Rooyen, Ernest 174-175
Vetten, Lisa 33-34, 63-67, 70
victim blaming 50, 52, 78-82, 91, 165
#VictimNoLonger 103-104
victims
  'ideal victims' 164-165
  incorrect details of, in media 83
vigilante attacks 35, 204-205
violence, extreme 3, 68-70, 76-77, 174-175, 197, 210-211
violin graphs of femicide victims 167
Volksblad 195-196

Weekend Post 53
WhatsApp 25-29
white people
    Afrikaans-speaking 34, 86, 94-95, 99, 172-173, 175, 178
    definitions 192
    elderly women 168, 170
    farm murders 171-179
    femicide-suicide and family killings 85-86, 94-96, 98-101
    intimate femicide 77
    media coverage 37-38, 194
    right wing 3, 11-12, 34, 84, 175-176, 178-179
    'white genocide' 3, 161, 172, 196
Whittlesea abductions 30-31
Witchcraft Suppression Act (1957) 151
Witches, Witch-Hunting, and Women 157-158
witch killings
    Apel-GaNkoane massacre 149-154
    burnings 149-155
    farm murders and 176
    media coverage 154, 158
    'muti killings' 154, 156-158
    police and 155-157
    Satanism 154, 156-163
    'social enemies' 154-155
    statistics 151-152, 155, 157-158
Women and Law in South Africa 63
Worden, Nigel 175
World Conference on Human Rights 63
World Health Organisation 14

Xakeka, Noxolo 146
Xingwana, Lulu 142

Zibi, Nandipha 'Carol' 105
Zozo, Duduzile 144
Zuma, Jacob 138